ADVANCE PRAISE FOR CLAN...

Ryan's dynamic prose blows a massive hole in the wall of cynicism peddled by indifferent hacks and weary activists. These tales not only drag you screaming to the barricades, they send you over them and beyond—into the unknown where glorious possibility begins.

—Mick McCaughan, *Battle of Venezuela*

These poetic tales of anti-capitalist resistance and autonomous spaces are as heartbreaking as they are filled with heart, and that is precisely their clear-eyed utopian beauty.

—Cindy Milstein, writer, and co-organizer of the Renewing the Anarchist Tradition Conference

This book is a map, allowing us to navigate the liberated zones of riots and festivals; late-night conspiring and pre-dawn revelry; alleyway escape routes and jungle hide-aways; parties in crumbling squatted buildings and tea ceremonies in rugged guerrilla encampments—always with a rakish raconteur at our side. At once celebratory and self-critical, *Clandestines* offers a geography lesson of the shadows, where borders are disregarded, revolution is in the air, and adventure is always just around the corner.

—Jennifer Whitney, co-author of *We Are Everywhere: The Irresistible Rise of Global Anticapitalism*

Tired of dry political analysis that leaves you wondering what's really happening in the world? Ramor Ryan's grassroots revelations beautifully recounts his own experiences, revealing the inside story of revolutions and contemporary movement scenes. No gods, no masters? Here's a book worth enjoying.

—George Katsiaficas, *The Subversion of Politics*

Ramor Ryan is one of history's great guys and in this book he manages to demonstrate that being a great guy can also be a powerful form of political praxis. In fact I'm convinced now that all we need is about a hundred more Ramors and the revolution would commence tomorrow. Actually, this book might help there, because one thing it surely shows is that no matter how bleak and how dangerous some of the places through which one must pass, to live as a rebel, in the constant awareness of the possibilities of revolutionary transformation, and amongst those who dream of it, is the best way one can live.

—David Graeber, *Fragments of an Anarchist Anthropology*

Ramor Ryan's essays are outstanding in that they read like good short fiction, while at the same time offering the news and analysis, the history and the drama of our contemporary times. He writes with an intimacy and close-to-bone-rawness that is reminiscent of Eduardo Galeano, and he never short-changes the lyric or his attention to craft. Ramor writes as one who has lived a rich life; one of adventure and struggles, fighting, writing, being on the front lines, and also one of stealing away under cover of night to reflect and find the words to tell the stories to those that will not make their way to the burning farms of Zimbabwe, the quilombos of Brazil, or the mountains of southeastern Mexico.

—Holly Wren Spaulding, Sweetwater Alliance

CLANDESTINES

the Pirate Journals of an Irish Exile

CLANDESTINES

the Pirate Journals of an Irish Exile

RAMOR RYAN

ak press, oakland, edinburgh, wv

Published by AK Press

ISBN 1904859550
ISBN 13 9781904859550

AK Press
674-A 23rd Street in Oakland, CA 94612 USA
(510) 208-1700
www.akpress.org akpress@akpress.org

AK Press UK
PO Box 12766 in Edinburgh, EH8 9YE Scotland
(0131) 555-5165
www.akuk.com ak@akedin.demon.co.uk

The addresses above would be delighted to provide you with the latest complete AK Press catalog, featuring several thousand books, pamphlets, zines, audio and video products, and stylish apparel published and distributed by AK Press. Alternatively, visit our websites for the complete catalog, latest news and secure ordering.

Library of Congress Control Number: 2006920692
Library of Congress Cataloging-in-Publication data.
A catalog record for this title is available from the Library of Congress.

Cover design by Chris Wright
Layout by King Tender
Illustrations by Simone Schmidt
Primary Photographs by Tim Russo

Thanks to the Institute for Anarchist Studies for financial and moral support.

Printed in Canada on 100% recycled paper by union labor.

—for Ixim

CONTENTS

INTRO-DUCTION

Like anyone who's known Ramor, I've heard bits of these tales before. Fragments stitched together in a never-ending conversation from San Cristobal to the Lower East Side, always on point as to wherever the discussion is going, but always also an enticement to a fuller telling.

This, then, is a long awaited book for those who have crossed or traversed any of Ramor's paths. But it will be just as much of a welcome revelation to those who may never have suspected the existence of these people and places. For not only are these great yarns, they are also the fleshing out of neglected histories, a filling in of some elusive blank spots on our cognitive maps. What was it like to be an Irish rebel at that "end of history" of the 80s and 90s? *Clandestines* is one answer to that question, and hopefully it will inspire others to tell their own stories and create new ones.

At times these stories are romantic, but they are never romanticizing, for unlike his kindred spirits from the barricades of 1871, 1919, or 1968, Ramor can find no solace in any arrow of history or tactical jujitsu that he can count on, in the last instance, to usher in the revolutionary dawn. By the time he makes it to Belfast, Berlin, and Managua, the magic bullets have all been spent, the parties are long over, and the dreams gone sour. But this diminishment of hope is accompanied by the fiercest of commitments, a determination not to succumb to the cynicism of the neo-liberal era, which scorns every unselfish gesture. The freshness of these tales lies precisely in their freedom from illusion and, paradoxically, disillusion, for Ramor's lowered expectations of "revolution" allows him to find beauty, humor, and resilience in unexpected places.

Some readers who have walked these same and intersecting roads will find these tales familiar—the rich descriptions of the social centers and subcultures of the overdeveloped world, the plundered, forsaken spaces and resilient humanity of the global south. But this twinge of recognition makes Ramors' tales all the more poignant, for they bring into relief the invisibility of so much political experience of the last three decades. Why are the 10,000 people who challenged the Democratic Party in the streets of Chicago in 1968 acknowledged as having changed history, while the 100,000 who shut down San Francisco in 1991 to protest the "first" Gulf War are all but forgotten? Why are the small clusters of anti-war activists in the US in the early 1960s remembered (rightfully) as visionaries while the ten million around the world who protested the impending invasion of Iraq in 2003 considered by many to be a failure? In many ways, the stakes were just as high as in the 60s, the tear gas every bit as stinging, the outrage and solidarity every bit as enveloping. And yet…the documentary residue of First World dissent in these decades is very slender, both in volume and in impact. These experiences are often shoehorned into a box of borrowed memories from other eras (when they are not erased altogether by the media). As a result, these recent histories are as clandestine as the precarious livelihood of many of the participants—and as unexamined. Ramor offers a reminiscence of this era without nostalgia, regret or doubt, and that is a welcome thing.

An even more poignant question addressed by this book is the following: why are almost all the struggles against colonialism and neo-liberalism in the global south in the past 30 years virtually unknown in the Western world? Ramor is of course an observer to one of the great exceptions to this rule: the emergence in the 1990s of a small collectivity of Chiapan Indians who changed the world without ever seizing state power. Yet the success of the Zapatistas in drawing attention to their struggle is contrasted tragically by the tens of thousands of indigenous Kurds, Acehnese, and Africans who have been slaughtered in the same period in almost total anonymity. Combine these people with the countless peasants, nomads, and slum dwellers of the global South who have been crushed by the neo-liberal project, and a gigantic iceberg of suffering and resistance is revealed to be hidden under the placid surface of "timeless" capitalism. Ramor contributes to the mapping of this iceberg, drawing connections, linking experiences, yet refraining from speaking on behalf of those he encounters. In time, many more voices of resistance to the new enclosures will emerge from the shadows of clandestinity and tell their own stories. This book is Ramor's story, and a window opening up unto this world.

One reason for the neglect of the Western radical milieu of the late 20th century is its lack of grandeur and heroism. Ramor's narratives turn this absence into a virtue, for it is his keen observation of the spectrum of resistance to intolerable conditions (which themselves range from boredom to deprivation) that give the tales their subversive inspiration. From the sublimated class war on the banana boat to the ritualized mayhem of Berlin Mayday, Ramor is able to draw out the absurdity, tragedy and, finally, persistence of social and political refusal. Here, too, Ramor is a creature of his time, as his political compass is guided by repulsion, not attraction, from most of the blueprints and models which guided his forebears. The lessons learned from history are mostly negative; roads better not traveled, certainties that should be questioned, stances and postures that are unsustainable. If anything, Ramor's only dogma is his diatribe against amnesia: by remembering past freedoms, he insists on its continuous possibility, however fragile.

This journey would not be possible, of course, without fellow travelers, and the stories here are testimony to the thriving anti-authoritarian, anti-capitalist, and broadly anarchist milieu which has flourished in the global North and Latin America in the last few decades. Not to say that all of the characters encountered in these pages are self-consciously ideological in all of their actions. In fact, it is precisely Ramor's discovery that so many "ordinary" people around the world are reinventing solidarity and mutual aid that is one of the book's most hopeful observations. In the course of his journeys, Ramor casts an unflinching eye on the human cost of counter-revolution in Central America, the catastrophic consequences of armed struggle in Turkish Kurdistan and the terrible disappointment of the PT in Brazil. But, surprisingly, we find that revolutionary defeat does not necessarily mean the end of all hope. In fact, for those on the ground, it cannot. The end of one story is the beginning of many others, for the quest remains, as Sub-commandante Marcos puts it, for "a world in which all worlds fit."

But enough with extraneous interpretations. Ramor is, in the best Irish tradition, a storyteller. What did it feel like to be a first world rebel at the end of neo-liberalism? This is one answer.

—*Eddie Yuen*

OLD WORLD

Old World
Norway
Sweden
Finland
Russia
Estonia
Latvia
Lithuania
Netherlands
Luxembourg
Ireland
UK
Baltic Sea
Denmark
Belarus
Germany
Poland
Belgium
Switzerland
Austria
Slovakia
Ukraine
Hungary
Moldova
Slovenia
Portugal
France
Croatia
Romania
Bosnia + Herzegovina
Italy
Black Sea
Bulgaria
Spain
Turkey
Serbia + Montenegro
Albania
AFRICA
Macedonia
Greece
N
W
E
S

SEX AND THE BERLIN WALL

Before they took down the Berlin Wall, we adventured there.

In its twilight years the Wall became an absurdity, a monument of ridicule and sad old history.

One year before it fell in 1988, a bunch of anarcho-squatters jumped east over the Wall, as a sound system blasted the Sex Pistols once-provocative song—*I'm gonna go over the Berlin Wall, bodieeeeees!* The West Berlin riot police pursued them, sticks flying. Everything in West Berlin was the carrot or the stick. The anarchists had been occupying a park to block the construction of a road. The Police had finally overwhelmed them, and so the squatters clambered over the ugly graffiti-ridden monstrosity and were welcomed by East German border guards with tea and biscuits. Shortly afterwards, they were smuggled back to West Berlin through quiet doorways in the great Wall. Rumor had it that some of the anarchists stayed in the east, but I doubt it, for the East was no place for lovers of any type of social freedom.

At a rowdy squatter party on Oranienstrasse, West Berlin, one year before the wall came down, my friend Damian met Simone from Slovcnia. Some terrible punk band played and the crowd was a drunken mob; wasted bodies littered the rough floor, mine among them. Simone was a teenage poet, ex-junky, trained in military matters by the Yugoslav army. In between poem recitals, she would warn of the prospect of terrible war in her country. We laughed, and adored her poems. She adored Damian.

Damian was a young Irish Republican who despised anarchists and the social degeneracy he witnessed around him in the decadent oasis of West Berlin. "These people have no revolutionary discipline!" he ranted, knocking back his umpteenth Hansa Pilsner beer—40 Pfennigs in the local Kaisers Supermarket, a mere pittance. Simone was an anarchist who abhorred almost everything, except Irish Republicans and Damian. At this time, the IRA was bombing the city of London, and each time a bomb went off they would celebrate by getting horribly drunk. And when they got horribly drunk, monstrous things would inevitably occur.

"Damian," she would growl-purr in her Slavic tongue, "Come to me."

She was about his height, but stronger. He would come sit on her knees and they would titillate each other. Drink would disorientate them. Misunderstandings would occur. Damian would be in the midst of explaining meticulously the tactical urgency for more no-warning car bombs in the middle of London to some random visitors. Simone would decide he was ignoring her, deceitfully.

"Dam-eh-ann!," she would growl-purr. "Come in here."

She would lead him into the adjacent bathroom. Presently we would hear the gruff sounds of a body being pounded about the place. She would thump him around for a few minutes, and then they would re-emerge—she looking haughty, he fuming.

"Never ignore me, *Dam-eh-ann,*" she would conclude.

The Berlin Wall divided the great old city. The colorfully painted facades of the West Berlin buildings contrasted with the iniquitous grey concrete of the East Berlin tenements. Capitalist spectacle, Communist utilitarianism. Both sides were chockablock with unhappy Germans. And on both sides the buildings were pockmarked with gunfire and bomb damage. But for us—the squatters, the *autonomes* and the anarchists—the Wall was a superannuated joke. We mocked both sides and lived in our free spaces and talked and fought for our own variety of liberation. Vanloads of riot police camped on our street corners, as they did on street corners over the Wall. We did not live in the ridiculous Cold War; already we were fighting the anti-capitalist struggle, against both state and market capitalism. The Wall was just one more wall—there were many.

"Come, Damian," said Simone one night, as we gazed over the hulking Wall from one of the tourist vantage-points dotted along the Western perimeter. "We shall cross the bridge to the East...."

I watched them as they set out, hand in hand, across the Oberbaumbrücke. This bridge was the historical crossing point where Western spies were exchanged for Eastern dissidents. The gates were low; they clambered over them easily. The watchtowers were unguarded. Soldiers seemed to be asleep at their posts. I saw Simone and Damian walk the length of the long bridge, passing through floodlit zones and barbed-wire sections. They disappeared from view, unscathed, into the East. A Slovakian anarchist and an Irish freedom fighter had clandestinely penetrated the defenses of the Eastern empire!

The Wall was a symbol of the arrogant nonsensical posturing of two appalling super powers, easily mocked. Simone and Damian crossed the Wall, found a quiet bench on the other side, and fucked each other with laughter and passion. A cop came upon them and arrested them—not for crossing the Berlin Wall, but for fucking on a bench. They got arrested for making love! East or West, said Simone afterwards, same fucking cops.

The Wall came down dramatically less than a year later; but it was already an irrelevancy, for the two powers, for Capital, and for the emerging *Anti-Capitalist* resistance.

MAY THE ROAD RISE TO YOU

BELLA
POLIZEI

Mayday is a celebration of all that is life-giving and free in this world. Long ago when Europe was still a vast forest, the people celebrated spring—the re-birth of the cycle of Nature—with festivals of dance, song, feast, and mirth. A pagan ritual in honor of Maia, the Mother of all Gods, it came to be celebrated specifically on the first day of her month. So it was, before Empire, before the Romans, before Christianity, that the people took this day to rejoice at the end of the long winter and the start of the bright, creative spring. The feasting was great, as were the games, the dance, the drink, the merry-making, and the inevitable lovemaking. Everywhere people "went-a-maying," a maypole would be erected for people to dance around, amongst other symbolic acts.

2000 years later we are still here celebrating. It is a sunny afternoon in Berlin, May 1st, approaching the end of the Millennium. In a tidy urban park, a few thousand locals enjoy picnics, music, drinks, and games. It is peaceful and lazy; a gentle breeze flutters the leaves and we are content. "Oh-oh, here come the Romans!" says Mayday. Mayday is his real name, and here he is with his can of Berliner Pilsner hovering around his lips and a look of concern on his sunny face. "I didn't go to work today," read the words on the chest of his red hoody, "I don't think I'll go tomorrow. Let's take control of our lives and live for pleasure, not pain." Indeed—it is the first of May, it is a holiday, and nobody works.

Except the Romans. Here they come like a sky full of wintry clouds—a van full of tooled-up riot police to disturb the peace, destroy our tranquility. Everybody knows there's going to be a riot—it is Mayday in Berlin after all. But the riot squad also had attacked the witches, gathering last night in Kollwitzplatz—a brutal, unprovoked attack on a large group of people performing a pagan ritual in a public park.

About a thousand years ago, the assault on Mayday began. Unable to suppress the popular pagan celebration, the Romans declared that Mayday would be a time to honor some Christian saints. This attempt to hijack the ritual was ignored and ridiculed by the people, and it didn't work. Around 500 years ago—upon the dawning of the Age of Conquest and the imposition of Capitalism, the nation-state and slavery—the real repression began. Mayday was equated with paganism; paganism with heathenism; and of course, whenever the authorities of the Middle Ages mention the word "heathen," genocide was not far off. And so the suppression of Mayday and all things heretical was executed with religious zeal and sadist fervor—witches were burnt at the stake, maypoles were used as whipping posts, and so on.

First they came for the witches of Kollwitzplatz, and now the *Bullen* are coming for the picnickers. Have you even seen a German riot van? It is a tasteful green and white design. The storm troopers are themselves decked out in fatigues—a lighter shade of military green, a pastel green suggesting a gardener or a park-keeper. Out they jump from their bright van as if to say—*Here we are! A bunch of friendly minstrels to join your party!* But it doesn't work—oh, wolves in sheep's clothing. The heavy armor on the vehicles, the helmets, the shields, the big boots and the sticks don't fool anyone—it's a bunch of Nazis, or indeed Romans, back again to fuck up the peace of freedom-loving folk! It's a fierce provocation. We begin to gather up our picnic and beverages, and the *Bullen* advance in tight "turtle" formation (a Roman tactic!) while beating their sticks against their hard plastic shields.

Like a band of merry outlaws from a black-clad Robin Hood flying column, the Black Bloc emerges dramatically from a little wooded bower. They pour out in gleeful ferocity, two dozen masked crusaders, and counter-attack the surprised *Bullen*. They shower the gaggle of cops with a barrage of missiles and by sheer force of energy, with the surprise attack and the flying stones, the cops panic, turn in confusion and flee—bolting like, well, bulls—up the street, pursued by a band of almost frolicking masked miscreants and the howls of laughter and abuse from the assembled multitude.

Mayday is a ritual that has been, throughout history accompanied by bonfires. As the flames engulf the abandoned riot van, the people dance around like a band of festive Celts of old. Here we are, history dancing with us, the heathens of the ages resisting the suppression of our day of leisure, our day of carnival, our merry-making.

The history of Mayday turned around some time at that point, 500 years ago, into one of resistance. In the spirit of outlaws, the rituals took on a new, more mischievous and intrepid countenance. The "Lord of Misrule" presided over the proceedings; the "King of Unreason" and the "Abbot of Disobedience" took court. As a free expression of autonomy, Mayday came under increasing repression as the authorities attempted to discipline the people into a "workforce." It is in this element we are more familiar with Mayday. And it is this kind of mood that prevailed in Chicago in 1886, as a group of militant workers organized their Mayday demonstration at Haymarket.

It was an epoch marked by laissez-faire Capitalism (a forerunner of the Neo-liberalism of the 1980s and 90s), the depopulation of the countryside leading to migration on a massive level (this also sounds familiar today) and Capitalist expansionism. In response, the growing proletariat was beginning to organize strongly in urban areas as Industrial workers, forming unions and espousing political philosophies such as anarchism and revolutionary socialism. At Haymarket, someone lobbed a stick of dynamite into the police ranks, all hell broke loose and six workers were shot down. Later eight anarchists were convicted in a farcical show-trial and so the Haymarket martyrs—as they were to become known—became a symbol for workers' resistance on May 1.

So Mayday—the symbol of spring, rebirth, joy and festivity for a rural peasantry—became transformed through repression as a symbol of class struggle and revolutionary aspirations for the oppressed proletariat. Despite the change of perspective, Mayday still—whether rural or industrial, celebratory or subversive was rooted in the same notions—namely, a refusal to work, rebellion, disobedience, and the spirit of anarchy.

The modern history of Mayday in Berlin follows this model. Mayday is a ritualistic confrontation between rebels and authority. As West Berlin became a haven for those avoiding the military draft, so an oasis of civil defiance, a pirate utopia, a *quilombo* of sorts was created by the dispossessed youth and the resident bohemian artists. The theatre of confrontation became Kreuzberg, traditionally a workers' and migrants' neighborhood now colonized by a multitude of politicized squatters. Anarchists, *autonomes*, punks, Turkish, and Kurdish youth fought pitched battles with armies of riot police. Burning barricades, tear-gas-filled streets, fierce combat, mass arrests, and police brutality became standard fare for Mayday in West Berlin.

So this day in East Berlin, the conflict has kicked off early. As the convoys of police vans descend on the park to witness the smoldering ruins of the burnt-out carcass of this dead beast, we have all already taken off. Now is the hour of the Black Bloc, the insurrectionary anarchists, the Maoists, the Trotskyites, the political hooligans, the *casares* (a reference to French rioters) and the drunken punks.

Mayday and I, aligning ourselves with one of the above categories (not sure which), cycle down to Oranienstrasse, the heart of historical Kreuzberg. There is a full-scale riot in progress and we arrive on the wrong side, behind the police lines. The sky is filled with flying objects raining down upon the besieged police lines. It is a truly astonishing sight as paving stones, bottles, cans or whatever beat down like a medieval barrage. The lines and lines of riot cops are under intense pressure and occasionally one cop or another is carried behind, nursing an injury. "A handful of skilled stone-throwers can fend off a whole battalion of cops," explained Ringrose, my elder sister's boyfriend, years before when I was still a kid. He was of the earlier generation of Berlin Anarchists, who had raised the stakes in the early 1980's by taking to the street with combative resolve. And today, years later, his words resound as we witness maybe 50 stone-throwing militants holding off this street-full of riot cops. The tight street is a chaotic boiling pot of bedlam and as usual, the press is out in force, cameras everywhere, vultures stealing images to sell.

Mayday is gripped by a surge of rebel passion. "Come on!

Come on!" he beckons, "Let's go to the right side, get stuck in!" The right side is the Left side, which is the wrong side according to our guardians and law enforcers. The bikes secured, we roam around Kottbusser Tor to catch up with a mob chasing a convoy of police vans down Skalitzer Strasse. It is an extraordinary sight. An ecstatic horde of maddened youth flings half the pavement at the fleeing vans. The sidewalks in Berlin, inexplicably, are made of millions of small hand-sized stones that are easily dug up and make perfect ammunition for the urban insurrectionary. A barrage of pavement stones are flying through the air, battering the armored vehicles.

I watch my homey Mayday join the fray. He picks up the nearest cobblestone, rushes down the street, and flings it with all his might at the last of the retreating vans. It clangs against the metal grate covering the back window, bouncing aside harmlessly enough. Disappointed, he frantically locates another rock and that follows the first, this time smashing into the back door and leaving quite an impressive dent. "May the road rise to you, fuckers!" he cries. I look at Mayday and he is radiant with rebel joy. He seems 10 feet tall, his arms thrown up in celebration and his face radiating pride. He exhibits all the rapture and rage of someone who has cast aside all the shackles of inhibition and demonstrated forcefully—"I am alive, I am filled with passion, and I RESIST!"

It is contagious and addictive. Hooded-up, masked-up, a glance of an eye is enough to know who is a comrade and who is otherwise. But we are all comrades here today, no agent provocateurs or undercover cops. A bevy of stones later, the pigs have retreated further—but proletarian revolution does not seem to have materialized yet, so we retreat for a beer. Despite the widespread riots and the fog of tear gas, many bars and cafés are still open for business—like a sign of solidarity with the thousands in the heaving, battle-weary streets.

Our eyes streaming from the poisonous gas and blazing from the excitement of engagement, we rest and gather our senses about us. "This is brilliant!" says Mayday, luminous. "This is like a carnival of resistance…" Mayday is an ebullient person. He was brought up in a tiny rural community in the back of beyond. His father was a day-laborer, a bricky, dry-liner, laborer, whatever scarce work there was. From that background of poverty emerged Day, as he was called then. Not for him, the technical college or an apprenticeship. "I want to pursue my real desires, I want to travel, I want to make art and I dream of living in a completely different world…" he said. "You're mad," they said. "'I am," and off he went on his high horse on his quest for knowledge, enlightenment, pagan celebration and heathen sex. It took him to London, then Paris, then New York, and finally to Berlin—a squatted house in Duncker Strasse, an artist-bohemian dwelling filled with fiery radicals and illumined creators. Inspired by this wild subterranean scene, he embraced anarchy and total freedom. With neither a penny nor a fear in the world, he vagabonded and thrived, attracting friends like kids to a circus. A brick to the head at work brought him $10,000 injury damages, a princely sum that he spent with characteristic munificence and garishness over a six-month period, lavishing upon friends and acquaintances bountiful gifts and myriad beverages. Six high months of anarchy and luxury, of kindness and generosity. Then he returned to penniless vagabondage, once more immersing himself in art and politics, living and breathing both equally. He took his art and stunts into the streets.

Aghast at the straight thinking of the business community in the financial district, one day he mischievously set off to "work" dressed in the finest stock-broker's suit (borrowed, or maybe stolen) carrying a handsome brief case. As he marched regally down the main thoroughfare, the perfect image of the ideal city gentleman, he would suddenly let out a hoot, fling the brief case high up over his shoulder into the air, back-pedal wildly to catch the descending bag, and then…recover his composure completely, and continue his stride as if he was lost in thought.

This little stunt would have gone down wonderfully in the dada-ist journals of provocative street art, perhaps even made a few people think—who knows? Only it went sadly wrong, as these things sometimes did for Mayday. One more time he hooted, flung his briefcase high in the air and backtracked speedily to catch the bag—and there was a little old lady struggling along directly behind him, who took the full force of the flailing 6-foot tall Mayday. She screamed her face blue and the cop's dragged Mayday off, charging him as a public nuisance. Which he was and continued to be, proudly.

"Fucking Romans!" says Mayday, bringing us back from our fond reveries into the present moment. A bunch of *Bullen* have just burst through the door of our little sanctuary, this little café on Wienerstrasse. They overturn a few tables, whack a few coffee sippers, and all chaos is unleashed. The customers and owners gang up and conspire to push the rampaging pigs back onto the street. Clearly it's time to leave. We bail out onto the darkening street and the riot is in full swing.

It's early evening and Kreuzberg is burning. At this point it's worthwhile to have a word about tactics and strategy. What exactly are we trying to achieve by our belligerent actions? Why are we building barricades? Why are we engaging with a force far superior in arms and strength—the police? This question can be answered on multiple levels. If one would care to question each of the—how many?—5000 people in the street, one would get a kaleidoscope of diverse responses. Some would argue that this is a simple rebellion against power, a fight that should be taken to the authorities on every presented occasion. Others would frame it in terms of the ongoing Class War. Others still would insist it is a fight for the right to party because the *Bullen* were repressing the Mayday festivities. However, one thing is clear: the occupation of our civil living space by thousands of aggressive riot police is an intolerable situation. And this must be resisted.

The aerial view from the cop helicopter hovering over the barrio at this moment would look like this: ongoing running battles between squads of cops and rioters. Occasional barricades going up in flames, usually short-lived, as the water cannons quench the fire. Long convoys of cop vans snake around, generally being assaulted from all sides by missiles and stones. There are people crouching in every corner, in every shadow; every green space has a band of plotters. And most of all, rioters are taking advantage of the geography of the *barrio*. The streets are lined by enormous tenements, each of which has a doorway leading to the *hinterhaus*, the inner courtyard and usually linked to another courtyard, whereupon it's possible to enter one apartment building and exit through another, usually onto an entirely different street. Suffice it to say, it's a labyrinth of connections and an urban insurrectionary's playground. Add to this that the roofs are easily accessible and offer a temptation to drop things onto police vans five stories below. All in all, the geography and architecture makes for very favorable guerrilla terrain.

So who is taking on the cops? The masked, hooded, and rowdy hordes in the streets and the alleyways—building barricades, fleeing the snatch squads, hiding in doorways, sheltering in cafes—who are they? Well, this kind of operation excludes, obviously, the elderly, the infirm, the panicky, and people with large families depending on them…So no surprise, it is predominantly youth—although not necessarily male, and not necessary white. Critics from the more pacifist wing of the movement will say this kind of urban warfare excludes the population, alienates the masses. That it is no more than football hooliganism.

But just as it takes a whole village to raise a child, it seems it takes a whole community to host a sustainable riot. The local population here in Kreuzberg is generally not hostile to the street insurrectionists; the local left-wing Berliners have a gripe of their own with the *Bullen*, and the Turkish and Kurdish communities are certainly no friends of the state. Indeed, a good proportion of the youth engaging the cops are Turkish and Kurdish—probably militants from Dem Sol or PKK, two radical left groupings strong in this neighborhood. And then you have a good network of sympathizers, activists, ex-squatters, ex-punks, students, artists, and old communists who will actively support the rioters—offering refuge, opening doors, allowing their dumpsters to be used as barricades, helping the injured, hassling the cops. One thing is sure—if the local community is hostile to the people in the streets, then it's unsustainable. And this is one reason why the Mayday insurrection has occurred ritually in these very streets (or across eastwards in Prenzlauer Berg)—because there is a sea in which to swim, as Mao would have it.

Mayday and I have re-emerged from the café onto the street intersection and it is a tumultuous theater of pandemonium—squads of riot police are running around attacking random individuals, while objects are showered on them from every direction; indeed people are running in every direction, as the police and rioters seem to have gotten their coordinates mixed up or crossed and everybody has arrived in one spot, converging haplessly from all directions. If Charlie Chaplin had been here, he couldn't have made it up. In the middle of all this turbulence, familiar eyes behind ski-masks pull us aside. It's some of our neighbors—Irish, Spanish, and Brazilian *compañeros*. "Watch out!" they call, and we are dragged into a doorway. Sure enough, a half dozen Molotovs are launched from a second floor window upon an armored water canon, causing it to reverse from the intersection at high speed, in flames. As the *Bullen* go berserk, we run through the courtyard of the tenement, over a little fence, and out onto Naunynstrasse, safe—or at least for a moment. We run down as far as the plaza at Heinrichplatz. Bad move. Another armored water canon is speeding into the open space, spraying everything in sight with its powerful jet. First it shines its massive beam of light at the target, then it unleashes the water current, then the squads of mobile storm troopers running behind the truck sprint after the target, sticks flying. These guys are the dangerous ones—they are fast, mobile and vicious; they don't take prisoners; they dish out beatings and leave you in a pool of blood. Maybe afterwards some other bunch of cops will pick you up and haul you off to the van for arrest. Meanwhile the storm troopers have moved on, beating all and sundry in their path.

It's one of those moments of horror like when you realize your car is about to crash, or your bicycle has gone out of control. So it is when the searchlight blinds our eyes and the gush of water smashes into us like a piano falling from the sky. We are about a dozen people crouched in a doorway. The door springs open, both from the force of the water jet-spray and because we fall against it. We tumble in, and I glance back to glimpse the most terrifying sight of a gang of riot police sprinting across the plaza towards us, silhouetted by the searchlight. Suddenly I realize that we are with a group of locals—a couple of old folks, some teenage kids, a really young child, a family maybe just trying to get home, maybe out watching the sports. Anyhow, now they are in trouble. We all are. The kids scamper down steps to a darkened basement, and we split in various directions across the inner courtyard, as the first of the storm troopers burst through the outside doors. We are in their sights as we dash towards an eight-foot wall the other side. Glancing back again, I register that the cops are coming for us, which means they won't go for the kids down the steps. For some reason this comes to me as a relief, as I face the daunting wall. It is said that total fear, absolute desperation and the death instinct give you momentary superhuman powers of strength and perception. In that very moment I clamber over the enormous wall like a cat—I could not do it under any other circumstances. I fly over the wall as the first baton strikes the wall some inches behind. Mayday is not so lucky—they hit him as he struggles over; I pull him over from the other side. A half dozen *Bullen* are whacking away at him as he reaches the top of the wall and throws himself over, head first, onto the ground on the other side. The cops can't climb over because of their burdensome body armor, and Mayday and I scrambled away, his nose gushing blood.

It is a feeling of indescribable jubilation to escape from the clutches of the *Bullen*. I think about the kids and the old folks and hope they are ok; at least the pigs would have quieted down a bit with their frenzied attack stalled at the eight-foot wall. As for our *compañeros*, I hoped they have gotten away; but they know the score, the risks, they are not spectators. They go to the streets masked up; they have a legal number written on their skin, a phone number; they know what the deal is.

We emerge onto yet another street mad with violence, with heaving crowds, with fire and smoke and gas and the sound of discord and clamor as two armies clash by night. Mayday is in trouble, bloodied and disoriented from landing on his head. I want to get him out of there. "This way!" I gesture, and we begin running in the opposite direction from the conflict. We run blindly into the darkness as fast as we can. Mayday goes down hard to the crunching sound of splintering bone. I look back. He has crashed into one of those metal street bollards, groin height—like being kicked in the balls by a horse. He is rolling around in excruciating agony clutching his balls, his face bloodied, groaning frightfully. To stop myself from laughing—for fucks sake, the ignominy of it all! I picked him up roughly and dragged him away "Come on! Come on!"—as he suffers untold pain.

We collapse into a quiet Turkish *Imbiss* away from the din of the maddening crowd. I clean the blood off his face and we drink the most wonderful bottle of Beck's beer imaginable. We are out of harm's way here, unless they start doing sweeps of the surrounding areas. When Mayday has recovered enough to continue, we hit the street scurrying along in the shadows like hunted fox. Police vans filled with prisoners scream by, ambulances blare in the distance. Fresh groups of youth head towards the theater of unrest. And I think—who gains from this Mayday ritual? Certainly the cops get an opportunity to test out the latest riot-control techniques in what is, more or less, a controlled real-life situation (in-so-much as the resistance is never intensified, no arms or explosives are used, and nobody gets killed). The young novice rioters get a chance to learn street resistance and hone their tactics and strategies, to feel the strength of solidarity and become skilled at watching each other's backs. Nevertheless, it becomes a ritualized confrontation, full of sound and fury, signifying—well, if not nothing—at least business as usual.

With some relief, we finally arrive home, back into the welcoming old crumbling East Berlin squat that shelters us, protects us. Home after the battle, home from the wars. We fall into the *gemeinschaft,* the house café/bar, where we are surprised to discover a full-scale party raging. Oh yes, it's Mayday, of course there's a big celebration. The people are all dressed up and dancing around a pole decorated with ribbons and party decorations. It's a delight.

The strobe light exaggerates Mayday's injuries—he looks well fucked-up. The people surround him, showering him with sympathy, shock, and questions. "Did the *Bullen* do this to you?!" they demand angrily. Oh God, I hope they don't all decide to do some retributive "action" in response—I'm tired, I want to drink and dance and fall into easy embraces. Before I have to sabotage the moment by announcing that he merely fell off a wall and ran into a post, Eva the peacemaker intercedes with gentle force. "No, give him space. Sit down, bring drink...Questions later!"

While Mayday gets pampered by the Compassion Brigade, I wander around the gathering. It is quite a spectacle! On stage they prepare for some theatrics and a drag show; on the dance-floor people are swinging around high as kites—must be some Ecstasy in the house—and the rest cluster around dark smoky tables. The babble of excited conversations fills the room, the retelling of the day's adventures while throwing back beers and smoking joints. The German *autonomes* and Anti-fa, the Spanish anarchists, the Sudanese exiles, the Brazilian queers, the Egyptian pot-heads, the Slovakian DJ's, the Irish drinkers, the Polish hippies, the Kurdish outlaws, the visiting Japanese commies—all the clandestine multitude sharing tables and space and their lives and coming together and making a new little world, right here. There are no bouncers, no security, no managers, no staff; we are not customers, this is our space—self-run, autonomous; here there are only *compañeros* and respect, and it is beautiful. I am filled with a sudden feeling of happiness. It's only a big old squatted house but we really are doing it. This is something worth fighting for, worth defending.

"Ya, Ramon, they must turn down the music, I am asleep upstairs." This from Horst, the house grouch, an old artist who grumbles about everything. "I must go to work tomorrow!" "Yeah fuck off, Horst." This is not the night of the grouches and the jaded and the corpses. It is Mayday, it is our day; and now the battle has passed and it is time to dance around the Maypole, make merry, and celebrate everything that is good and free in this sordid life.

As Bacchanalian nights go, it rates. Mayday was soon back to his mischievous creative self, taking to the stage during the drag queen show. I am really hoping he won't do a repeat performance of one of his more talked-about shows in Duncker Theatre. That one entailed walking onto an empty, silent stage, naked, with a bucket. He proceeded to piss into the bucket, pick it up, and then pour the piss all over himself. Finally he bowed gracefully and walked off, to much critical accolade. No, this time he gets into the boisterous mood of the evening, paints dashing figures dancing on the stage wall—masked Zapatista insurgents performing boleros with, I'm not sure, some variety of drag queens. Or maybe portraits of Eva the Pole, or Jessica the American, or Rocio from Madrid, Mayday's favourite *compañeras*. Either way, they all love it and he is pulled into the swell on the dancefloor, engulfing him in a loving embrace. And I lose sight of him, carried away by the heaving tide of dancing figures.

Around dawn, as the sun appears stealthily and dramatically over the high tenement roofs—a still time of day that lends itself to mystery and illumined hyperbole—I walk into the silent street. The party is over, the people have gone to bed—in groups, in couples, alone, but they all seemed content. Mayday has fallen playfully upstairs with one or three of his inspirations. Now it is silent, and the dawn air light and refreshing. There she is sitting alone on a discarded couch on the edge of the sidewalk—she who I had been looking for—the fallen angel of Siegessaule in Kollwitzplatz. She who, I had wanted to approach, to engage, to embrace. But she had disappeared into the maddened crowd as the *Bullen* charged. Andrea Maria smiles at me, I sit down, we touch, and I find the last element of Mayday that had been missing—magic.

THE LAST OF THE AUTONOMEN

Portrait of a Rebel from the East Berlin Squats

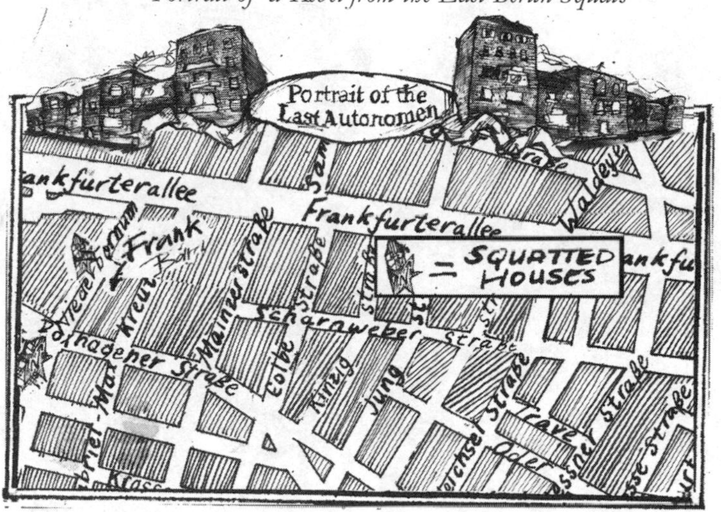

REVOLUTION
IS AN
ENERGY
NICARAGUA
AFRO - LATINA
MASTERP

Society produces all the criminals it deserves. And what if the criminal is an intellectual of high caliber with a revolutionary axe to grind against institutional society? Woe to that social order. Western Europe is so clearly unable to deal with the social brigand which its bourgeois liberal Capitalism replicates generation after generation. Hence, the political prisoner: an old *auto-de-fe* idea dressed up in new technological clothes. But this kind of miscreant won't go away; they are indigenous to the system.

Servant Einstein—"Ein" to his homies—is one such character. I have not known him long when he comes around to my place one night. He is fuming. While he was waiting for his falafel to cook at the local *imbiss* earlier that night, the Kurdish worker had begun to complain about the problems they were having with the Grey Wolves—the Turkish Mafia. Apparently the Grey Wolves were demanding protection money and threatened the Kurdish owners. Maybe the price of the falafel—a mere 2 *deutsche* marks, cheapest in all East Berlin—would go up as a result. Ein is typically enraged. Any injustice, however obscure, is a cause for immediate direct action. Here in the militant squatter scene, we are very fond of the beleaguered Kurds and reserve a special hatred for the fascist Grey Wolves who act as paramilitaries against the Left in Turkey.

This is a clearly a case for meting out some righteous revolutionary justice.

"We can get a weapon off Brick. He's got an AK stashed, Russian military leftover, like." Ein is breathless, conspiring. "I found out where the faschos hang out, like, an *imbiss* on Warsghauer Strasse, like, fuckin' Grey Wolves cunts, fuckin' shoot them up..."

Ein is Scottish. He speaks good German with a heavy Glaswegian accent, punctuated with "fuckin," every few words, as in "Vas ist deine fookin' problem, arshelocke?"

" He will get us all in terrible trouble!" said Niels the prudent German when Ein first moved in with us. It wasn't so much his wild unconstrained energy that was troubling, nor his sharp overactive mind that spilled over with venomous satire and hilarious depravity. The troubling side of Ein was the inferno of rage within him that was unleashed occasionally in the form of lightening violence.

"Let's go, "commanded Ein. " The car's outside. You drive, I'll use the fuckin' gun."

My savings grace is, I can't drive. I'm off the hook this time. Ein leaves the room, momentarily disgusted, off in search of a more willing comrade. No doubt Brick gets dragged in on the mission; Brick being a big favorite of Ein's because, as the story goes, he once dropped a fridge off the roof of a tall building upon a police car. Direct hit.

★

Ein had suffered the marginalized, dysfunctional formation of many who are drawn towards the vast Berlin squatter "community." In his twenties, with more than a fleeting resemblance to Andreas Baader, he came here to escape the horrible claustrophobia of his home country. If some flee political repression, and others flee economic hardship, Ein was of the "psychological refugee" category. "They were fucking messing with me head, man," he would say.

The East Berlin squat scene in the 1990s was a pirate's utopia, a temporary autonomous zone; a haven of anarchists, *autonomes*, punks, left communists, bohemian artists, *clandestinos*, exiles, migrants, idealists, sex-workers, the certifiably insane, hard drug users, and criminals in general. With nowhere else to go, we congregated there—the flotsam and jetsam from the margins of capitalist society. We distinguished ourselves from wholly criminal underworlds—we organized ourselves politically.

Ein had also been in trouble with the Scottish constabulary. The specific reasons changed, depending on the amount of hard liquor he had consumed and the current company he was keeping. It was a heist, or else it was armed assault, or else it was some revolutionary act that he "couldn't fuckin' say, you know what I mean, like..."

Ein was orphaned at an early age, and brought up by some uncaring relatives. He went from school to school, getting in trouble and getting expelled. He left his guardians as soon as he was old enough, only to land in reform homes for "troubled" youth. His childhood and teenage years were an unending struggle against the authority and insanity of the state institutions that attempt to control recalcitrant youth. A life of crime was all very fine, but soon enough young Ein realized that the problem lay in the structure of the state and a paradoxically permissive and repressive, by turns, society. He got involved in some armed revolutionary outfits—dangerous gangs of malcontents with a smattering of ideology, a lifetime of rage and courage enough to directly confront the perceived forces of repression. He eventually washed up in Berlin on the run, or running, where one of his girlfriends had a room in a squat.

Beautiful, fucked-up women seem to have a penchant for dangerous revolutionary men, and Anna was no exception. From Bosnia, she was a refugee, and as maddened and damaged by the chaos of war as anyone. I recall an anti-fascist demo in Alexanderplatz that was attacked by the German riot police. We were in tight Black Bloc formation, and linking my arm was Anna. With martial art moves worthy of Teenage Mutant Ninja Turtles, using my grip as a launch-pad, she drop-kicked the *Bullen* with astonishing power—accompanied by wild shrieking and devastating results.

Anna sheltered Ein. They were Bonnie and Clyde, Sid and Nancy. They beat each other to within an inch of their lives and returned to each other's embrace; *amour fou* and the impossibility of love in an unfree world. It was not uncommon for us to be basking outside our squatter bar on the street corner as things flew off their balcony five stories up, the cacophony of primal screaming alerting us to another Anna-Ein argument.

Meanwhile, balanced with that violence was their tender, immeasurable love. They would retreat for days to their warm nest to sing each other's joy. And when Ein gathered his people to his apartment, wild was the revelry and great was the celebration—like a band of Fianna from feral and heroic ages. Ein's capacity to embrace life was immense; whether thrilling in political street action and the excitement of battle or subdued in melancholy at the dearth of day, Ein burned and conspired and inspired—for good or evil—all who were around him.

Those majestic East Berlin tenements were riddled with bullet pockmarks from World War II. The cobbled streets were filled with a resonance of the crazy history that had engulfed them. From the hedonism of the Weimar republic to the revolutionary aspirations of Rosa Luxemburg and the KPD; to subjugation by the Nazis and the invasion of the Russians; to the imposition of the Soviet satellite regime and the fall of the Wall, followed by the unleashing of the floodgates of raw neo-liberalism—those streets teemed with tumultuous spirits. Perhaps that is why we were all there: a tumultuous historical spirit having enveloped and embraced its chaotic, youthful reincarnation.

★

I awake late; to some commotion outside the window—raised voices—the ubiquitous rude awakening. I immediately assume it is the police—a week earlier they had awakened me as they pulled my Kurdish flag from its perch on my balcony. The Kurdish flag was inexplicably and insanely banned by the democratic German state at this time. The amusing thing is that my room is situated on the second floor of the building—the *Bullen* had driven their van up on the pavement, and a cop decked out in the most fashionable riot gear was perched on top of the vehicle, reaching up to my balcony. I walked out in my underwear, smiling politely at my unexpected visitor. He barked some ferocious curses at me and ripped down the offending cloth.

But on this occasion it is not the cops; Ein and Anna are outside the corner shop across the street. Ein is screaming his head off—"*fucking sheissen arshelock*" this and that. Anna is being held roughly by the *Frau* shopkeeper battle-axe, who is responding to Eins' excitements with her own variety of expletive. A regular beat cop, possibly the only cop I have seen on the streets in this *kietz* (neighborhood) not in riot gear, is attempting to take notes.

By the time I have dressed, assembled some support, and arrived on the scene, Anna has been hauled away in a big snot-green riot van and Ein is being restrained by a variety of meaty young *Bullen* who look like a group of woodcutters just arrived from the Black Forest. By pure strength of critical mass, the gathered local squatters release Ein from the brawny grips of the arresting officers.

Apparently Anna had been accused of shoplifting by the *Frau* in the corner store—the irony being, although they were on their way—as was customary, to shoplift at the supermarket, she wasn't trying to rob here; squatter shoplifting etiquette excludes local shops. Nevertheless, the fearless *Frau* had made a big fuss and grabbed hold of Anna, and Ein had gone ballistic.

"She's a fucking refugee with a fucking criminal record, like, for fuck's sake, and she'll get fucking deported, like, by the *scheissen* fuckin' *Bullen* for this..." explained Ein in desperation. "She'll go fuckin' mad in jail, she'll fuckin' kill herself, she's been through too fucking much, like, shite!"

It's a serious situation. We call up some lawyers. While waiting to hear back, Ein hits the vodka. "She'll fuckin' die in there, she can't take it..." He paces the bar nervously, phantoms in his head working overtime; a long criminal life has made him paranoid and pessimistic. He stomps about and then changes the music—this is our own squat-bar, with cheap booze and a good sound system—and puts on Atari Teenage Riot. This is a bad sign, they being a local hardcore-techno mayhem and destruction outfit. "Start the Riot" blasts from the speakers.

He throws back the last of the vodka, and storms out.

We presume he has gone off to sort out the cash crisis, to get more hard liquor. Ein's renowned generosity means he would share every last slice of cheese or, as the case sometimes was, line of coke. One oft-told exploit resonated in the bars and cafés: how, the house having run dry, Ein had decisively taken it upon himself to supply the party. He leapt upon the U-Bahn to Alexanderplatz, whereupon—having spied his foe—he gave chase to a rich gent walking down Karl Marx Allee and ruthlessly stripped him of wallet and cash. Exultant, Ein joyously rejoined the surprised party. And so the people feasted long and merrily and their glasses did not run dry again. Such were the legends of Ein's generosity, and daring. So we are not unduly concerned by Ein's overly tempestuous exit; so he is, and it is lauded.

Some time later, the Polish hippy Magdalena runs in. "Is very bad. Front window Frank's Bar smashed," she says. "Too many police, violence."

We rush out of our squatters bar to the local "prole" bar down the street just in time to witness the cop van pull off, sirens blaring. A heavy black boot smashes out the side of the van window from the inside, as bodies heave about.

Frank, the affable local bar owner, a friend of the squatters, explains what happened with some confusion.

"This Ein-man, *ja*, passed by, looked in the door, shouted at two of my customers—one who had a German flag on the sleeve of his work-jacket—and Ein-man pulled out an air gun, *ja*, shot my window and jumped on the man, screaming about *Scheiss Faschisten* …Then the police came and took him away. He fought them, *ja*, like a madman…"

This is very serious. Ein has a criminal record and he'll go down for a long time for this. Squatters gather; we despair. "Fucking Ein," says Niels, one of the concerned squatters from No. 23. "He is mad bastard. We are sympathetic because of the Anna situation, but he's off his fucking rocker—we like Frank. His customers are not fascists."

★

Is every act of violence against the forces of repression a revolutionary act? In every revolutionary situation, it is surmised. We live like outlaws in squatted spaces, our *kietz* under a state of virtual siege, riot cops camped out on every corner night and day. Individuals like Ein are at war against the state every minute of their waking life. Such is the discussion amongst the assembled, predominantly German, squatters as we decide what course of action to take.

"Ve must to break him out!" shouts a drunk-punk as he dramatically bangs his fist on the bar.

"Ve should bang his head off the fucking toilet for being such a fool!" says another.

"Maybe will do him good, be quiet some time in jail," suggests the Polish hippy Magdalena.

"I think someone should, like, get some bread to bail him out," says Jessica the American, while breastfeeding her kid.

I am dispatched to fetch his passport from his apartment; we reckoned that was a good start. I burst into his room on the 5th floor. It is a large dark room decorated with metal bars and graffiti, NY subway style. Anna is lying on the raised bed. Fucking great—while all this has been going on, she has been unexpectedly released from jail.

She is silent, staring blankly at the ceiling. I notice she has a black eye and her eyes are moist. I begin to tell her the emergency, but she turns away, disinterested. Oh dear, Anna is having one of her episodes. I locate Ein's passport, assure her it'll all be ok, and return to the assembly in the squatter bar.

They are discussing whether they should take a collection for Frank's broken window, or just send him a letter explaining the inevitable consequences for windows located in revolutionary areas under siege from the forces of the totalitarian state.

"We must call a *Kietzplenum,*" insists one particularly boring *autonome.* The solution to every problem—a General Meeting attended by every lunatic and didactic theorist in the neighborhood. I am all for direct participatory democracy myself, but things are taken to an extreme in East Berlin. Like the time, after a marathon 20-hour *Plenum*, a group of hardcore feminists donned their ski masks and marched down the street to firebomb a neighboring squatted house—collective punishment for an alleged local misdemeanor. (The occupants of said house—anarchist brigands—had assumed they were under attack from Nazis, successfully counterattacked, and an unmitigated horror unfolded.)

Aghast at the idea of a *Plenum* right now, a small group of us break away and head towards the local police barracks. What we shall do there, we are unsure, but it seems urgent right now to get away from these fucking pedantic ideologues and establish some details on the ground.

It is early Sunday night, and the old cobbled streets are quiet. The uselessly weak communist-period streetlamps cast eerie shadows. We move swiftly with some purpose down the very center of the street—we are so many in this neighborhood that a certain lawless abandon informs our daily behavior. It is cold and most of us pull up our hoods. It goes without saying we are all clad in black. It's impossible to keep any other color clothes clean living in the rough squats. (Q.E.D.—the short story of the humble origins of the Black-bloc.)

An old *trabant* car pulls aside, intimidated by our presence. Groups of hooded squatters roaming in the night always means trouble in the eyes of the locals. They despise us; despite it being a staunch PDS (ex-communist party) borough, this conservative working class district understands the squatter and anarchist milieu as just another alien invasion. Indeed, so entrenched were we with building our autonomous zone with its peoples' kitchens, free cafés, cheap bars, workshops, gyms, vegetable gardens and what not, we had quite overlooked the absolute necessity of including the established local community. Then again, quite a few of the locals seemed far more interested in the newly-opened Burger King on Mainzer than our vegetarian *Volksküche*; even our nightly vandalistic reparations to the burger bar storefront didn't appear to convince them of the folly of their choice.

★

We spot him stumbling along the middle of the street towards us. He staggers from side to side like a drunk on mentholated spirits. But the contour is all wrong; he resembles a crumpled rag-doll, a misshapen puppet. Then he falls in a heap on the cobblestones. A darkened car that has been trailing him turns around and speeds off.

We pick him up. He is unrecognizable from the beating—his head is swollen enormously and grotesquely; his face masked in blood, hands double their usual size, are bruised and blackened. His clothes are soaking wet from blood. We pick him up and he collapses. He is sniveling and his breathing is erratic. When he eventually realizes who we are, he begins to sob. But not sorrowfully or pathetically—he sobs in relief that they will not begin to beat him again.

Ein had been saved from a long prison sentence because the *Bullen* had beaten him so badly that they realized he could not appear in the courts the next day without questions being raised. Such are the random delights of a criminal life.

We carry him back to the bar. He is shaking uncontrollably. We wash the blood off his face and hands. His face is disfigured and the bruising streaks in lurid colors. His nose is broken and several teeth are smashed.

Anna walks in. Her thousand yard-stare does not change much as she looks upon her broken lover. They stare at each other vacantly. Then her stare moves to the woman who is holding the wet cloth before Ein's battered face. It is Calamity, a squatter with whom Ein had a brief affair recently.

"Bitch!" Anna spits viciously, and runs out of the bar.

We lost contact with Ein a while after this. He was on the run again, having been sentenced to four years in prison *in absentia* for some action in support of the Kurds. Ein always had a great sympathy for the plight of the Kurds. The police came looking for him one evening: the street was blocked off, a convoy of police vehicles clogged the old street, and legions of riot cops surrounded the house. Standard raid stuff. A powerful beam of light flashed up and down the façade of our beautiful old crumbling building. A harsh voice barked orders at us over an extremely noisy loudspeaker. The undocumented migrants from the Sudan prepared to evacuate via the secret basement exit. The anti-fascist action militant hid her computer files, the Egyptian pothead hid his scales, the Slovakian DJ hid his stolen decks; all over the house clandestinos scrambled to conceal things, while the anarchists and *autonomes* blockaded the exits and prepared to resist the assault.

But Ein was gone. He was gone and nobody knew where. Even the fearless and loyal Brick had had a row with Ein. Ein claimed Brick was a police agent and Brick claimed Ein had taken liberties with him; either way, Brick, the stronger of the two, emerged with a couple of black eyes, and Ein lost another mouthful of teeth. Anna disappeared and pitiful rumors abounded as to her whereabouts—that she was a bombed out junky on Kottbusser Tor, that she was hanging out with Serbian skinheads or worse, that she was dead. Disintegration was complete. People claimed Ein had joined the "underground," but there was no "underground" to join in Berlin in the 90s.

He departed as he arrived, in a chaotic delirium of subterfuge and mystery, the better to fight.

TWILIGHT OF THE ARMED STRUGGLE

Fear and Loathing in Kurdistan

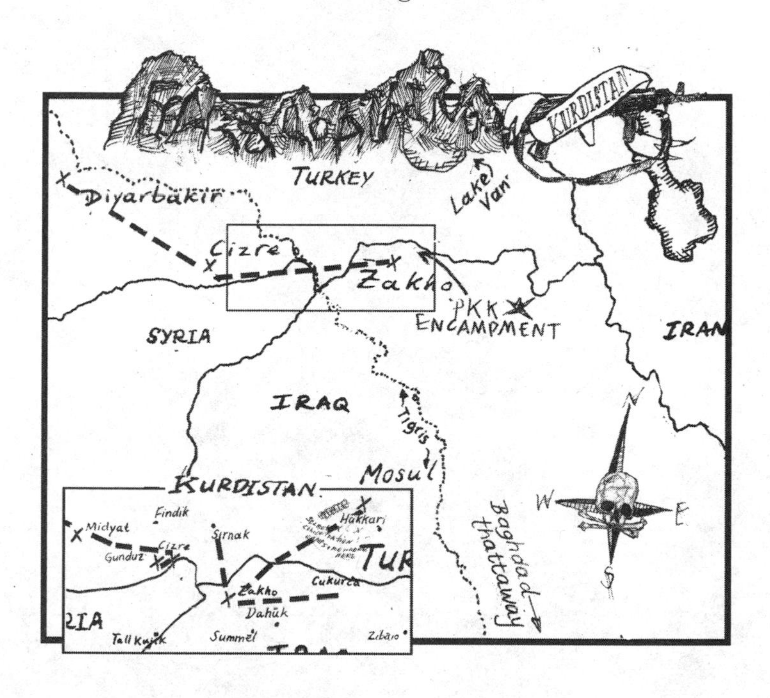

Kurdish refugees flooded into Europe during the 1990s, fleeing the brutal counter-insurgency war waged by the Turkish military in the southeast part of the country to put down the PKK (Kurdistan Workers' Party) rebellion. Many of them found sanctuary in Germany, particularly Berlin, and some found their way to the squats.

So it was there in the east Berlin squats that I heard first-hand accounts of the plight of the Kurds and the repression they suffered at the hands of the Turkish military. Everybody had lost members of their family or had their homes burned or suffered indescribable torture. The Kurds were well-organized politically in Germany, so the German state banned the PKK and any symbol of Kurdish nationalism, including the Kurdish flag. Kurds were also targeted by the security forces. Almost every pro-Kurdish demonstration I attended in Berlin was broken up violently by the riot cops.

It seemed a hopeless cause. A nationless people persecuted by the occupying Turks, Iraqis, Iranians, and Syrians, the Kurds were also bitterly divided amongst themselves into three warring factions—the PKK, PUK, and the KDP. It was said that the Kurds had no friends but the mountains, and even the snow-covered Kurdish mountains offered little sanctuary during the long, harsh winters.

As the tenth anniversary of the PKK uprising approached—1994, August 14th—our Kurdish friends asked us to help organize a delegation of international solidarity to witness the situation on the ground during this tense period. We agreed—not because we were supporters of the PKK, a Stalinist politico-militarist organization led by an old Marxist caudillo called Apo (Abdullah Öcalan), but because the situation was clearly so appalling in general and the war was almost ignored in Europe. Ultimately it was a human rights mission—against the state aggressor and for the downtrodden people. Unfortunately, the politics of the Kurdish resistance movement embraced the worst of both nationalism and authoritarian communism, as exemplified by an interaction we had with two young militants in Istanbul.

"Are you Marxists?" they asked. "No," we said, "Our political outlook comes from the Anarchist tradition." "We kill people like you," they answered, "but you're Irish, and we like the Irish."

I returned to Ireland from Berlin and organized a small delegation comprised of some activists and journalists. Chaperoned by a PKK cover group, we set off for the southeast part of Turkey, the Kurdish region, on the eve of the tenth anniversary of the armed uprising.

Our objective was to penetrate the militarized zone of southeast Turkey in order to locate and document an alleged concentration camp set up by the Turks to intern some 20,000 Kurdish civilians. Failing that, we were to report on the scorched-earth campaign being perpetrated in the region and collect eyewitness reports from the Kurdish Refugee Camps located in the UN-sponsored Kurdish Safe Haven in northern Iraq. The obstacle to overcome in this task would be the Turkish Military and Intelligence Services which, would go to any lengths to prevent the presence of foreigners in the region. Previous delegations had been harassed and intimidated from start to finish and had their film and documentation confiscated. Most were detained, and some were imprisoned. One German reporter was murdered by suspected Turkish agents in northern Iraq.

The Ancient City of Diyarbakir

Landing in the Diyarbakir airport is a wake-up call—the runway is flanked by long lines of military aircraft: F-16 jets, CF-104 Starfighters, US Army Black Hawk helicopters, and field artillery. On debarking, most of the passengers from our flight group themselves in military formation before the waiting army officers. This airfield, headquarters of the Turkish Air Forces, is host to the notorious Second Tactical Air Force Command—responsible for three airbases in the east of Turkey, and with an infamous record of indiscriminate bombing of Kurdish villages and Refugee Camps.

So we have arrived in the warzone.

Here we are met by Burhan, a representative from the Kurdish organization, who will be our guide. An urbane man, well traveled, and fluent in English, French, Turkish, Kurdish, and probably a few other languages, he comes across as a strange but fascinating clandestine figure. He is a man who has lived many lives, and his current role as our guide seems a little below his status as an international Kurdish Gadfly. And it is a potentially suicidal mission for him—he's risking his life to take a bunch of activists and journalists into the warzone. Is the situation really so desperate for the Kurds?

Attired in a journalistic flak jacket, Burhan strikes a very shady pose and is noticeably nervous. This comes as no surprise as, surrounded by the military, he is as conspicuous here as a hare in a field of coursing dogs. Nevertheless, he hustles us out from under the suspicious gaze of the airport security officials. According to our story, we are an Art and Historical Society inspecting Mesopotamian ruins and this historically rich region, and he is our official guide. Southeast Anatolia is, after all, one of the cradles of civilization.

Situated on the banks of Tigris (Dicle) river, Diyarbakir carries a medieval air, with its old walls encircling the city. Ramparts symbolize an eternal state of siege. The route to our hotel is dotted with military checkpoints; the streets are filled with armored personnel carriers, tanks, and jeeps. Although officially designated an *emergency situation*, this is really a warzone, with the Turkish Military—patrolling the streets with guns pointed at the citizens—as an occupation force.

The city has the hysterical atmosphere of any third world metropolis: horribly overcrowded, people hawking goods on every sidewalk, and lots of loitering unemployed youth. The population has exploded in the last five years—from 200,000 to over a million—as the dispossessed Kurds flock in from the depopulated countryside—a result of Turkey's scorched earth policies.

Tea shops occupy every corner; multitudes of men sit around on low chairs playing board games. Women are inconspicuous although not many are cloaked in *burkas*. The place appears to be swarming with secret agents. They immediately begin following us around the bustling streets—we are conspicuous, being the only Europeans in the city. Our lodging, the Diyar Buybuk, is a fine hotel with the atmosphere of a Kurdish-style Casablanca. Some none-too-discreet secret agents loiter in the lobby pretending to read newspapers, just like they do in spy movies. We assume our Art and Historical Tour roles; we all transform into bit-actors playing our parts. We discuss things from our dog-eared *Rough Guide to Turkey,* while each trying to keep a straight face. "You know, the Hasan Pasha Ham Mosque we passed is a *caravensari* in the typical Ottoman style of the 17th century."

In the hotel we hook up with a larger group of British human rights activists, and now we are a dozen in total, including Burhan the guide. Our first visit in Diyarbikar is to the local Human Rights Office, a place clearly under siege. There we interview a Kurdish shepherd who had been tortured, buried, and left for dead by the police. The man begins to tell his story, translated by Burhan, his testimony is typical of the dozens we would collect during our brief visit:

We were taken to the Hacilar barracks and were kept for four days without food or water or sleep. We were subjected to the most brutal torture: electric and water torture; being hung from the ceiling, beaten. In the same place there were many other prisoners from the villages near Cudi Mountain and Silopi. Most of them were elderly people. The screams were frightening. The police were demanding to know from them where the PKK weapons and ammunition were hidden.... After four days of continuous torture they pushed us in an APC and took us away. They beat us with their rifle butts. They started cutting our ears while calling out the names of killed Turkish soldiers...After about an hour we arrived at a deserted place from where a dreadful smell emerged. We were pulled out. Our hands and feet tied with chains were freed...They pushed us into a grave-like pit which they had dug. They pushed us in one by one and began shooting. They fired hundreds of bullets. The bul-

lets were falling around me. That is why lots of soil fell on me. Then the guns became silent. The soldiers left... I waited for a while in the pit and then I got out, no matter what happened. I struggled for about an hour to get out. As I raised my head I saw a light. I lay down in the pit pretending I was dead. I waited but then I got out. The lights which I had seen were from the Kreiyares barracks about 300 meters away on a hill... I checked the others but they were dead. The corpses were dismembered, the blood had turned the soil into mud...I ran and the blood was pouring from my ear and other parts of my body. I ran on and on and by dawn I met a shepherd. When he saw me he was speechless...

A Kurdish Village Burnt to the Ground

Early the next morning, we leave Diyarbakir and head for the mountains. With a few maneuvers we lose the secret agents trailing us in crap cars. We are feeling daring and courageous as we pass through the first handful of roadblocks. We are still near enough to Diyarbakir and its myriad archaeological ruins to pass as the Art and Historical group. The soldiers we encounter first are young and probably conscripted; they accept the proffered bribe, a packet of cigarettes. The police roadblocks take a bit more persuasion, but Burhan has a British passport and we appear such an unlikely bunch that we get through. While the British human rights people are all older and respectably presented, we (the five Irish) are younger and look more like a grunge-rock band on tour. There are roadblocks every 15 km or so; the security forces at each are understandably confused by our strange group. We have negotiated a good half-dozen stops before we even get close to our first port of call, a Kurdish village that has been reportedly attacked by the Turkish military.

Burhan orders the driver to make a turn off the highway onto a back road. We trundle along the dirt road for a good while before we finally drive into a small, old village called Gunduz, population several hundred. Tractor-trailers full of the villager's possessions are heading out of the village towards the main road. Most of the old stone houses have been hurriedly evacuated. We speak to some of the remaining inhabitants and learn that the army has given them 24 hours to leave or face the prospect of being killed. The reason, they say, is that they have refused to become government paramilitaries, to take up arms in the conflict against the PKK. A villager gives us this account:

The Turkish army came three months ago and asked us to become village guards. They said we were supporting the guerrillas. But a guerrilla never even passed by our village! When we refused to become village guards, they smashed our furniture...They burnt this house weeks ago to teach us a lesson.

Most families are heading towards the sprawling shantytowns on the outskirts of Diyarbakir, where the population has tripled in the last year. But not everybody is leaving.

"*We would rather be shot than leave our village,*" says one couple with eight children who are staying put. Their family history goes back centuries on this land. We promise we will return the next day to maintain an international presence and to be witnesses to any attempt to evacuate the remaining families.

We can't get through the next day, as the whole area has been sealed off by the military. Witnesses report that some villagers who refused to leave have been killed by state forces. The rest have fled, the village has been burnt to the ground, and the water well has been poisoned and mines buried to dissuade anybody from returning. Gunduz has become the newest addition to a growing list of two thousand villages that have been cleared out and burnt down in southeast Turkey.

Detained in Hakkari

The next day we go in search of a route to the reported concentration camp near Hakkari. We pass through the Kurdish town of Sirnak, which has been fairly well destroyed by Turkish artillery—buildings are scarred with gaping holes through concrete gable ends. So too the towns of Hakkari and Cizre show evidence of mortar fire and aerial bombardment. Cizre, in particular, has clearly been the scene of intense street fighting; buildings display bullet marks, rocket holes and signs of attack by heavy artillery. With the loss of civilian authority, the area is policed by the military as well as the paramilitary *Gendarme.* Their role is officially one of law enforcement, but in reality they function as a counter-insurgency force.

The secret prison camp, holding some 20,000 inmates, is located 12 miles outside Hakkari. Its presence has been well documented by human rights groups, but no media or international observers have ever gotten near it. Sure enough, the road is obstructed by a sizeable *Gendarme* roadblock. A tall officer steps forward and speaks to us in English with a German accent. "Ve know exactly who you are, and ve have had enough. Come vith us."

He orders all twelve of us out of the minivan, and we wait on the side of the road surrounded by police with guns as they search the van. A couple of hours pass and we are still waiting on this isolated road deep in the mountains. More time goes by and we are worried now because it is getting dark. Darkness and the military don't go well together. They have a plan for us.

"You are returning to Hakkari with us," the officer informs us. "Oh, no," we say, "We are an Art and Historical Tour Group and we would like to continue back to our hotel in Diyarbakir... "No, it is too dangerous. We must escort you to the *Gendarme* barracks in Hakkari, for your own safety," says the officer, "This is terrorist country." We file back into the van and a guard climbs in too, holding an Uzi—for your own safety—he says, but then he points it at us.

We set off in a military convoy as the sun sets. Armored tanks and APCs ahead and behind us are all driving along the valley road in pitch darkness without headlights, and we are the only vehicle with lights on. We are rumbling slowly through guerrilla territory in the dead of night, with steep enclaves overlooking us as we snake along the bottom of the deep valley. We are a sitting duck for any guerrilla who might be up in the hills with a rocket propelled grenade.

The headlines would make splendid propaganda for the Turkish government: "PKK massacre twelve International Human Rights Observers!"

We wind through the dark mountains slowly, the silence permeated only by the rumble of the tank engines. We curse the dastardly *Gendarme* for their fiendish little game. Fortunately, the PKK are quiet that night, and we trundle into the small town of Hakkari with some relief. The convoy pulls into a little provincial *Gendarme* barracks. High concrete walls enclose us. The courtyard is filled with military vehicles: Hummers, APCs, and a small tank.

"We are a Historical Tour Group," we complain. "Are we formally under arrest, officer?" This is all the resistance we have, the invisible clothes of human rights. With their rifles the guards gruffly indicate the direction, as they are in no mood for human rights games. We are led past the entrance and around a dark corner to the back of the building. We are prodded with guns to indicate that we should descend a staircase into the basement. A heavily fortified door leads into what, for all intents and purposes, appears to be a dungeon—or, in our frightened minds, a torture chamber. We create a big ruckus and refuse to enter and try to force our way back up the stairs. The guards relinquish. Maybe it is all a joke on their part, to terrify us. Anyhow, their little game works—our nerves are shattered.

We return and enter the front door of the barracks. Even the front desk of the place smells of blood and urine. You couldn't invent a better location for a good torture scene—it's dark, dank, and filled with armed men who emanate brutality. We are briefly interrogated and all our details written down, then the officer informs us that we are to be held overnight "for our own safety" in a local hotel. We are afforded the ubiquitous armored car convoy for the trip to the hotel. It is late at night; the streets are empty and the town is asleep.

Past midnight and the lobby of the Hakkari equivalent of the Holiday Inn is filled with heavily armed military and Special Police. We are all exhausted, and confused as to why they have brought us here instead of detaining us at the jail. Maybe they are still uncertain as to who we are. We file upstairs to our allotted rooms. While the lobby is heavily guarded, they allow us to wander freely in and out of our rooms. We look out the window and see a tank stationed in the hotel car park, with its turret pointing at us. We couldn't have made this up. Someone picks up the phone and discovers that the international operator can be accessed! So we resolve to call Ireland and alert our emergency response network to cover our backs. But then the problem emerges: how will we alert our people without alerting the Turkish cops who will, of course, be monitoring the call—why else would they allow us the liberty of a phone? It's an obvious trick, we decide. How can we say what we want without revealing who we are, without implicating ourselves?

In a moment of inspiration, we remember that our contact man in Dublin is a fluent Irish speaker. So we can communicate in Irish and the Turks will never know what we are talking about! They may have an English translator listening in on our line, but an Irish speaker? Never. The only problem is that the five Irish here know all of ten words of Gaelic between us. Nevertheless, we write out a message as best we can to be read over the phone in Irish—"We are in a hotel in Hakkari, and are surrounded by men with guns. If we don't contact you tomorrow morning, it means we are fucked, and call in the support network."

We all gather around. I make the call. Our man in Dublin answers the phone groggily, awakened from his sleep. "Howya, pal," I say, "it's myself, ringing from Turkey." I am trying to impress upon him the urgency of the situation by the tone of my voice. Our man doesn't get it immediately, and starts on a cheerful line of questioning. "How's it going, man?! How is Turkey? Are yez getting places you wanted?!" But before he says something that will implicate us as human rights workers, I interrupt him. "Listen, pal, here is a lad with a message for you—listen carefully, ok?"

So another member of our group takes the phone and reads out the message somewhat nervously. But we have made a couple of mistakes in the translation—we've confused the word for "gun" with the word for "dress." And, at a loss for the Irish translation of "*support network*" we've substituted the word for "supporters" which can also be colloquially understood as "fans." So what was read to our somnambulant Man in Dublin translated to something along these lines: "We are in a hotel in Hakkari. We are surrounded by men in dresses. There could be trouble. If we don't ring you tomorrow morning, call our fans." I take back the phone. "Did you get all that, pal?" "Has your lad there had a few drinks?!" Our Man in Dublin chortles. "Very funny lad, that. Men in dresses, ha-ah! Yous sound like you're having a ball there..."

But despite ourselves, it doesn't matter. The next morning the guards and tanks and armoured vehicles have taken off, and the officer comes to us and tells us to return to Diyarbakir and not to return to the emergency zone. We're off the hook.

Into the Kurdish Safe Haven

Back at the Diyarbakir Hotel, we decide to drop the search for the concentration camp, and the decision is made to get to the refugee camps in northern Iraq instead. There are reports of Turkish air strikes on the civilian camps, and we, like ambulance-chasing lawyers, feel compelled to follow the action.

We take the international highway from Diyarbakir to the Iraqi border, passing the scenic Lake Van, talking and bribing our way through countless military checkpoints. A huge line of oil tanker trucks congest the border crossing, openly violating the UN sanctions on Iraqi oil.

"Welcome to Free Kurdistan," says the sign as we cross the Turkish border and enter the Kurdish safe haven in northern Iraq. This is a zone set up by the US, the Brits, and the French after the Gulf War to protect the Kurds from Saddam's troops. There is an element of autonomy here but the zone falls under the jurisdiction of two opposing Kurdish factions. Artillery and missiles can be heard in the hills behind us, as KDP (Kurdistan Democratic Party) and PUK (Patriotic Union of Kurdistan) cadres lob stuff at each other.

We cross the border and enter Zakhu, the main Kurdish town in the region, which is under the control of the KDP. We are escorted to a KDP military bunker. By now we have dropped the Art and Historical Tour guise and feel we can safely say we are a human rights delegation. This is OK with the KDP, who have suffered at the hands of the Iraqis and control their own refugee camps. But they are at war with the other Kurdish factions—the PUK and the PKK—so they don't want us to fall under the orbit of anyone but them.

We are awarded a "guide," a *pershmerga* guerrilla carrying an AK-47, to accompany us during our stay. He's not hostile, but he annoys Burhan, who hates the KDP. "They work for the Americans," he says bitterly. Before long, we give our *pershmerga* the slip and head to the hills, towards the PKK-controlled area.

First, though, we pass through PUK territory. This is marked by a roadblock guarded by a bunch of young men and women guerrillas, who looked more out of the Spanish Civil War. They are cooking around an open fire and wearing irregular military gear and red and black neckerchiefs and cradling old machine guns. They greet us cordially and allow us passage into the PKK territory. At this time, there is a truce between the PKK and PUK while they both fight the pro-American KDP—the irony of course being that all three groups arose in the 1970s from the same Marxist-Leninist ideological background. But ideology no longer plays a part, explains Burhan, and now the PUK and KDP are just tribal. "Tribal," he spits. "The PKK are the only ideologues," he says proudly.

A Refugee Camp under Siege

We climb into the sparse mountains, higher and higher, and many hours later arrive at an enormous UN-run refugee camp. Here 16,000 people live in tents, spread across a rocky valley without electricity or running water. The inhabitants appear to be predominantly kids and older folks. Many families are sheltered in makeshift huts constructed from branches and leaves. The only sign of the UN is their name written on the side of the plastic toilet walls. They deliver monthly supplies of food and some medicine, but the camp is largely autonomous, run by the refugees themselves. Their biggest worry is the approaching winter, when the temperature will drop dramatically and the mountains will be covered in snow.

We are welcomed like kings—a carpet is laid out, tea poured, and lamb kebabs served. The people are relieved that outsiders have made the effort to come visit them, and they line up to tell their stories. Ali Aslara, an elderly man who has fled from his village Horsik, Sirnak, tells a typical refugee story:

The soldiers came to our village at dawn. People were still sleeping when the bombardment started. Everyone was running in different directions. I ran back and I looked for members of my family but I couldn't find them. Five members of my family are missing. Since the village was bombarded in March I have had no news of them. No guerrillas ever came to our village, we were treated like that because we were Kurds. We're Kurds. The guerrillas are fighting for us and we have sympathy, and we refuse to be village guards for the military.

Later they show us evidence of the aerial bombardment that has occurred a few days previous. Eight people have been killed as the result of an intrusion by the Turkish Air Force into the UN-sponsored No-Fly Zone over northern Iraq. Two weeks earlier, according to refugees, two Cobra helicopters had launched a machine gun and rocket attack on the camp, leaving several dead and many more injured.

"There's nowhere left to run," a centenarian refugee woman tells us. "The Turks want to destroy us everywhere we go."

A PKK Guerrilla Camp

We leave the refugee camp shortly after dawn, heading towards the guerrilla camps. A dozen people load into a pickup truck. Our guide Barhan looks a lot happier cradling a well-worn AK-47 than persisting in the guise of the disgruntled translator for an irritating bunch of foreigners on an Art and Historical Tour of southeast Turkey. Nevertheless, that outlandish cover has gotten us here, further into the war zone than any other recent delegation. And now we have crossed the frontier into Iraq, negotiated our way through countless roadblocks and finally arrived in the PKK-controlled mountains.

Higher and higher into the bleak, sun-burnt mountains we go, deeper and deeper into the unmapped environs of guerrilla country. Four men emerge from a bush at the end of the track and greet us warmly. Distinguished-looking men who could have just stepped out of a University lecture hall. These guerillas are our guides for the three-hour trek along mountain paths. In single file, beneath the scorching 100-degree sun, we begin the grueling hike.

The sun beats down unrelentingly, we talk amiably to the guerrillas as we march—about the struggle, about the hardships and the sacrifices, ultimately about their own deaths. An image would remain with me later—the purpose and grace of the guerrillas making their way along the rough tracks, their tracks, the first liberated territory of free Kurdistan. It is an historical image: the guerrilla, the liberator, the vanguard of the new world struggling to be born. The clandestine history-maker, inevitably the martyr, sacrifices everything—a violent death assumed—but is fully assured of the righteousness of the struggle.

Down in the valley, we come upon some shepherds tending their flocks. Like the numerous people dotted throughout this area, the sheep are hidden from our eyes. But they are here somewhere, probably scores of them, they too accustomed to living clandestinely. In contrast to the urban look of our guides, these guerrilla shepherds are rough in appearance with dark, rugged faces etched deeply, like the mountains, by the hardship of outdoor life. We meet our first woman combatant here, and our group assaults her with a thousand photo shots; she looks shy and flees. By mid-afternoon we approach a makeshift guerrilla hospital. I had pictured it as something resembling MASH—it turns out to be a hole in the mountain, just a dark and dusty cave. That's the men's section; the women's is a large clump of bushes below.

The mood is cheerful among the twenty or so men convalescing outside the cave. The guerrilla doctor talks, unsurprisingly, of medical supply shortages. Down the cliff, a bunch of teenage girls sit among the bushes. They are in varied states of damage—mostly from bullet wounds. These combatants had held their surrounded position for three days without food. They are silent and sullen; we get only a mute response to our awkward questions. They are shy and in pain, our intrusion is unwanted.

An hour's hike later (and with some of the older members of our group now being virtually carried up the mountains because of exhaustion) we finally arrive at the main camp. Looking down the long, scrub-covered floor of the valley, one sees nothing; and to look over the expanse one would hardly notice any sign of activity. But here and stretching for a few miles up the valley, some six thousand PKK soldiers reside. We descend the hill and gratefully collapse out of the sun, under a hedge roof. Some smiling guerrillas bring us glasses of tea. Even here the Kurdish tea etiquette is upheld—a thimble glass is served on a saucer with a silver spoon.

Seated upon a beautiful old woven carpet, we are served a lavish lunch. They have slaughtered a sheep in our honor. Polite introductions are made all around, to a variety of guerrillas—the cook, the provisions man, and a couple of very young combatants with a spattering of English—all attired in PKK military fatigues and carrying sub-machine guns slung around their shoulders. We are the first foreigners to enter this new camp, and for the guerrillas it is a victory that we have even gotten here at all.

After lunch, we are taken on a tour of the clandestine camp. First call is the munitions store, where a few men mend and clean the armaments. AK-47s are the mainstay of the guerrillas, but here we see bigger machine guns and a couple of sniper rifles. SAM-7s and mortars litter the floor of the cave dug out from the side of the mountain.

Further along the mountain path, dug into the boulders, is a room-sized garment factory. Here, half a dozen young guerrilla women make the soldiers' combat gear on sewing machines hooked up to a small generator. Like any factory in the world, it is hot and noisy and unpleasant. I ask the workers how they feel about joining the PKK, only to be stuck here in a sweatshop all day.

"Each of us has her own role in the struggle," responds one.

They explain how the army attacks their position regularly. A helicopter leaps over the mountain and there is little chance to react. Casualties are taken and the camp location has to be changed. Up and down the mountains endlessly, year after year, go the clandestine and nomadic combatants.

We are invited to participate in target practice. The target is a large boulder across the valley. One member of our group, Niamh, greatly impresses the assembled guerrillas with her steady hand. Maybe it is because she looks sexy handling the AK or maybe she really is a sharpshooter. I had assumed that Niamh, an ambitious reporter from a small Irish newspaper, had come with us hoping to make a killing from an exotic trip, but maybe I had underestimated her. Perhaps there is more to her than meets the eye. Seamus is undoubtedly our top marksman, effortlessly hitting the boulder with a volley of shots. I miss not only the boulder but also the mountain itself, sending a bullet off into the next valley and hopefully not hitting some wandering sheep. Noel the photographer snaps away merrily, promising to present us all with portraits afterwards to give to our grandchildren (these photos will, of course, cause us a lot of grief later in the trip). The sun shines, the mood is light, and we laugh warmly with the Kurds, sharing a moments reprieve in a warzone amongst the walking dead.

Nighttime in the Guerrilla Camp

As dusk approaches, we hear a military exercise taking place below us on the valley floor. We stumble down the hillside and come upon a small clearing totally shaded by trees where about a hundred guerrillas, both men and women, stand in formation. All over the valley, battalions will be lining up for a kind of roll-call before evening dinner. When they breakup, I find myself surrounded by smiling faces asking me in broken English what I think of the camp and the PKK. Some look like students, some like farmers; most remind me of my friends in Berlin.

Darkness falls, and the valley is calm and meditative. The full moon casts a soft blue haze over the mountains. The murmur of voices floats across the cool night air. There are no lights and no fires. Guerrillas approach us shyly and give us melon to eat. They ask us questions through the translator about the situation in Ireland. Like the radicals we had met in Istanbul, they're big fans of the IRA. Seamus has mustered his basic French to explain to a group of quite clearly mesmerized young guerrillas the essential details of the last 800 years of struggle in Ireland. I don't think its lost on him that half these young men will be dead or captured within a few months of active service, and he talks to them with an appropriate respect. The guerrillas are all set for a long, deep discussion into the night but we are all exhausted and must sleep. The delegation retires under a large bush, sleeping in a line on the ground covered by a white sheet.

But the white sheet is a problem. If the camp is attacked during the night, the white sheet will be the most obvious target. We are briefed on the procedures for attack. If it is aircraft, follow the guide to the nearest cave or dugout. Take absolutely nothing and keep low. If it's a Cobra helicopter, don't move; its heat-seeking missiles will target anything that moves. But if it's a Cobra we won't have a chance to move anyhow—its stealth and incredible speed will render all defenses useless.

The chances of an attack are high; they've been attacked several times in the last few days. With this sobering fact in mind we fall asleep, while being eaten alive by mosquitoes. The poets are mistaken—the guerrilla's life is not romantic.

Breakfast with Dizre

A women's battalion has been marching all night to reach here. They think they're heading for active service, and come heavily laden with arms and supplies. They are completely pissed off to hear that they've come all this way to speak to a bunch of international observers. We had made a special request to speak to them, not realizing the trouble we were causing. At dawn, we clamber up a hill and join them at their camp. Thirty young women are lining up for a roll-call. We shake hands with each of them, timid smiles and wide-eyed interest all around.

The guerrillas fall out, and six join us for the interview. We sit among the rocks at the edge of a deep crevice, and the dawn sun creeps over the next sparse mountain. They serve us the ubiquitous tea (somebody had packed these glasses and saucers and silver spoons along side their SAM-7s and missiles). Planes pass high overhead, out of sight, and the guerrillas clutch their AKs.

Commander Dizre speaks eloquently and with conviction. She is still a teenager and yet has the gravity and wisdom of someone many years older. But then again, she has been fighting with the PKK for four long years. The average lifespan for a guerrilla on active service is 6 months—Dizre has lived many lives. Our translator, Burhan, becomes unusually taciturn. He had served under Dizre in another unit some time ago, and is quite in awe of her. He might even come across as a little lovestruck.

The interview that follows takes on a pattern. We ask Dizre questions that probe her personal life and her experience as a woman with the guerrillas, but her answers pass over these aspects and concentrate on the PKK and their struggle, strategy and tactics.

"My family were patriots and my whole life I was brought up as a patriot... My past life is over, let's talk about the campaign."

And on the women's struggle?

"Because this society is backwards, so too is the position of women. Women find inspiration through the Party; liberation for women will be achieved through national liberation."

As she talks about the struggle, Dizre becomes wholly animated and speaks at length about the current situation. She praises scientific socialism and quotes Mao, she mentions Vietnam and Cuba as influences; she insists that despite the New World Order, a socialist Kurdistan could be managed alone in the world if necessary.

17-year-old Nalin wears a metal Lenin badge, the kind you see being sold where the Berlin Wall used to stand, along with other Soviet bric-a-brac. She carries a particularly large machine gun. We ask her to describe the daily life of a guerrilla.

In winter, she says, they wake at 5 and then drill and exercise until breakfast. From 8–12 they undergo political training, and from 2–6, military training. Dinner is from 6–7 and then there is an open forum for discussion. Bedtime is 10. That's during the winter, when the climate—cold and snowy—puts a brake on most active service. The summer is different. They have no routine, for they go where they are called; they engage in combat or they act as backup for other units. Does she find the guerrilla life difficult, we ask "No, I don't find any of it hard."

I ask Dizre about *Apo*, Abdullah Ocalan, General Secretary of the PKK. "Apo" means Uncle, echoing "Uncle" Ho Chi Minh. He has been compared to Fidel Castro and to the Shining Paths' Chairman Gonzalo. He stands high as the undisputed

Leader of the Party, and has acquired a cult following among the Kurds. Dizre's eyes light up, a warm smile crossing her face. The assembled guerrillas let out a collective laugh. The translator curses me quietly, "We'll be here all day with the answer!"

Audience with the Regional Rebel Commander

That afternoon we receive a very special visitor. All the guerrillas around us become giddy and the sense of excitement is palpable. Saladin is the Commanding Officer for the region and a member of the Central Committee of the PKK. An almost religious hush descends on the assembled as Saladin and his entourage descend the mountain track. He is a regal-looking figure, around 40 years of age, with dark, handsome features and an athletic physique. He has about him an air of grace, something quite princely, a natural dignity and poise. Despite the rough fatigues, his dress is also quite stately—perhaps it's the richly woven cummerbund that adds the touch of luxury.

An engaging smile lightens his charismatic face as he offers us each his hand. We are all humbled before him and almost bow in return. There is a touch of magic in the air. A genuine Kurdish Prince!

He squats comfortably, cross-legged on the rug, and begins to speak softly and firmly. Our translator has become uncharacteristically nervous, and blushes as he trips over his words.

Your visit is very significant as it falls on the tenth anniversary of the beginning of this war. It is important the things you report from your visit here, for this stage of the war is very harsh; things have escalated somewhat…Ten years ago the Kurds were oppressed by the imperialist state and the path of resistance chosen was armed struggle. Armed struggle, the only resort left: by the people, with the people.

The reason was because the Turkish state was attempting to destroy the Kurdish people. It was our duty to respond. Armed struggle was a step forward for the liberation of the Kurdish people but it hasn't stopped the Turks. For ten years they have burnt our villages and murdered and tortured our people. Only those villages that become village guards remain untouched. The state is using all means necessary to crush us. Their tactic is to destroy everything, absolutely everything. Anything living, anything worth destroying. We have lost so much, so many people.

And therefore we have responded with an escalation of the rebellion. Our continued rebellion will lead to an end in Turkish atrocities. Our people sacrificed so much but their sacrifice has developed the war.

And so the princely Saladin continues his monologue, constantly referring back to the sacrifice of the people and the PKK's historical role in resisting the Turkish state. He recites the words like a familiar poem, but a poem told with controlled passion and assured righteousness.

...But the PKK protects the people, both materially and spiritually. We have proven we are capable of winning the war. We have endured ten years of sacrifice, but now the people have an army they can depend on and who can fight for them. Our people are no longer isolated; they now know how to fight for freedom. We have established an organization that guarantees democratic rights and freedoms. We believe in ourselves. We have lost much. But now we are organizing ourselves into a modern army to protect its people."

Commander Saladin is a man who inspires trust and respect. A look at the attentive cadres listening in the background proves that his presence is awe-inspiring, his words sublime. But what he is suggesting sounds outlandish—to build a "modern army," a standing army, to confront the Turks militarily straight on, across a battlefield? The Turkish army counts on 600,000 troops, a formidable arsenal, and strong support from the US, Germany, Britain, and France. The PKK remains a raggle-taggle guerrilla band of lightly-armed insolents who are also fighting in their own backyard against the Kurdish *peshmerga* of the pro-American KDP. As a guerrilla force they are under pressure and cornered. The only way out is political, not by creating a standing army. This sounds like a suicidal strategy to pursue.

Suddenly the illusion of Saladin crumbles...Maybe he is just some pumped-up warlord after all.

Return to Zakhu.

A man is busy unloading dozens of RPG rockets from his Land Cruiser onto the rocky roadside as we descend from the mountains. He gives us a mischievous grin as we walk by. It's a pleasant sunny afternoon, the mood is relaxed; there's a lone man unloading a massive arsenal of destruction onto the side of a deserted mountain and this does not seem out of the ordinary. We've come a long way.

Back at the refugee camp, we are greeted warmly, fed and sent on our way with a performance of traditional Kurdish dancing. Is there no end to these people's hospitality? "Tell the world!" is all they ask in return. I fear we will let them down.

We bounce down the rugged mountain road—the last of the liberated territories—returning to Zakhu, the run-down wild-west town controlled by the KDP. On the outskirts of Zakhu, marked by rough shanties and crumbling burnt concrete houses, we're joined by an unexpected guest. The KDP *pesh-merga* "guide" clambers aboard our minivan. He has been wait-

ing here since we departed 4 or 5 days ago. He is not so friendly this time, and orders us to the bunker military headquarters of the KDP. There's only one person in the sandbagged office—a smart dressed, short-haired American. He's remarkably friendly, asking us jovially what we think of the place and who *exactly* we are and where we have just come from. His manner annoys me in the same way Jehovah's Witnesses on the doorstep do.

"And what are *you* doing here?" we ask him. "I work for an international agency," he says, then changes his mind. "A religious organization. Are any of you Catholics?" Catholics? This is a new line of interrogation. But it becomes clear with the arrival of two British army personnel. They introduce themselves as part of the UN coalition overseeing the Kurdish Safe Haven.

"Rather hot, isn't it, what? Not like home, eh?" says the first. "I used to live in Dublin, you know!" says the second. "Any of you chaps from Belfast?"

Having ascertained that none of us are IRA, and that we are indeed in all probability a harmless human rights delegation, they relax a bit and chat about their role here. They acknowledge that they know about the Turks' bombings of the UN Refugee Camp. But, they ask, what could be done? Turkey is a key member of the coalition overseeing the area and monitoring the

No-Fly Zone. However, they add in hushed tones ("and this is of course, you understand, off the record..."), Britain is going to *have a word* with them about it.

Northern Iraq—the Kurdish Safe Haven—has been for a short time, a UN flagship endeavor; Operation Provide Comfort is to guarantee the Kurds freedom from the molestation of Saddam and his formidable Republican Guard. The No-Fly Zone is enforced by Britain, France, the US, and Turkey.

However, these four countries are members of the NATO military alliance and so the UN operation assumes significance in terms of NATO's strategic ambitions. Turkey is a NATO lynchpin in the Middle East, a bulwark against fundamentalist and Arab power. Turkey has NATO's second-largest army and is supplied by every European arms-manufacturing nation, but mainly by the US and Germany. Former British Foreign Secretary Douglas Hurd, answering a question about Turkey's human rights record and arms supplies from Britain, once declared, "What Turkey does with its weapons is Turkey's own business."

Under the cover of its peacekeeping role in patrolling the No-Fly Zone, the Turkish Air Force launches attacks indiscriminately against guerrillas and Kurdish refugee camps. The Turks are given a free hand in carrying out these attacks while their NATO allies turn a blind eye. Meanwhile, the Ankara regime insists that the conflict is strictly an internal one.

We come to monitor human rights abuses perpetrated by Turkey on the Kurdish minority and now find ourselves witnesses to an international conspiracy. This has been a journey into the heart of darkness created, overseen, and perpetuated by the New World Order.

Suddenly we are keen to get out of the Kurdish Safe Haven and into Turkey. Turkey seems a Safe Haven when you've got the KDP, British military intelligence and possibly the CIA on your back (or worse—the Jehovah's Witnesses!). It's six o'clock and the sun begins to set as we're marching across the long, dusty bridge back to Turkey. Here we come, loaded down with film and video and notes of testimonies and documentation and things very damaging to the Turkish state. Here we come, fresh from the refugee camps, the guerrilla camps and the Kurdish Safe Haven diplomatic and security circus—experienced, weary and unprepared.

Another Turkish Police Station.

"They've arrived!" the Turkish border guard announces into his radio. All our passports are taken and the interrogation begins. My stomach takes this most inappropriate moment to declare war on me. The untreated water we've been drinking for the past week is finally catching up with me. I feel like fainting and all my insides are poised to splurge out.

There is no situation on earth that is not made worse by the arrival of a police man on the scene. And here he is now, poking his hand about in my bag. He flicks through my grubby, scribble-filled notebook, scrutinizing it page by page: he calls over our translator. Suddenly it occurs to me that we might be in very serious trouble.

Burhan returns and worry is written all over his face. "He's spotted references to the PKK and Commander Dizre. They're sending for a translator. We're OK, keep calm." Everybody panics about the notes in hidden places, secret pockets, stuffed down the front of their trousers, in their shoes, everywhere. A competent search would net everything.

Back at the local police station they begin the search. I make a bolt for the toilet—firstly to allow my tortured insides to flow out violently, and secondly to shred some offending notes. With much anguish I tear them up, page by page—all the testimonies, quotes, analyses, feelings and emotions shredded, and poured down a little hole in a police-station bathroom.

Back in the lobby, the pile of confiscated material on the table grows. Notebooks full of notes, hours and hours of written interviews and testimonies necessary for the newspaper articles, ten hours of High 8 video recording for a proposed movie, a hundred rolls of camera film. At risk are the identities of those who talked to us, those who sheltered and fed us—all of them on film, all the names and places and dates recorded in print. At risk are those in the human rights Offices, in the refugee camps, in the newspaper offices, and any others who made "unpatriotic" statements or criticized the government. At risk are all our contacts comrades in Istanbul and Diyarbakir, and even those in Dublin, Berlin and London.

The horror continues. There are even, in that pile on the table, photographs of us handling weapons, as we were playing around in the guerrilla camp. If anyone cares to present us as dangerous subversives, as international PKK cadre, it's all there on film. If the Turks need an excuse to detain us, to incarcerate us, or to sentence us, it's *all* here. Our foolishness knows no bounds.

The Special Police arrived—tough, hardened cops in casual clothes with state-of-the-art pistols by their sides. Bastards with tight faces and heavy moustaches, they are grim and menacing, torturers smelling of death-squads. They immediately get heavy and start manhandling us, pulling at the women's bras in their search for hidden material. One of the British women is taken aside and strip-searched. "Traitor!" they accused our translator, Burhan, as they slapped him around the place.

It's past midnight, we've spent hours and hours in this hell-hole. This place of misery that is haunted by endless anguish—the pain and suffering of the Kurds who have been tortured. Those who have been beaten, burned and electrocuted, hung by their arms until their back muscles rip and had their ears severed. We've heard all the testimonies, the blank descriptions from those that survived the sadistic beatings, their harrowed eyes saying a thousand tortured words. This police barracks in Silopi is a place of unmentionable brutality and suffering.

But something we've said, or that someone has said, has impressed on the military officials the idea that we are not to be incarcerated or further mistreated. We are dispatched to a shabby hotel, and armed guards are posted outside our rooms. In a stroke of luck, one of the British women manages to get out of the hotel to a phone, and rings contacts in Ireland and England. This time there is no messing about. Our emergency network kicks into action. Suddenly a variety of friends, politicians and human rights representatives are calling all the relevant authorities in Turkey to denounce the "kidnapping" of our group. We make the front page of the national newspapers the next day, and the news on television. It's all too much pressure for the Turkish officials and they order our release. We are driven to the airport and flown to Istanbul—minus all our confiscated film, notebooks and tapes. We are relieved, but devastated. What a fucking disaster.

Upon our return, the Irish delegation acts with the appropriate tactical urgency—we wrote articles, we make presentations in public or before governmental committees, we speak to the press and television, and we consolidate our solidarity group. We do the usual solidarity things, but it feels like we are pissing in the wind as the Turkish military destroys the armed resistance and hammers the civilian population.

A Disaster Foretold

The Kurdish Workers' Party was a politico-military organization that emerged in the 1980s in response to a murderous Turkish dictatorship intent on wiping out any Kurdish nationalism in its midst. They grew in the 1990s to being the largest Kurdish revolutionary movement, counting on tens of thousands of militants and a support base of hundreds of thousands with an expansive network throughout Europe. The authoritarian, vanguardist guerrilla movement that emerged, however, developed a strategy of engagement that achieved little beyond inadvertently getting a lot of people killed.

The just cause and righteous struggle of the Kurdish revolutionary movement was squandered by the flawed strategic and tactical thinking of the PKK leadership. Armed struggle when it is the State that has all the arms? The bizarre leadership cult around leader Abdullah Ocalan further debilitated the Kurdish struggle. *Apo*'s capture in Kenya in 1998 sealed the fate of the resistance movement. All the shortcomings of a revolutionary movement plagued by a leadership cult and implacable hierarchical structure became apparent. In a history similar to Peru's *Sendero Luminoso*, the Kurdistan Workers Party collapsed once their leader had been captured. Ultimately, some cultural gains were made for the Turkish Kurds, like recognition of their language, so that Turkey could appease their European human rights critics.

It was not for this that the 30,000 died.

CIVILIZATION AND ITS DISCONTENTS

A Rainbow Gathering in Croatia

Life before domestication/agriculture was... largely one of leisure, intimacy with nature, sensual wisdom, sexual equality, and health. This was our human nature, for a couple of million years, prior to enslavement by priests, kings, and bosses.

—John Zerzan, *Future Primitive*

Un mundo donde quepan muchos mundos
(A world in which many worlds fit)

—Sub-Comandante Marcos

In this spirit I will approach the Rainbow Gathering. I have never gone before. It is said to be a bunch of hippies drugged out on remote mountainsides with a lot of bongo drumming and ohmming. The worst excesses of peaceniks and pacifism, vacuous illusions of love and community; celebrating privileged autonomy and freedom in the belly of the whale while all around is chaos, war, disintegration, and injustice. "Naive," "hopelessly idealistic," and "profoundly counter-revolutionary" are the criticisms thrown at the Rainbow idea.

At this moment, the Rainbow Gathering sounds like heaven. It is a few days after the G8 riots in Genoa and we are being hunted down by the Italian police force. The cops are exacting revenge on the lingering protesters. On the sea promenade I meet a bunch of German anarchists. They are clothed in the uniform of the Black Bloc, hoodies and boots and combats, and report constant harassment from cops as they search for their van that has been lost or stolen. Harassment? Better to say a broken arm, black eyes, and a variety of bruises. These kids have been pummeled by Berlusconi's boot-boys.

We are lingering here for Carlo Guiliani's funeral. I am with my road companion Cervando, a filmmaker from Big Noise

Films, and a random traveling bronzesmith—who was passing through Genoa and got caught up in the spirit of the events, loved the riots, and is currently a "star" of the Big Noise rough cuts as she indulges in spirited resistance at the front line of the people's insurrection.

The bloke from Big Noise and the bronzesmith go to the central railway station to retrieve goods from a locker—bad idea. The cops jump them there and they are locked up for a few days. Cervando and I congratulate ourselves on our counter-repression guile as we take a local bus to the next train station along the line, making a clandestine getaway.

It is a relief to be out of the control zone that was Genoa. We have a contact in Florence, one "Big Tony" who spent his time in Genoa policing the Black Bloc. Any time some of them got a little carried away and damaged locals' cars or small shops, Big Tony would be there with his big stick to ward them off. He meets us at Florence station with a bottle of Castro beer and the bad news that we can't stay at his apartment because, he explains somewhat sheepishly, his mother is coming to stay. It's 10 p.m. on a cool summer evening in central Italy, and we have nowhere to stay and no plans. Tony mentions a Rainbow Gathering in Croatia. "Ok," says Cervando, always ready to run with the bulls, "let's go."

We while away a few hours in a small park in front of the train station waiting for the 5:30 a.m. train. As we throw back our wine, the nighttime park fills with sleepers; beside us are some polite dudes from Algeria with exemplary upper-class British accents, over there some Moroccans and a large group of noisy, drunk Eastern Europeans. A band of African musicians from Lagos serenades us quietly through the night—the migrant masses, the *clandestinos*. Some cops arrive before first light, and a lot of the people surreptitiously move away. We watch as a couple of Danish backpackers have their belongings robbed by fleet-footed teenagers at dawn, and so we board the train.

The port at Ancona is another cosmopolitan rendezvous—a hybrid of global people coming and going. This ocean, the Adriatic Sea, is a graveyard of clandestine corpses who have fallen short in their efforts to reach the European shore. Kurds,

Iraqis, Albanians, and Chinese in the thousands offer blood at the altar of Fortress Europe. It's a melancholy place.

And balanced with that sorrow is a small random act of kindness—a Nigerian woman gives Cervando and me (who are quite lost as usual) a lift in her car to the ferry terminal building. She is happy to talk in English with a couple of scruffy hitch-hikers. Her 7-year-old daughter sits with us in the back seat and sings a lovely song. "Do you boys have enough money?" the mother asks as we thank her and wave goodbye.

Gone To Croatia

The all-night ferry to Croatia is filled with a mixture of spirited young Italian vacationers and migrant workers returning home. We're heading to Split, where we plan to catch a bus to the northern point of Pula, the supposed location of the Rainbow Gathering. Studying a map for the first time, we realize that Pula is about 500 miles from Split. Croatia is a lot bigger than we thought. Cervando reaches for his wine and comments "This is not good." But his focus is broken by the large group of young, beautiful Napolese communists nearby who are gulping back straight gin and chanting football or communist songs.

We sip our wine on the deck under the starry night sky and join in the singing with the communists from Naples as the ship rocks gently, cruising across the calm Adriatic sea. Two amiable women join our table and conversations ensue. As luck would have it, they too are headed to the Rainbow Gathering. The Bosnian, Ines, is returning from Genoa, where she ran with the Black Bloc. Indeed, she is still clad in the ubiquitous uniform of the street insurrectionists—black hoodie, big boots, dyed hair and lots of metal things stuck in her face. Danchi from Croatia looks like she might be more affiliated with the ranks of Starhawk's pagan crew, with her tie-dyed dress and long blonde dreadlocks. It is not strange that a Bosnian Black Blocer and a Croatian Rainbow head would randomly strike up a conversation with us—these things always seem to happen on the road. It is a fortunate meeting, too, as they inform us that the location for the Rainbow Gathering has been changed at the last moment. Now it will be held in the mountains of Velebit, a lot closer to Split than Pula. Cervando and I wonder why the Rainbow people hadn't advertised this important point on their web page, which we had perused at the port.

"Because they don't the want the wrong people to know that its changed," explains Danchi.

Very mysterious, we muse, *these Rainbow people.*

The wine flows and the night stretches into the wee hours, and the Communists are still singing away—although by now extremely drunken and bawdy and one girl has achieved a very impressive projectile vomit over the rails. Danchi and Ines are enjoying the wine and plying us with questions about the situation in Genoa after the riots. Cervando and I respond with questions about life in ex-Yugoslavia. Ines is a war refugee who fled Bosnia with her family when she was six. Danchi is born and bred in Split (a Splitter?)—disdains the war, Croatian nationalism and Catholicism. Ines is a hardcore anarcha-feminist, and Danchi is a bit of a hippy with a cocaine problem.

Split is breathtakingly beautiful, a mish-mash of architectural styles and cultural influences. The medieval ghetto section of town is a magnificent labyrinth preserved like a vast living museum. Split has been spared from damage during the recent war but is nevertheless a bastion of Croatian nationalism. Everywhere we go the walls are covered with a poster of a man draped in the Croatian flag giving the victory sign. It's very iconic in a fascist way, and I presume he's some war hero or political leader. But it turns out that he is merely a local javelin thrower or cyclist or something who's won a competition—they must be short on heroes here.

Danchi invites us to stay in her mother's house deep in the ghetto labyrinth. Her welcoming mother pampers us with strong coffee and pastries. At the house we meet Jennifer, from Sweden. Another veteran of Genoa and an anarcha-feminist, Jennifer appears to be involved in some kind of relationship with Ines—one that does not please Danchi.

It's time for a swim. President Tito's summer palace is now run-down and abandoned. We clamber over a wall and find ourselves on a lovely sea-side promenade framed by a Spanish hacienda-style palace. A rusting Armored Personnel Carrier with machine gun turrets sits vanquished in the long grass. Danchi informs that this is where Tito entertained guests like Chairman Mao, Che, Ho Chi Minh, and even Stalin. Accompanied by the ghosts of all these veritable Communist leaders, we all strip and jump into the delicious sea.

As we bask luxuriously in the hot sun, I am not surprised to notice Cervando lazily throwing his arm around Danchi's bare shoulders as she whispers provocatively in his ear.

Cervando is a Tex-Mexican on a European tour. Ostensibly a filmmaker and political activist, he is more like a larger-than-life character from a Hollywood movie. Sporting a wide-brimmed straw cowboy hat he purchased for a peyote hunt in the deserts of northern Coahuila and a Top Gun leather jacket (in the European summer!), he handsomely slouches around with a rakish grin and mischievous demeanor. He is most fond of the ladies, and they of him, and so it is that he and the fiery Danchi discover that they are kindred spirits within 12 hours of our random encounter on the ferry. Ah, road life.

Planning to set off for the Rainbow Gathering in the morning, we wine and dine and explore Split's engaging nightlife. In a low-life fishermen's bar, a heavily scarred fisherman ex-soldier buys us drinks. "I love the Irish," he says in gravelly, barely discernible English. It appears he loves the Irish because they are good Catholics and good at blowing things up.

"You like Croatia?" he asks.

This Croat is a scary character who gives the impression that he might glass you if you give the wrong response. He is wavering dangerously between cantankerous solidarity and spontaneous ultra-violence. The veins in his forehead bulge unsettlingly as he toasts the Pope one more time. He eyes me suspiciously, in doubt of the piousness of my Catholicism. A potentially ugly moment is averted as Cervando steps in to regale him with Texan charisma. Fortunately he has a love for Texas too—the Bush Family, it seems.

Meanwhile outside the fishermen's bar, things have blown up between Danchi and Jennifer. It's something about fish. Danchi wants us all to enjoy some of Split's finest maritime culinary delights, but Jennifer is a strict vegan. She is appalled at the notion of eating sister creatures. Danchi explodes, attacking Jennifer's righteousness. Ines plays peacemaker, holding back the not-so hippy-now Danchi as she looks like she might thump Jennifer into the sea. Split is a beautiful place, but everybody seems to be on edge. The long night ahead still has to be negotiated and there is a distinctly unsettling feeling here that anything could happen. Suddenly the prospect of a Rainbow Gathering chill-out zone seems very alluring

We continue the night's revelries at an open-air sea-side disco populated by mean looking local gangster-mafia types and hordes of supermodels. Fights break out now and then, but no one seems at all concerned. Huge amounts of alcohol are being consumed. Around 4 a.m. as the disco winds down, Danchi and Cervando disappear into the night, arm in arm. Jennifer, Ines and I decide to scramble over the fence to the adjacent sports center and join the people skinny-dipping in the Olympic pool. Jennifer, who has had a few drinks too many and is still upset from the fracas with Danchi, decides a group of lads are mocking her as she swims and decides to confront them. She is one short, blonde, naked drunk against five burly, clothed macho lads; the odds are against her. She takes flight, into the night screaming wildly, pursued by Ines.

A silence descends around the pool. Fun is over. People pull themselves out of the water, quietly pull on their discarded clothes, and slip away into the night. I find myself alone.

It's 5 a.m. I am cold and lost. I have no idea where I am or where Danchi's house is, deep inside the impenetrable maze of Split's ghetto.

A figure moves about in the shadow of the deserted sports complex. I approach him to ask directions. He speaks a few words of English and does indeed know where Danchi—the famous Danchi of Split—lives, and he promises he will take me there in his car. Only first, could I help him do little a job? It appears he is a thief, and tonight he is creeping around the shadows to relieve the People's Sports Center of the fancy hi-fi speakers draping the walls. We pass a guard, sleeping contented in a hut, and the guy shinnies up a wall to unhinge the speaker boxes from their position with a screwdriver. He hands down the heavy apparatus, and when we have secured two I follow him sneaking across the car park to his car, buckling under the weight of the large speakers. The things one must do to arrive home safely at night! Danchi is awake when we arrive at the house, and is unfazed by the amplification apparatus blocking her doorway. "Where is that shit Jennifer?" she growls in her guttural tone.

What has all this got to do with the Rainbow Gathering? Nothing, other than that all these people are headed there, even the clandestine robber.

Darko of the Croats

Cervando and I sip wine on the back of the late bus to Zagreb, discussing his previous experiences of Rainbow Gatherings in the USA. "Crusty heaven" he calls them, uncritically. We debark in the middle of the night at a place called Gracac. The bus conductor knew where to leave us—all the hippies, weirdoes and drunken hobos have exited there for the last week. It is a late-night rural restaurant on the side of the road, surrounded by absolute pastoral emptiness. There are two locals lingering at the otherwise empty bar. They beckon us over, we sit at their table and they buy us liquor. Without a word of English or Croatian to share between us, we are soon splitting our sides laughing at everything and nothing. The two local men like their drink and are wonderful hosts. They understand "Rainbow Gathering" and indicate that one of them will drive us there, a few miles deeper into the mountains. Wonderful. Everything falls into place. Even at 3 a.m.

Darko, the appropriately named young toothless skinhead takes the wheel of an old military truck powered by a squealing two-stroke motor. Off we set on a dirt track into the dark mountains. Suddenly it hits me that this is a potentially dangerous situation, as we are bouncing along a quiet mountain path with a clearly deranged backwoods Croatian nationalist going fuck knows where. "Cervando!" I hiss. "What's going on?"

"It's fine, man, relax," he assures me.

Darko is banging the roof of the decrepit old military vehicle while chanting football songs, mad drunk. The engine is squealing wildly and we are crashing along a rough track at a dangerous speed. Suddenly we stop in the pitch darkness. Darko motions for us to get out. Uh-oh.

We've stopped at a rustic mill in the middle of nowhere. We enter through a heavy wooden door and Darko switches on a light. We are in a bare room with various woodcutting materials slung around the place. Darko indicates that this is his home and workplace; he is a miller. He hands us some beer, the quaintly named Zlatorog Pivo, and hustles us into a side-room. The walls are covered with drying grass plants. We swoon in wonder and inhale the deeply aromatic jungle of potent weed. Darko grabs an abundant handful and humbly requests us to roll up. Cervando is in his element, and obliges with extravagance.

The weed gives Darko great expressive powers. He explains with cutthroat action, that his mother, father and five members of his family were killed by Serbs in the war. "*Mater*!" he says with a dramatic swipe of the neck. "*Pater*!" he continues with same brutal cut. Then he pulls up his shirt to reveal a ghastly bullet wound—he, too, was a soldier.

Nevertheless, the problem remains that it is 4 a.m. and we are in the middle of nowhere, still miles from the Rainbow Gathering, all profoundly bollixed—drunk and stoned. So, off we set into the deep night in the old truck. Darko is high as a kite and bangs away on the roof as we jaunt along, his toothless smile and his strange tongue singing Croatian nationalist or football songs. He is about as happy as I have ever seen anybody in my whole life, and it is probably because he is so devastated by the war and life and everything. High up in the mountains, Darko stops the vehicle and commands us to start walking. The night is pitch dark and the air thin and cold. But the silence is piercing. I realize I have not heard such silence in a long time.

We stumble down a rough hill, and descend into a thick fog (I am relieved that it is not poisonous and disabling like the last fog that enveloped me—the suffocating volleys of tear gas engulfing the streets of Genoa). We walk a long time, stumbling along and giggling a lot about nothing; soon the distant echo of drumming becomes discernible. As we descend from the dark mountain plateau we arrive in a valley spotted by little campfires flickering in the translucent pre-dawn light—the end of a long night.

The Rainbow Gathering, At Last.

We approach the first campfire excitedly. About 20 morose people huddle in blankets around a couple of djembe drummers. After our long adventure to get here we expected fanfare and adulation, but nobody greets us, nobody stirs, nobody even registers our presence. Or at least not until Darko pulls out his cigarettes and lights up. Suddenly four or five people demand their share. Having stripped Darko of all his cigarettes, they turn their backs on him. Darko leaves a while later to return to his cabin—nobody has spoken to him and he feels ill at ease. No love for Darko at the Rainbow Gathering.

Cervando and I stumble around in the semi-darkness, suddenly exhausted. We find an empty space under a canvas tarpaulin, crawl into our sleeping bags and sleep properly for the first time in days.

We are woken the next morning by a naked hippy asking us not to sleep in the "temple." A temple? It looks like a few sticks and a tarpaulin to me, but we're not here to upset anybody, so we drag ourselves out and search for a new nest.

The valley is teeming with people. Teepees, tents and huts of all kinds are littered around the green valley. I have never seen so many naked people in all my life, and it startles me. People of all types, ages, and descriptions wandering around scratching their arses as they collect wood or fetch water or chat in the easy sun. But it is a happy thing; people like to be naked in the sun. Cervando loses no time, I notice, in getting "native."

"The Rainbow Family of Living Light: a place where people cooperate, not compete," says a sign on a notice board. Other notices advertise drumming workshops, meditation, prayer, healing, family events and the location of the Shanti-sena, a "peace-centre." "No Alcohol!" reads another sign, and a warning—"Chemical intoxication of any kind is dangerous to the spirit of the gathering."

We relocate into a large collective tent, where we are delighted to discover a bunch of Italian pizza-makers who had been at Genoa. A light, cheerful mood abounds as Cervando and I nurse our hangovers. People are remarkably friendly and we are addressed as "brothers," although we feel a bit out of fashion without any psychedelic tie-dye items or flamboyant scarves to tie around our bodies. I do my best by wrapping my Palestinian kafia—last seen cloaking my head during the riots—around my hips, Tarzan style. I feel a bit more disguised and part of the assembly until I walk into an Israeli peacenik camp with Star of David flags fluttering in the breeze.

A howl goes up from a clump of bushes and begins to echo across the valley. Suddenly the howl is taken up from all four corners as hundreds of voices unite in a long, drawn-out roar. Jesus! What the fuck is this? "Food Circle," a Russian hippy informs me, "Time to eat." Ah, yes. I listen closely and sure enough, the bedraggled howl raising the heavens is indeed "Fooooood Ciiiiiii-rrrrrrr-cle." The people gather in a massive circle in the center of the valley. The majority of people seem to be western Europeans, with German being the most prominent of the languages I hear. Yet the *lingua franca* is English. I have not heard or seen anything in Croatian anywhere.

Now comes the bit I have been dreading. All the people gathered—over a thousand—form two vast circles, stand up, and hold hands. Then a grumble begins. They have begun their interminable ohmmming, and it continues for a good ten minutes—all these people ohmming away, some quietly and others ecstatically, before they all burst into some happy song of thanksgiving for the food. The finale is reached in a crescendo, and everybody raises the joined hands in the air and begins to clap others' hands, which seems to me, quite a ludicrous action. The naked hippy holding my hand claps so dramatically, that I fear the rule about chemical intoxication has been violated.

This is, unfortunately, all very reminiscent of the awkward ecumenical retreats I was forced to attend in my youth by my

Catholic educators—places of religious inculcation and spiritual and ideological orientation. Peace, love, the philosophy of nice-ism, and an esoteric ritualism. I smell a fundamentalist sect.

The food is dragged out of the hedge kitchen in enormous cauldrons and haphazardly served to the hungry hordes. The feeding of the thousand (quite miraculous) by a bunch of Jesus look-alikes in loincloths screaming "First serving!" and "Second serving!" is all conducted in delightful chaos. The sun shines, the children play, the people munch away on their soy goulash, and the hum of conversation fills the peaceful valley.

When the food is finished, the drumming circle begins—the pervasive beating out of the primitive rhythms. Joints are passed around generously, some people dance, fire-eaters and jugglers do their tricks, and others engage in Capoeira combat exercises. Announcements are made about the various workshops, talks and activities organized for the afternoon, and everybody seems either busy as a bee or lethargic as a cat. Here is a space without electricity; without cars, computers, and television; without technology or machines. The void left by the absence of these devices is filled with interaction between people, by simple creativity and leisure. I am reminded of John Zerzan's notion of future primitives and a society premised in leisure, intimacy with nature, sensual wisdom, sexual equality, and health. It is all here.

In a world marked by struggle, violence, injustice and exploitation, here is the Rainbow people's response—to retreat to relative wilderness and create a utopian temporary autonomous zone based on spirituality, healing, peace, and love. It's all good, except that we are three miles from the front line of the Croatian-Serbian war; less then ten years ago these same mountains were knee-deep in blood. The surrounding villages are pockmarked with artillery damage and bullet holes. The Rainbow Family recognizes this by holding a "light meditation for peace" at sundown, an hour of silence and prayer. Would any of the warring parties of this conflict have joined in the light meditation for peace, I wonder—the Croatian Ustashe Nazis or the Serb Irregulars? How about the Bosnian Muslims, resident NGO, Al Qaeda? No, I don't think so.

The Gathering is about as anti-capitalist as is possible. Commerce is prohibited in favor of bartering; money does not change hands. Everything is free, from the food to the joints passed around, but in the spirit that in receiving one must also give. All work, as in cooking or cleaning or collecting wood or digging shit-holes, was voluntary and everybody gives a hand—mutual aid and leaderless collectivization in practice. A hat called "The Magic Hat" is passed around for donations to pay for food bought in bulk at local markets. An elected financial committee ensures the transparency of accounting to ensure corruption does not occur.

There is no central authority and no leadership, but instead a process where decisions are taken by a general Council. Anybody can attend Council meetings and participate, and decision-making is by consensus. This is not such a utopian idea, as millions of people in the world—from the indigenous communities of Mexico to tribal societies in Africa—currently use similar structures to make decisions. Here, practiced by a very tight group of predominantly white, middle class, well-educated Westerners, this system of participatory democracy works—at least insomuch as the three week Gathering thrives, and has done so in various locations around the world for almost 30 years.

Peace and Love.

She is a remarkable sight and a powerful talker. Tania is from Estonia, and a Rainbow militant. "I hate the industrial-petro-chemical nuclear society. This is my revolution," she says. She's worked as a masseuse on the beaches of Ibiza, satisfying the desires of tourist clubbers whose joints and muscles were destroyed after too many nights of raving and ecstasy. With this ample income, she's traveled the Rainbow circuit and lived the nomadic lifestyle. "But I am lucky. Many of us must work full-time as well as belong to the Rainbow Family." She introduces her friend, a carpenter from Slovakia, who describes himself as a pure Communist and says his goal is to live in Cuba, working as a carpenter and spreading his "anarchist" ideas. Unlike the majority of the men here, he is not clad in hippy fashions;

his hair is short and neat, he has no tattoos or piercings and he wears only a fashionable pair of Levi 501s. The feral Tania, it should be noted, is wearing a big knife hanging from an African belt, and nothing else. Her cropped, bleached hair is held in a leopard-skin scarf. Her short, muscular body, tanned and slim, is Olympian in its proportions; and her quick mind has been trained in Philosophy and Music at a Moscow university.

She is a strident defender of the Rainbow faith. In response to my criticism that the Gathering is a bourgeois indulgence peopled by those who don't have to work for a living, she responds in perfect English.

"Nobody here escapes the agony of survival, but in a mad world of material surplus, most of us get by scavenging and by working in the informal or illegal economy. Many are rebels from the bourgeoisie, but many more of us are rebels from the working class."

Capitalist globalization and neo-liberal policies are causing massive impoverishment and misery; if the Rainbow Family wants to change the world, why don't they fight the structures of power and organize in solidarity with the oppressed?

"We are creating a model of a new world here and we invite everyone to join us. We are idealists and we are pragmatists; look how it works here. We don't fight power—we create alternatives. We don't confront—we circumvent and move forward. We are creative, not destructive. Capitalism will be beaten by peace, co-operation and love of the Mother Earth."

As to my observation that the quasi-religious aspects of the proceedings is reminiscent of fundamentalist indoctrination, she seems baffled.

"I grew up in an atheist society. I was starved of spirituality. The Rainbow spirituality is wholesome and beautiful and allows my spirit and soul to soar to heights I never knew existed."

I am not convinced, but I am not going to deny anybody her celestial delights, so I return to one of the campfires. The endless litany of guitar players singing John Lennon hippy period songs "Imagine," "Give Peace A Chance" has me aching for MC5 and Underworld, but fortunately Cervando is on the ball, snatching the guitar before another white-robed Jefferson Airplane accolade can begin. In his cowboy hat and Texan drawl, he sings some Townes Van Zandt songs about killing and loving and melancholy and having no remorse. It's wonderfully subversive, and his impudent act of rebellion is not lost upon the younger, more impressionable elements among the assembled.

After five days I am thoroughly bored at the Rainbow Gathering, and as I wander the valley to find something to do, the smiling faces and well-wishing vacuousness of the multitude is reminding me of my visit to a Jehovah's Witness compound in Colombia where the legions of the brain-washed wandered about in a similar stupefied reverie. Here it might be the effects of the holy herb, but nevertheless, it is affected and indulgent. I have stopped eating at the food-circle, as my protest against the absurd ohm and hand-clapping ritual, and if another naked yuppie computer programmer from Munich calls me "brother" I will rudely lecture him on the evils of the back-to-nature tendency of the Hitler Youth in the 1930s. There is no sign of Danchi and the crew from Split, and I really could do with a bit of their corrosive humor and unpredictably explosive presence. Even the dodgy thief from the sports center would brighten up the proceedings. Rainbow "peace" has become bland for me.

Cervando is in no mood for taking off. He and his newfound friend, a young actress from the Munich crowd with a proclivity for nudity, are at this moment beating out the rhythm of the swamps in the communal tent as people go about their business. I wander over to a nearby Vision Council meeting where there is discussion of the location of the next World Gathering.

"Has anybody here been in Brazil?" asks a dreadlocked man clutching a feather. They have decided to hold the next Gathering in Brazil, not because they have been invited by a group of Brazilian hosts, but because people want to go to Brazil.

I've been to Brazil, to the Zapatista *Encuentro* hosted by the Workers' Party, but I feel uncomfortable saying this, as if it's way too political.

A shy woman says, "I've been to Brazil, to the Amazon."

"And can you share your experiences there with the Council, sister?"

"Well, I stayed with a Healer."

"And was the territory a good location for a Rainbow Gathering?"

"I don't know, because I never left the hut." She blushes.

"Well how about the situation with infectious diseases, sister?" asks the man with the feather.

"I think it's quite safe," she informs us. "I got no infectious diseases while there."

An older man wearing a loincloth takes the feather. "If you drink your own urine every morning, you will have no worry of infectious diseases." he says.

"Thank you, brother," says the Scandinavian Rasta man. "I think we have learned a lot today concerning the Brazilian Gathering."

I walk away, contemplating the potential taste of piss and the arrogance of imposing a Rainbow Gathering on an unsuspecting Brazilian community. I pass the Italian pizza makers, some Black Bbloc-ers in repose, some Barcelona squatters playing chess, a group of Russian musicians, the Israeli peaceniks, a bunch of screaming kids, a group of nudists parading about, a juggler, a trumpet player and the Hare Krishna tent. I notice that the Romanian bongo-drumming hippy that Cervando befriended earlier has now shaved her head and joined the Hares, for fuck's sake. The Munich yuppies are preparing coffee and smoking joints and one of them says to me—"peace and love, brother." And I don't think so—yuppies and love don't go. And this is the crux. The illusion of peace and love, of intentional communities, of utopian spaces created outside of society—it can only end in a Jim Jones-style massacre or dissolution. And it's not enough, it's never enough. Rainbow Gatherings are all right for your holidays, but one more push, idealists, if you want to be revolutionaries.

THE MAKING OF A REBEL

A Graveyard Massacre in Belfast, 1988

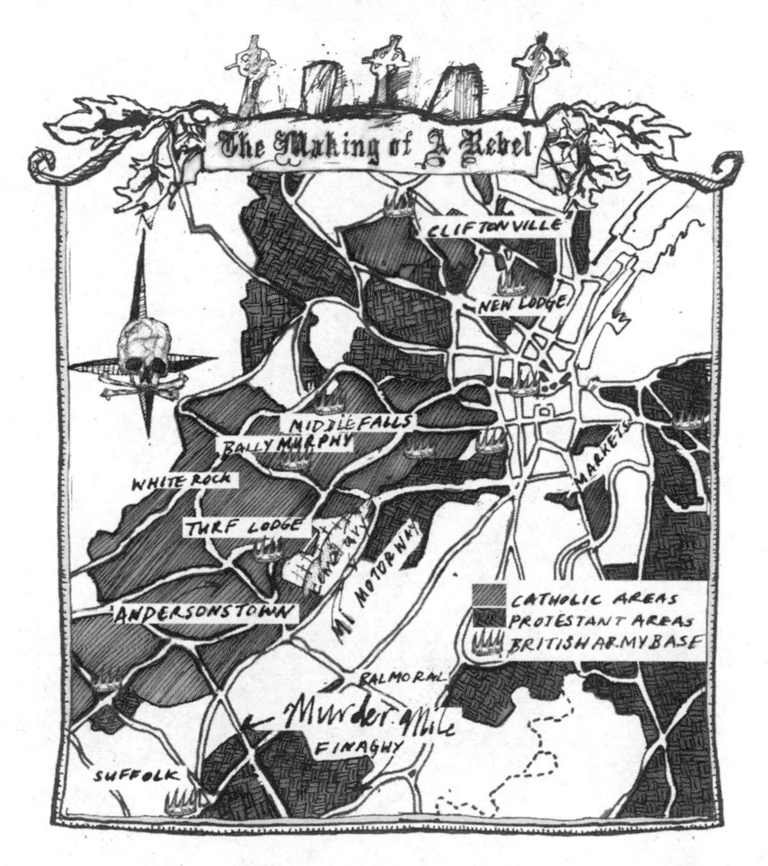

Rainy Days

Two idle Dublin youths, we are dispatched up to a funeral for three IRA volunteers who have been shot in Gibraltar by the British Army.

"There are some job vacancies for yez now," says Joseph's father caustically, "Yez useless unemployed louts." He has a point. Unemployment in the south of Ireland is hovering around 20%, emigration is a rite of passage, and we live in a backward little conservative statelet run by gombeen politicians overseen by the Catholic Church. Dublin is a grey, depressing place—populated by cynics and alcoholics, soggy from the relentless drizzle. A funeral in war-torn Belfast sounds like a holiday. We buy some flagons of cider for the bus ride and off we set, going jovially over the border, our spirits undampened by the sheets of filthy rain beating down on the weary old city.

Despite the fact that we have crossed an international frontier, we find Belfast indistinguishable from Dublin—except that the Queen's emblem decorates public buildings instead of Gaelic symbols, the mailboxes are red instead of green and the street signs are not bilingual. Minor details, trying (and failing) to impress upon the populace that they are closer to Manchester than to Dublin. Belfast is as Irish as any wretched, gloomy, rain-sodden scumbag of a town from Limerick to Cork, Mullingar to Monaghan; places inhabited by a similar variety of unhealthy, disparaging begrudgers.

The single dramatic difference is that Belfast is a town under siege, with extensive military fortifications and bulwarks everywhere. Belfast plays host to a massive British Armed Forces garrison. The continuous presence in the streets of armored vehicles, Saracens, and police and army jeeps with machine gun turrets inspires mitigated obedience, as do the gangs of machine-gun-toting English troops roaming the thoroughfares with fear and itchy trigger fingers. Nevertheless we had looked upon it all passively, unmoved by what now seems like a complete descent into insanity. This madness had been normal to us; as "Troubles" generation children we had grown used to these images and this reality, although quite absurd, had become familiar to us.

We set up shop at a friend's house in Finaghy, a relatively salubrious neighborhood bordering the hardcore Republican, working class Andersonstown. Our host Katey, a young Belfaster sporting a luminous green Mohawk, is delighted to share our flagons of cider but is slightly uncomprehending as to why we want to attend the Republican funerals. While she vaguely supports the national struggle, like most youth from the subcultures, the Republican movement is "other;" it is a thing of the Catholic ghettos, of the Fenian proletariat and the traditional small farms in rural badlands like South Armagh. For young punks like her and her ilk, it represents a tired old world of endless conflict, strife, and vengeful cycles of internecine violence. The heavy militarization of the city is her main gripe, the saturation of troops and cops rendering any freedom in the city null and void.

"What's it like?" said Katey having a *gurn*, "You can't even take a wee dander in the park without some fuckin' peeler having a sniff up your hole looking for explosives…"

The truth is, I'm not sure why I'm going to this funeral. Three IRA Volunteers, Mairead Farrell, Danny McCann, and Sean Savage, were on active service in the British Protectorate of Gibraltar on the south coast of Spain, and as they walked in the sunny afternoon, a group of British Special Air Service (SAS) soldiers gunned them down in cold blood. True enough, the trio was not monkey spotting, but there was something disturbing in the manner of the implementation of the sentence—a death-squad execution, a political assassination reminiscent of those carried out by mobsters or the Tonton Macoutes. Instead of arresting them or even attempting to arrest them, the SAS simply filled them with bullets. So I'm not sure why I'm going to this funeral, but it feels necessary. I grew up somewhat unconsciously an Irish "patriot,"—instinctively supportive of the Hunger strikers when I was a kid, against Thatcher; against the British occupation. I had unconsciously assimilated the line—pushed in the media (and the general Irish consensus at the time) that Brits Out was tolerable but the IRA's armed struggle, specifically the bombing campaign that targeted citizens, was way out of line. The media routinely labeled them the IRA "murdering thugs," but I questioned why the British forces—who also killed lots of Irish people—were referred to benignly as "security forces."

Communities in Resistance

So here we are in front of the Saint Enda's Church on the Andersonstown Road in West Belfast with 10,000 mourners watching the three coffins draped in Irish Tricolors being carried down the steps. Gerry Adams is over there at the front, looking characteristically dour and unflinching. The soft rain falls incessantly, and everyone is wrapped up tightly, hoods pulled over heads, and the entrenched dress of the multitude reflects the defiant, resolute mood. Here is a crowd that has seen more than its fair share of funerals.

West Belfast, the battered enclave of the Republican Movement, is an old working class district whose archaic Victorian architecture is both superannuated and oppressive. Terraced houses crowded with large Catholic families festoon the tight labyrinthine streets. Deprivation intensifies as unemployment levels reach 50% of the working population; the housing crisis goes hand in hand with the health and education service crises. Military occupation and a constant state of siege contribute to making it the most appalling place to live in Western Europe. A veritable hell.

There is an expectant mood among the mourners outside the Church. This is a very significant gathering of Republicans, and anyone who is anyone is here—all the top commanders, all the soldiers on the run, all the militants, all the well-known infamous figures and forefathers of the movement. The dead were, after all, important members of the GHQ of the IRA, the General Headquarters, which presumably means they were on the Army Council, the supreme decision-making body of the clandestine army. We should be graced with a Color Party shortly, a furtive military display by a group of armed, masked guerrillas who will give full military honors to the martyrs with a gun salute. That's always an exciting spectacle at paramilitary funerals.

Katey is approached by a sinister figure sporting a philosopher's beard and quite unfashionable fisherman's clothes. He is introduced as "Shane" and his pal, a shifty-eyed civil-servant looking type wearing a shoddy brown suit, is introduced as "the accountant Fergal." A few murmurs later they depart, and Katey explains that she knows them from her school days in Saint Mary's on the Falls Road. They were two of the local lads who went on to join the IRA. They are on the run now, and it's the first time she has seen them in a long time. And Fergal actually is a trainee accountant, she assures us. Shane, clearly a man familiar with clandestinity, is not a fisherman.

"Were they surprised to see you?"

"Ach, sort of," says Katey, "they were unimpressed with me mohawk and told me I should cop meself on and get involved..." She gives one of her punk rock sneers.

"And this is one thing about some fucking Republicans," she continued, "If they're not getting their rosary beads in a tangle over the Saxon foe, it's always some sanctimonious, holier-than-thou lecture on morality or why you should sacrifice everything for Mother Ireland."

The funeral procession sets off slowly, and the crowds move in to follow the hearses. A lone bagpiper plays haunting laments and all is hushed in that reverent church manner, except for the shuffling of boots through the puddles. We move slowly up Andersonstown Road and I notice that from every lamppost hangs a black flag; the occupants of almost every house are on the door-step solemnly paying respect as the coffins pass, and each and every man, woman, and child is wearing a black armband. There is a forbidding strength here, one you can feel in the air and see written on the faces of the people—an entrenched spirit of resistance and determination. The few stifled tears fall beyond the people's hearts into their clenched fists.

These people are the backbone of the Republican Movement, which at this time—the late 1980s—is going through one of its bleakest periods. The armed struggle seems interminable and is going nowhere. Politically, Sinn Fein has been losing ground since the electoral gains post-Hunger Strikes. Sinn Fein means *We Ourselves* in Irish, and never has it been truer for this outcast community. The pariah of Ireland, these Republicans are reviled and loathed by the mainstream media, considered a "terrorist community" by the rest of the island, and criminalized by the judicial system. Being from West Belfast means being vulnerable to attack by Loyalist paramilitaries at any time, and subject to arrest and detention without charge by the police. It means suffering discrimination when dealing with state services like housing, education, or health; it means the British Army occupying your streets, sudden nighttime raids, and helicopters hovering overhead. A good proportion of the youth are serving prison sentences in the H-Blocks or on remand in Crumlin Road Prison. Subjects are tortured in the notorious Castlereagh Interrogation Center. Activists are stalked and murdered by undercover death squads. Yet still they resist. Still they cover and favor the IRA. While the enormous machine of State counterinsurgency attempted to separate the guerrilla's from their support base, the community steadfastly stands up for their beleaguered clandestine army.

At the foot of the sublime, terrifying Andersonstown Barracks, a towering fortification of sheer wall and enclosed gun turrets, we veer right into Milltown Cemetery. Behind opaque, bulletproof slits of glass, British Army Soldiers observe us coldly, the enemy, the terrorists; maybe they have even written triumphantly on the wall—SAS 3, IRA 0.

It takes a long time for the 10,000 to file into the cemetery. A lone helicopter stalks the cloudy sky. It is unusual that the British military presence is so extraordinarily discreet. Republican funerals are usually an occasion for the military state to employ overwhelming force—to "police" the occasions. Normally there are dense lines of armored vehicles crowding in the mourners; long columns of riot cops wielding plastic bullet guns and sticks; fleets of Helicopters, tanks, and armored personnel carriers—a formidable display of the full armory of the state. The strange absence of the military makes everyone, paradoxically, a bit more nervous. Everything out of the ordinary has these people suspicious.

Milltown Cemetery's Republican plot is choc-a-bloc with gravestones: no shortage of martyrs here. I pass the Hunger Strikers' plot and feel history resounding. The names on the tombstones are all familiar from the television, from the newspapers or from the history books. Many graves are adorned with Celtic crosses. The mood is resilient, and the flowers are fresh.

We crowd around the recently dug graves and crane our necks to get a view of Gerry Adams leading the graveside oration. He is all leader now, and strikes me as an extraordinary figure; his command over the assembly is absolute, and his manner is severe but utterly assured. Here he is, this nobody, this nothing man, a trainee barman from the Falls Road born into a large working class Catholic family; a man who has gone through it all, from his days as part of the urban guerrilla to his incarceration as a political internee, rising to be commander of his contemporaries in Long Kesh Concentration Camp. When he was a young IRA leader, the British flew him to London for the secret 1972 peace talks with the Heath Government. Here he is now, years later—leading a fledgling political movement as the supreme commander of the clandestine Irish Republican Army. Soon he will be fêted, wined and dined by world leaders, including the President of the USA.

His politics may be reformist and socially conservative, and his political methodology suspect; but he is undisputedly a remarkable figure, and the most outstanding politician of Ireland's modern era.

And he is of the people. They revere him, and in turn he repays their faith by trying to act in their interests. As the first bullets ring out in the still afternoon and the first grenade shatters the gravestones, I see him in slow motion. He does not duck and flee, but takes command. "Get down!" he shouts, as he pulls bodies close by him to the ground. Now he is like a military commander, and this is the hour of the secret army.

Death in Belfast

Michael Stone, a scruffy fatso from the ranks of the UDA

(The Ulster Defense Association, a pro-British paramilitary unit) has just snuck up the hill from the adjoining motorway and opened fire on the multitude with a gun and grenades.

As the first burst of gunfire destroys the funereal peace of the afternoon, I remain calm and watch the pandemonium evolve around me as if I'm removed and elsewhere. This is not happening. When the first explosions resound nearby, I still do not react. It is when the self-described "accountant" and his buddy the fisherman philosopher appear on the scene looking extremely agitated that I finally realized it was for real. "It's a Brit attack," they say with some authority. "We're away, off to Divis to get our guns."

Suddenly injured people are all around. The ominous crack of the gunfire continues and the soft thud of the explosions throws up shrapnel and debris from random places. The multitudes heave and duck; some people dive to the ground and others hover behind gravestones and everywhere people scream and shout and it seems we are being attacked by an army, or maybe from the air, or maybe it's mortars. The sheer volume of the crowd limits the view, and the hilly graveyard hides the truth—a lone gunman is waging war against 10,000 unarmed mourners.

All this has happened in less than a minute. A wave of movement is now gathering in the recoiling multitudes. Young men begin to head in one direction, like a river breaking its banks. The trickle becomes a flood and as the terrifying sound of gunfire continues and the explosions persist, a cry goes up of frantic voices—"This way!" "Over here!" "Get them!" "Charge 'em!" Amongst the confusion and bedlam, these youths seem like they know exactly what they are doing. They move swiftly, with intent, through the crowd; they flow in a single swell down the hill, in the direction of the gunfire.

Joseph and I look at each other. We'd come as observers, as Southern tourists to a Republican day of mourning. Now we are confronted with a very real decision. In one direction people retreat, carrying their wounded, scrambling away from the melee; in the other direction flows a small but determined group of predominantly youth towards the theatre of conflict, towards the unseen gunman. Unarmed, running into the unknown, they act with resolute conviction, with dogged bravery and a strange passion.

We run with them. Into the fire, into the clash, unthinkingly but instinctively. We run with them into the indefinite, the danger, the conflict—we enter the struggle.

Michael Stone retreats back down the hill, still firing his guns, still chucking grenades. The youths pursue him, crazily and heroically confronting him—he has his guns, they have their hands. Three of them fall: Caoimhin MacBradraigh, Thomas McErlean, and John Murray, sacrifice themselves to protect their community from murderous attack. Many others are wounded as they close the gunman down, but eventually he is caught, disarmed and subdued.

At the moment they begin to beat him to within an inch of his life, British Military suddenly arrive on the scene. Throughout this whole episode, not a soldier or policeman has been seen—only that lone ominous helicopter hovering in the cloudy sky, monitoring every second and every movement. But now a van comes blasting up the adjacent M1 motorway, soldiers charge out and bale into the lynching crowd, violently rescuing the battered gunman from his peril. They push back the Republican youths and pile the beleaguered assassin into the safety of their unmarked undercover van.

Back up on the hillside, the scene is ghastly. In addition to the three people killed, scores are heavily injured. People languish amongst shattered gravestones. An epic endeavor of community action and mutual aid kicks in. Spontaneously, people form human chains and pass the injured from person to person down a long line as far as the road. On the road, cars are stopped and commandeered to take the wounded to the hospital. All this happens in the shadow of the great hulking monstrosity of the British Military Base, whose massive steel doors remain bolted shut. The soldiers inside watch coldly and detached, while their fleet of emergency vehicles remains idle. This is an occupation army, not a rescue service.

A woman with her eye gouged out passes through my arms, then a young boy with blood pouring from his head. A tough-looking middle aged man next to me, looks me in the eye as I pass the boy along and says, "That's it, comrade, hand him here." For the first time in my young life I was called "comrade" and it meant something. Me, an uninitiated youth from the ubiquitous sheltered streets of Dublin, occupied mostly with the everyday concerns of a banal existence. So I suppose I become someone else that day, with a new awareness of life-and-death struggle.

The lone helicopter lingers in the empty sky and monitors every instant, offering no assistance. We find ourselves alone in these tempestuous times, with only the community left to fall back upon. And somehow the community prevails, holds strong, and we evacuate in a group, retreating from the graveyard like an army retreating from a vanquished battlefield, and we watch each other's backs and make good our flight.

Suddenly there are troops everywhere. They pop out from alleyways and bushes; their APCs come trundling down roads, and armored jeeps appear on every corner. Itchy soldiers materialize in gardens and bushes, and each and every one has his gun pointed at us. Everywhere we turn as we retreat in fear and in shock, guns are trained on us, rifles trail our movements. This traumatized, retreating multitude is now being targeted by the state forces. Here we were, carrying our injured and dead—unarmed, fleeing, and the Brits were targeting us. My disgust becomes anger, my anger becomes rage, that rage became honed and directed, and the British occupiers have created another Irish rebel. A rebel who will, instead of looking away, stare them back in the face and say with a clenched fist, Tiocfaidh ar la!

Streets and Police

West Belfast burned that night. The streets filled with barricades and petrol bombs, plastic bullets, and the din of two armies clashing by night—we with our hands, they with their guns. The riot raged, buses burned, plastic bullets ricochet treacherously in every direction, and the night air filled with fumes and smoke and gases and violence. Joseph and I find ourselves on the Andytown Road once more, and this time it is engulfed not with bereavement and grief, but with rage. The

Brits try to contain it, to hem it in by blocking off West Belfast with their armored vehicles, and they eventually succeed. This eternal rage is closed off and contained within its own locality and rendered ineffective. Northern Ireland is not ungovernable, just the Republican ghettoes.

As if by magic, there appear some masked men in guerrilla fatigues. They order the youths off the street. "Away with yez now, lads!" With surprising discipline and haste, everybody disappears into the houses, into the alleys and down terraced streets away from the main road. Joseph and I are left in eerie silence, disturbed only by the crackle of a burning line of buses and debris and the noxious fumes of burning gasoline from the barrage of Molotov's. Suddenly we are very alone. Through the haze of smoke and fumes we can make out the distant shapes of the Saracens and tanks and armored vehicles of the Brits. A masked man appears dramatically before us; he may or may not be armed. "Get the fuck off the street! Go on away home with yez!" he said, "There's an operation about to go down!" Fuck, an IRA rocket attack or something is imminent and we are in trouble now. We don't know where to fucking go. We don't know where we are and everybody has disappeared; we are stranded, marooned and nervous. We approach the masked man, who is now telling a petrol station owner to turn his lights off.

"Hey, Mister!" says Joseph. "Could you tell us the way back to Finaghy?"

The guerrilla is most helpful and instructive in his directions. "Ach, it's a bit of a walk, lads. Take your first left there by the burning bus, continue down that road until you come to the Murder Mile, and follow that all the way through."

"Thanks, Mister…" And so the man takes off, a cinematic figure in combat fatigues, silhouetted by the smoldering ruins of the barricades.

The Murder Mile. I've heard of that, from an Elvis Costello song. Some kind of interface between two tribes where the Shankill Butchers or some other killers operate with impunity. Great, I think, it's night-time, Belfast is in upheaval and we are wandering down a treacherous, ill-lit stretch of road dotted with abandoned and burnt-out little houses on either side—a post-apocalyptic lonely landscape. Joseph is philosophical—"At least there's no peelers…"

As if on cue, a helicopter moves into view, shattering the night sky. We walk on intrepidly and the lone helicopter lingers above us ominously. Its powerful spotlight floods us with a spectacular sea of bright, blinding light. It is like being on a big stage in a vast, darkened desert. We continue to dander along listlessly, as if unconcerned that a helicopter is bearing down on us, flooding us with its hypersonic light rays. "I think we've got a kerb-crawler on our backs, Joe…"

And just as abruptly, the lights go out and it flies off, leaving us like night-flies floundering in the sudden darkness.

Now a darkened car has appeared behind us. It trails along slowly, and as we glance back we can't see the occupants because the windows are tinted. Murder Mile. We have just walked from the fenian Andytown. The helicopter. Our minds run riot; we are in trouble. For what seems like an eternity, the car trails us from a short distance. There is nowhere to run, as all the houses are boarded up and closed off, no escape route. I keep imagining a bullet lodging in my back or penetrating my skull. "What if they kidnapped us ?!" I think, beginning to panic.

A loud crack and we jump to the ground; we lay there, stricken on the pavement, as the car drives by. Nothing has happened.

Manufacturing Propaganda

With some relief, we finally get back to base in Finaghy. We fall in the door, filled with a newly discovered bravery and implacable revolutionary zeal.

"Fucking hell, wait until you hear what happened to us!"

Katey is waiting for us with her arms folded sternly across her chest. "Oh yous made it out alive, did yez? And us here, shitting ourselves thinking you fucking tourists would be riddled with bullets out there." This is her way of caring, in a Belfast kind of way.

On the RTE 9 o'clock News they show a different reality from the one we have just lived through. They present Stone as a lone gunman and suggest that the people brought it upon themselves by attending a "terrorist" funeral. The notion of collusion is excluded, thereby exempting the guilty through omission. It is as if they are telling the story as seen through the eyes of those who were watching down from the Andersonstown Barracks.

On the other channel, the BBC, it's the same propaganda. All the channels seem to use the eternal calm of their news studios, their impeccable accents, their suits, the respectability of their corporate backers, and our confidence in them to sell their version of the truth.

As would emerge later, Michael Stone had been, predictably enough, using arms supplied by British military intelligence laundered through the South Africans; he had been released like a rabid dog by his British handlers who had full knowledge of the security set-up for the funeral. Indeed, later Stone would go so far in implicating the military as to state in his trial that he had read intelligence files from the Crown Forces. And the undercover van that spirited the hapless fool away? Military backup. This is the real story of the day's events.

Of course, Sinn Fein representatives were banned from speaking on the airwaves at this time, so nobody from the protagonist viewpoint could be heard. Not just Sinn Fein spokespersons were banned, but anybody suspected of being a Republican, or holding views sympathetic to a Republican analysis ("Hush-puppies," was the strange term given to this variant by the witch-hunters, the anti-Republican inquisition). A conspiracy against Republicans, and against presenting the truth as it really is? Absolutely.

Against Occupation, But Not For Social Revolution

Joseph and I return to Dublin, a mere 100 miles from Belfast but another world in terms of consciousness. Life goes on as normal, the rain falls, people fumble in the greasy tills. The welfare line is interminable, and the cattle boats sail out twice a day to take the emigrants away. The mad war and the ferocious injustices are lost in the usual media cacophony of "IRA murdering thugs" and "terrorism." The British military occupation doesn't hold any significance, nor does the Orange Statelet founded on discrimination and Unionist supremacy, nor the collusion of the state with the Loyalist death squads. The complacent and cynical state of the southern Irish establishment, in the face of the euphemistically entitled "Troubles" is inexcusable.

Joseph's family seemed disappointed he had not joined the IRA. Now he would come down for breakfast in the morning to discover no place had been laid for him at the table. "Oh, are you still here?!" his father would exclaim sarcastically. "Bernadette! Set another place, our son has not yet gone to join the struggle!"

The IRA wouldn't be very interested in the likes of us anyhow. Joseph is clearly more enamored by the writings of Stalin and Kim II Sung than Padraig Pearse and Eamonn DeValera. And what with my problems with authority and penchant for the philosophies of the Situationist International, we wouldn't have made very disciplined volunteers. I don't understand how the anarchist McGuffin ended up in the ranks of the IRA—a protestant to boot! Our ilk in Republican circles was definitely confined to the margins, amongst the desperadoes of the Irish Republican Socialist Party or the Irish People's Liberation Organization—radical groupings that, after lofty ideological disputes over Marx and the National Liberation question, would get down to business by eliminating each other over the years in appalling feuds. Years later, a left-wing journalist charged with subversion and membership of the IRSP would rest his case with the argument, "How could I be part of that organization? I'm still alive!!"

This was, in any case, the dying days of the armed struggle. Ireland emerged into the tremulous light of ceasefire and a fragile peace. It was not a peace with freedom and justice, but a peace that was preferable to war. The Republican community were weary of the sacrifices of struggle and the British were weary of the economic damage wreaked by the conflict. The late eighties heralded the twilight of the gunmen; Gerry Adams led a secret political initiative formulated between political businessmen behind closed doors. As the monumental steps were taken towards the compromising Good Friday Peace Agreement of

1994, the IRA became a carefully honed tactical device for negotiation. Sinn Fein entered the murky swamps of politricks. The People's Army became the "guns under the table," and street politics were re-construed in terms of electoral strength.

Republicanism, as it entered electoral politics, revealed its revolutionary limitations. Socialism was sacrificed for nationalist aspirations. Community action became the Party Machine. Gerry Adams became a slippery and tricky statesman. Sinn Fein welcomed US multinational investment (even arms manufacturers) into the newly legitimized Northern Ireland. Gerry Adams was inside negotiating with the World Economic Forum instead of out on the streets of New York with the thousands of protesters. Constitutional Republicanism sacrificed its radicalism for a negotiated solution—an eventual United Ireland, safe for Capitalist investment and business as usual.

Post-Republican Fenians?

We never joined the IRA, but we learned what it is to be a Fenian rebel. Instead, we look about us, our own lives, and we begin to resist where we are. In an instructive way, we do not embrace Republicanism, but the Republicans inform our rebellion. Nationalism and Anti-imperialism have their limitations, but the lives and actions of these people from the Republican Movement inspire courage and action—people like the Hunger Strikers or the political prisoners with their implacable struggles for dignity in the brutal prison system. Or the struggle at the grassroots level, the communities and the neighborhoods resisting the brunt of the repression—how they organize, how they defend themselves. These everyday people, nobodies, nothings; people who rise from their fucked-up situations, capture a bolt of lightning and wield it against the oppressors. They offer inspiration by their deeds and allow us to realize that empires can be overthrown. These humble people born among us, admired and cherished—Irish Fenians, proud rebels.

Throughout history, Irish warriors have fought for freedom against tyranny, injustice, and occupation. Most rebels won a few battles; all lost the War. Today's Republicans are finally winning battles, and have their final victory in sight. The British will eventually withdraw and the Unionists will integrate into a United Ireland. But still tyranny, injustice, and a more subtle form of foreign occupation remain.

The battle is no longer against British imperialism but rather a nebulous form of neo-liberal Capitalism known colloquially as the Celtic Tiger. Now Ireland is part of the European Union. What does the idea of a United Ireland mean in the shadow of the great European state? That they paint the post-boxes celtic green instead of royal red? That all the street signs will be bilingual? Irish nationalism no longer provides revolutionary responses to confronting capitalist globalization or the demand for grass-roots democracy. The struggle continues, because even within the prospect of a united Ireland, there is still a long way to go. It is not time for rebels to sheath their swords.

INTERMEZZO

HIGH SEA ADVENTURES

Ocean Crossings in Search of the Revolutionary Atlantic

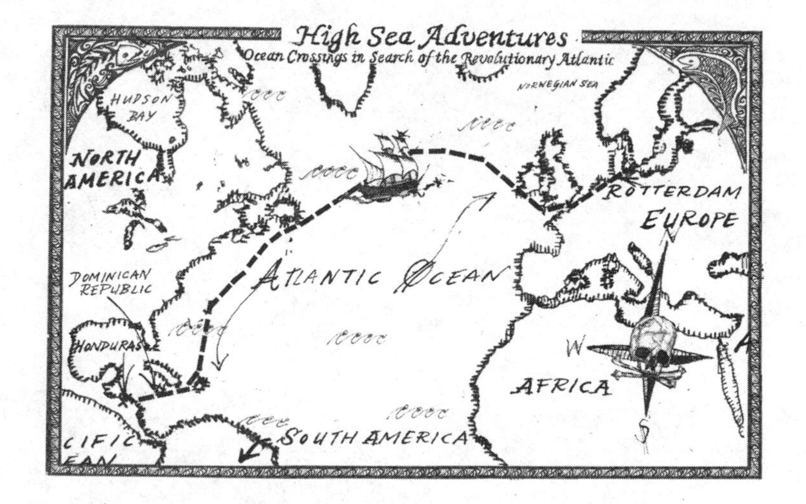

BELÉM
PARÁ

I've only been at sea two months and already I am sick to the bottom of my heart of the sailor's life. Not the seaman's life as such, but the sea-faring environment—the regimen on board the banana boats, the slave-like labor at the ports, and the immorality of the global banana trade, which is pure naked exploitation, a pillaging of the South. My daytime activities of painting or chipping rust and my nighttime shift on watch are both occupied by fantastical notions of violent mutiny, hoisting the black flag and setting sail with my crew of fellow newly-initiated pirates.

But such musings fall on absolutely uninterested ears.

I approach one of the Filipino deck hands—the most disgruntled of the lot—as we share a few beers in his cabin. I ask him why, if life on the ship is so fucking miserable, doesn't the crew organize to change things. "You know," I suggested jokingly, "Like an old-school mutiny!"

Manuel, a young man in his early twenties like me, laughs so hard that beer foam came out his nostrils. "Why would any of us think such a thing! In 254 days I will be finished with all this hell and I will return to Manila, buy my land and farm with my wife and children. For us Filipinos this is the best job possible. Two years labor at sea and then we are set up almost for life. There are many who would do anything for this job." He changes the subject, pressing a photo of a young woman into my hand. "She's pretty, isn't she? That's my sister. You could marry her, take her with you to Europe. She's a good cook, and tidy." I'm not making any progress here at all, so I take my leave.

Bananas

So we've been doing the rounds around the Caribbean, picking up bananas at a variety of ports. Heading towards the

Dominican Republic, our ship, the MV Suriname—a four thousand six hundred metric-ton refrigerated cargo carrier, known as a reefer, flying under a Panamanian flag of convenience—cuts through the breezy tropical sea at a steady eighteen knots. Despite the infuriating working life on board this floating gulag, there is still an indescribable joy in walking the deck as we sail the gorgeous Caribbean Sea on flawless sunny days like today. As the sun sets resplendently on the immense horizon, we pull into the small port of Manzanilla. "Half astern! Slow astern!" shouts the Captain as the huge ship careens dangerously towards the short, antiquated pier. "Dead slow!" Despite the choppy sea and the difficult undercurrents, we berth gently. The mooring lines are secured to the rusty bollards, and we are docked once more.

Hundreds of thousands of freshly harvested green bananas are to come aboard and be put in the cavernous refrigerated hold, a job that will take a full 24 hours to complete. Most of the crew streams ashore, preparing for a night of drunkenness and revelry. I still have my 4 to 8 a.m. nightwatch, though, even when moored so I am spared the worst excesses of the night's revelries. From the quiet bridge I watch the longshoremen load the boxes by hand from the old banana freight train into our dark, mysterious bowels. It's tiresome work, this endless loading, and in case any of the workers get lazy, there are armed guards posted to watch over them. "What's with the guns?" I ask the Second Mate, who—more out of habit than need—continually checks the radar and the satellite navigator, despite us being at port. "There was a Dockers' strike here last month. They fired the leaders and are now making sure that the rest don't get any stupid ideas." The Captain comes onto the bridge at dawn. "Zer good!" he says, referring to the hired guns. "Finally, some security measures!" For him, the problem is the pilfering of the longshoremen and the hustling of stowaways onboard. For him, more guns is good news. And it's the same at all the ports where we dock. In Puerto Cortes, Honduras; Puerto Barrios, Guatemala; Independence, Belize; in Georgetown, Guyana; and Parimaribo, Suriname—always the same regime of guns and suspicion, waterfronts filled with resentment and fear. The longshoremen are badly paid, and their work haphazard, and when the big ships come in, their shifts last all day and night. As the disgruntled workers load the hold through the night, you get the feeling they would like to load themselves on too. A melancholy mood predominates the rigorous work, in the shadow of armed guards.

A few members of the ship's crew almost don't make it back in time. They come scrambling up the gangway with five minutes to spare and are clearly the worse for wear. The night-clubs and brothels of this little port town have taken on a mythical status in the eyes of some of the sailors. I hear the Captain command the Chief Mate to punish the latecomers. "Chipping rust with the lawnmower for three days," he says sternly. That means being dispatched to the nether regions of the vessel to dislodge rust with a heavy, lumbering, noisy machine called a deck scaler. Ten minutes pounding with that thing and you are ready to jump down the hawse pipe for good. It's a maritime nightmare.

The great engines hidden deep inside the belly of the vessel rumble into life, the hefty mooring lines are taken off the bollards and gathered onboard, men scurry around frantically on the dilapidated pier, and we are off, setting sail once more across the Atlantic Ocean.

Into the Deep Blue Sea

It is almost dusk and the sun is setting dramatically on the lush banana plantations surrounding the docks. From high up on the ship's bridge deck I can see far and wide. The tropical vegetation shimmers in a thousand shades of green, its pungent aroma mixing deliciously with the powerful fragrance of the fresh Caribbean Sea. The old rustic railway line runs out of the plantation and all the way up the pier. The decrepit train stands there almost derelict, its wagons bereft of their cargo. Dozens of workers stand around, exhausted after their grueling shift, relieved to see the bananas off. I spot the unctuous local Banana Agent, the only man in Manzanilla who wears a suit, waving us off over-enthusiastically. Young couples gather to watch the huge ship slide out to sea; not much happens in these small port towns. Parents have brought their children, who wave sadly at our departure. Everyone is silent, dreaming of other lands—of migration, exodus, or desertion.

The great hulking reefer ship turns 180 degrees in a wide, lumbering arc, and now the bow faces the infinite ocean. The quaint little Caribbean port town is left behind, becoming smaller and smaller as the horizon encloses it. The sea ahead is perfectly calm, a ravishing sapphire blue, sparkling and inviting, and dolphins leap joyously about the hull. We have two weeks of open sea before us, as we sail from the mesmerizing, translucent beauty of the Caribbean to the choppy, grey European North Atlantic. We have two weeks of monotonous factory work ahead of us—painting and chipping rust, doing watch, cleaning and gazing out to sea, haunted, melancholic.

We are sixteen men of diverse nationalities trapped within the steel confines of this floating prison, encumbered with an archaic maritime hierarchy, teeming with resentments and the petty everyday hassles of living in close quarters with a group of people not of your choosing. We may have rough weather, or engine difficulties; people will fall ill, and others will become overwrought by the homesickness or love-sickness of a year away from their families and homes. The sailors will cling to the fond memories of a couple of days onshore, the bustle of the port, the good people of Manzanilla, the late night beer and revelry, and for some, the delirious dawn shared with the tempestuous women of the Caribbean night.

"Yah, Irishman, move your fucking ass, do some work." This comes from the great German wit, unfortunately, our Captain. He is a big man with great ruddy cheeks and a thick beard. He has been a sailor all his adult life and is, as they say in the trade, confident of the sea. Typical of his class of European officer, his political persuasion lies somewhere far to the right of Le Pen. The Captain, the Chief Engineer, the First Mate, and perhaps the Second Engineer on any cargo ship of this line is European—German, Dutch, or English—while the crew is generally from the global south—Filipino, Chinese or Indonesian. The mid-ranking class is made up of Indians, Pakistanis, or maybe just un-ambitious Europeans.

I've had the misfortune of spending a lot of time around the officer class on a variety of banana boats. Most of these guys have been at sea 20 years or so; they are frightening specimens of stunted humanity. "It would be better if I could flog them," remarked one Dutch Captain, referring to his recalcitrant crew. An English Captain insisted on referring to the Irish, Indian, and Pakistani crewmembers as "Us Brits..." (Strangely, the Indian Bosun, Raj, loved this—he even hung a portrait of Elizabeth Windsor in the radio room to appease the Captain.) But our current Captain, the bulbous German, is easily the most obnoxious of them all. "One time we sailed from Madagascar," he boasts, while knocking back a brandy, "With ten stowaways in the hold. I ordered all the hatches locked shut and turned up the refrigeration. Those blacks froze to death!" His fellow officers chuckle away in an obedient chorus, as if this is a joke instead of a multiple homicide.

These merchant vessels seem at times like theatres for simmering class war. Class war and race war, both. The members of the European officer class, who all joined the merchant navy when these shipping lines were wholly white and European, resent the Asians who are employed because they are cheap labor—the *maquilador*-ization of the fleets. The Asians hate the Europeans because they are racist and unjust bosses. Language comes between the two classes—how can an English Captain order around a Chinese crew, demean them, whip them into line, or teach them obedience and the traditions of the sea if they can't understand one word he says? There was no common ground between the two.

Sailing with a Chinese crew one time, I tried to befriend them in the spirit of worker solidarity. I entered their dining quarters, bedecked with red flags and a portrait of Chairman Mao, and attempted to initiate an interchange of language, English for Mandarin. My efforts came to zero. They suspected me as a spy, an infiltrator that would only harm them in the end. They wanted nothing to do with me. I was white so I was ejected, quite politely.

The Filipinos are different. They are more Westernized.

Many are born-again fundamentalist Christians, Bible-thumping sailors. This doesn't stop some of them from filling in the boredom of off-duty hours with lesbian-hardcore porn movies. Others try to set me up with their sisters, proffering photos of pretty young girls and claiming they will do whatever I desire—if I marry them. It is a liability being white below deck. I work alongside them all day, chipping rust or painting; I drink surreptitious beers in their cabins (drinking is outlawed on the ship); we discuss the Bible, we share watch…and yet they always consider me "*other*." Maybe it's because I've been invited to eat at the officers' table?

The European officers have taken me under their wing as a cadet, as a young man who obviously needs guidance—probably because I am white. I've been invited to dine with them, which is always a traumatic occasion. These old fascist codgers always try to plant the old salty seadog number on me, as if they are wise old men who know the ropes. As sailors, as workingmen, they did—they know the boat, they know the sea, they know how it all works, and they get the goods there on time. This is understood, and this is why they are paid a fair wage for a job well done. The problem is beyond the old salty sea dog paradigm. We sit around a table three times a day for two weeks at a time, and when any other subject comes up—politics, culture, or sports—we have stormy waters. If the topic isn't their desire for more immigration laws, it is their admiration for Margaret Thatcher; if it isn't their desire to see all Arabs wiped off the face of the earth, it's their support for the loyalist Rangers football club, and here I am a Celtic supporter. Even though they are Europeans, white men like me, I feel extraordinarily ill at ease in their company. To complicate things further, I am a "man of letters," an intellectual in their eyes (I read books). They hate intellectuals, the liberal media, people of color, and most of all, feminists. They are angry and cynical men filled with hubris.

One night I get drunk in the lavish cabins of the German Chief Engineer. At 60, he is older than most of the other officers I have encountered, and a certain weariness informs his discourse, which makes him more tolerable than the more arrogant types. As the night wears on, and his more outlandish fascist statements are tempered by sentimentality and melancholy, he becomes maudlin and hones in on one overwhelming theme. "I want to be free!" he says. "I want to be free from this shitty ship and this shitty job, and the fucking engine room and this shipping company. I want to be free of my boring wife and my damned family and my suburban home; I want to be free to take off around the world and just to be free. I want to be free!" The tiresome old bore goes on like this for a long time, and finally we have found some common ground. It's not much, just a desire for the freedom to roam, to be unrestricted. We clink our glasses with grim complicity.

The Dawn Watch

Afterwards I go up to the bridge for my 4 a.m. to 8 a.m. watch. The kindly Filipino Second Mate intimates that I should drink lots of coffee to sober up. I explain to him what has happened, how I ended up drinking all night with the Chief Engineer. I tell him how I found the Chief Engineer, in the end, a decent enough man—even if he is a bit of a Nazi. The Second Mate smiles and uncharacteristically reveals a gem of gossip. "They say he has fallen in with a Brazilian mulatto in Suriname. He wants to marry her and live on the coast of Bahia with her. He is a new man now, repenting his dark past and his bad treatment of the Filipinos. The crew has grown fond of him."

The Second Mate, a soft-spoken grey-haired man in his 50s, abruptly returns to business as if he has let down his guard by speaking so openly with me. He turns to the radar, writes briefly in the log-book, and then retires to the chartroom.

I am left alone on the bridge in the darkness, the ship plunging through the deep night and the coffee percolating on the desk. The ship is rolling gently, as we steam full ahead at a steady 20 knots without a blip on the radar.

The 4 a.m. to 8 a.m. watch shift is the romantic shift—one gets to watch dawn rising across the vast horizon and it is a magnificent vista, changing subtly every morning, as we traverse the Caribbean to the Atlantic or vice versa. Every hour we note our position and the sailing conditions in the Chief Officers log-book, "pitching moderately," and I attempt to induce the Second Mate into conversation. But he is a wary man, and I get the feeling he doesn't feel he has much to say about himself. He has been at sea 8 years, does not express any great love for the sailor's life, although he considers himself privileged to have a well-paid job. His sole wish is to return to the Philippines, his family, and the plot of land he has managed to buy, and farm away the rest of his life. I get the distinct feeling that a sailor's life, for him, is one step up from a chain gang. Strangely, I never do get his name the whole voyage—everybody simply refers to him as "the Second Mate." On the door to my cabin is the title "Spare Officer." Do they refer to me colloquially onboard as "The Spare Officer?!"

How calm is the bridge in the depth of night! I check the various instruments and stare into the darkness, peering for whatever obstacle could be lingering in our passage—fishing boats, lumbering whales, or drifting North Atlantic icebergs. I never spot anything. I listen to the BBC World Service, sip coffee and, rocked by the gentle pitch and the somnambulant ocean air, fall into a calm reverie thinking about my favorite maritime topic—Pirates.

Passing a Pirate Enclave

During the Golden Age of piracy in the 17th and 18th centuries, crews of early proletarian rebels, dropouts from civilization, plundered the lucrative shipping lanes between Europe and America. They operated from land enclaves, clandestine ports; "pirate utopias," located on islands and coastlines as yet beyond the reach of civilization. From these mini-anarchies—"temporary autonomous zones"—they launched raiding parties so successful that they created an imperial crisis, attacking English trade with the colonies, and crippling the emerging system of global exploitation, slavery, and colonialism. ("Pirate Utopias," *Do or Die*, No 8).

The Caribbean teems with the ghosts of the pirate world, and the pirate utopias once dotted around the region remain part of the cherished folklore. There is still a tangible sense of piracy in the air, provoked by the great extremes of wealth and poverty starkly coexisting in the Caribbean. Haiti, the poorest country in the western hemisphere, is a short boat ride from the Virgin Islands, playground of the rich and famous. And it is here that I will get my first taste of the "threat" of latter-day pirates.

We have been delayed loading bananas at the Honduran port of Puerto Cortes, and the Captain has been acting edgy all morning. The task now is to make up time on the crossing. He could cut through the infamous Tortuga Strait, a narrow slipstream between the Haitian coast and the small island of Tortuga. The danger is that the channel is less than a mile wide and populated by a lively band of latter-day pirates in rubber dinghies equipped with powerful outboard engines and AK-47s. They would speed out in groups and seize a passing ship by throwing ropes up over the side and climbing aboard. The grand size of our ship makes it difficult to guard the whole length of the vessel. Pirates can climb aboard, break into the metal containers and steal anything that can be dropped into the rubber dinghies below. Alternatively, they can simply hold up the crew at gunpoint and do exactly as they please.

The Captain, after much contemplation, decides to go the Tortuga Strait route. "We'll save four hours," he says to the First Mate, "It must be done."

The crew is dispersed along both sides of the deck, some armed with handguns, to ward of the potential robbers. We enter the narrow channel and small settlements are visible on both coastlines—multitudes of little huts and not a large building in sight. The channel is a couple of miles in length. Dozens of little boats crisscross the channel: battered old fishing boats, rustic ferries packed with people, and the "suspicious" little inflatable dinghies. The Captain could go full speed, ensuring that we pass too quickly for any pirate to catch up, but that would cause havoc for the locals in the violent wake of the passing ship. Little boats might overturn, or we might simply run over slow vessels. Basically, by going a reckless 20 knots, we would be crashing through, causing untold damage—drowning even—just to stave off the pirates. The Captain, a real bastard, is tempted.

He discusses the dilemma with his buddy the Chief Engineer, another German. I don't understand German but it is clear that the Chief Engineer is talking the Captain down from his reckless path, and almost begrudgingly, the Captain orders a reduction of speed.

By this stage I am positively pissing myself with excitement. I would present any potential pirates clambering aboard with my assistance. This is the historical Tortuga, one of the earliest Pirate Republics! This little island off Hispaniola was once the scourge of the Caribbean. C.L.R. James documents in *The Black Jacobins* the groups of European clandestines who took refuge here in the year 1629. "To Tortuga came fugitives from justice, escaped galley slaves, debtors unable to pay debts, adventurers, men of all crimes and nationalities. Slaughter, internecine followed for 30 years..." James, no friend of the pirates and buccaneers, saw them as dropouts and criminals. Other historians frame the Caribbean pirate enclaves in more favorable and revolutionary terms. These "Pirate Utopias" were rebellious settlements premised in radical democracy and racial equality, oases of freedom in an increasingly brutal "civilized" world founded upon the slavery and exploitation of the "New World." While a good portion of the pirate community was comprised of mutinous sailors from the merchant privateers or the imperial navies, many others were "a melting pot of rebellious and pauperized immigrants from across the world—thousands of deported Irish... Royalist prisoners from Scotland, Huguenots, outlawed religious dissenters...captured prisoners of various uprisings, Diggers and Ranters, runaway slaves and rebellious proles..." (*Do or Die*). The original buccaneers got their name from *boucan,* the practice of the Arawak Indians of smoking beef. The Atlantic rebels "went native," and made common cause with the indigenous groups. The self-organization of these pirate communities—not just in Tortuga, but in Honduras, the Bay of Campeche and all over the Caribbean—represented a genuine alternative society in the seventeenth century. These were the clandestine autonomous municipalities of its day.

Disappointingly, we pass through the Tortuga Strait without even so much as a hint of a Jolly Roger gracing the horizon.

The Captain chuckles coarsely as we pull out once more into the open sea. "Yah, fucking assholes too busy screwing their mothers to take us on…ha-ha!" This Captain is a real comedian; he has us in stitches all day. He's forever shouting at Filipino crew, "Stop staring at your shoes like Imelda Marcos and get to work, ha-ha!" The workers shuffle away without a word. I suppose I wasn't expecting a motley crew of latter-day rebel sailors, but I also wasn't expecting such a brow-beaten obedient lot. What of the secret history of the revolutionary Atlantic, the treasured tradition of mutiny, and raising the black flag?

The romantic maritime, it seems, is dead and gone; it's with Anne Bonny in the grave.

Troubled Waters

The next afternoon, the sea is calm as I idly paint the starboard boat deck with a long roller. My peaceful daydreaming is disturbed by the Chief Steward summoning me before the Captain. Of all the Filipinos, this guy, a Jehovah's Witness, is the most dangerous. The other Filipinos distrust him and I have already had a bit of a run in with him. He's a big fan of the US military bases in the Philippines. His ambition is to open a McDonald's franchise in his hometown, Malabang on Mindanao. I earned his displeasure by laughing aloud when he waxed lyrical on the wholesomeness of the McDonalds menu.

The Captain is seated behind the desk in his office with impressive nautical charts rolled out in front of him. He is grunting to himself somewhat boorishly. Over his shoulder hovers the twitching Chief Steward, and through the portholes I can see the cargo stacked on the expansive deck tilting gently with the pitch of the ship.

I may be in trouble.

"Are you writing some kind of investigation about this shipping company?" the Captain asked directly, fondling his beard and looking like the meanest bastard one could possibly imagine. He continues that the Chief Steward has found, "while changing the cabin linen" some written notes I had left carelessly on the desk. I glance at the sycophantic Steward with a burning stare.

"I like to keep a journal, Captain, but it definitely wasn't written for the eyes of the Chief Steward..."

The Captain was clearly reveling in the whole situation. He could be his very own Gestapo! "Ve are concerned that the confidentiality of the shipping line has been violated." A company man, he goes on to outline how I have been taken on in good faith by the director, and I am abusing that trust by intending to publish an account unhelpful to the shipping line. "Are you a journalist?" he asked directly, his eyes burning into me.

And this is the thing: I have been doing a little research with the aim of exposing some trade injustices, but nothing about the shipping line or this man's sacred fucking Shipping Company. I'm looking into the bananas. My little clandestine concern is the bananas industry.

But I have an explanation. "Captain, I'm writing a short eclectic piece for the Seaman's Union magazine about life on board a modern vessel, comparing it to the old romantic idea of life at sea during the so-called Golden Age of shipping. I am writing an article that merely expresses the discontent of the crew, their lack of interest in the sailor's life, and how big ships are more like floating factories...But nothing damaging to the Shipping Company."

The Captain looks at me crookedly. His eyes narrow and he pulls at his beard. I have drunk with this man, he has told me his stories, I have shared his space, and I suspect he might actually have a soft spot for me. "You ask a lot of questions," he said. "You are a good listener. You are young and idealistic. I believe you." He broke into a cunning smile. "I will help you with your article and we will print it in the Company Bulletin too."

"That's great," I mumble feebly as I cast a nasty glance at the Chief Steward. Fucking scumbag rat. I will have a word with the other Filipinos about this—they don't like him either.

A Motley Crew

But they aren't interested. I tell my mate Manuel, the young disgruntled Filipino deckhand, what has happened and how the Chief Steward has ratted on me to the Captain. "The Steward is a dog," laughs Manuel, "We expect that from him." He changes the topic to the nocturnal delights in some seedy Manzanilla brothel. Another crew member enters, a guy even younger than Manuel, and his line is that the Chief Steward did no wrong—"He was only doing his duty." Later that night on watch, the Second Mate chides me, "Don't worry about these things. You should keep your head down and do your work." That is what he says about every problem. It drives me crazy—Why don't these people stand up for themselves?

I find an excuse to leave and make my way to the very bow of the ship, as far away from the bridge and the rumbling engines as possible, past the lines of freight containers, past the stored mooring lines and various accoutrements, down to the end of the forward deck. Like a world apart, here at the very tip, the forecastle of the ship is a little platform that hangs over the water. The hull drops at a sharp angle below, so when I'm sitting perilously on the edge, grasping the metal bars and dangling my legs, it is as exhilarating as a fairground ride. The ship pitches more dramatically at the bow, and the tumultuous sea churns about lasciviously ten meters below. The spray of surf wets my face and the delicious aroma of the salty sea overwhelms my senses. Sometimes dolphins chase the ship here, leaping delightfully about the hull. I'm sure this place has a name, as everything has a nautical term, but I don't know what they call it. For me, it is my place of wild solace, alone as I can be on the ship, plunging through the dark sea in the deep of night.

A Valediction to Imperial Hydrarchy

I'm chipping away at rust with a handheld jackhammer on the port side bridge wing. The work is monotonous and the scraping noise is driving me nuts. I've been at this all afternoon. I suspect this is part of the Captain's punishment for my misdemeanors. Suddenly the whole horizon fills with a great wall of water, several hundred feet tall, as an Extreme Storm Wave sweeps in from the winter North Atlantic…

The Captain's guffaw interrupts my dream-time flights of fancy. "Yah come on, Irish scholar, lets see if you can write even with all those blisters, ha-ha!" He beckons me into the chartroom, where a computer sits idle. "Use this to write your fantastic article!" he says, rubbing his hands together merrily, maybe expecting some whimpered excuses. "Now!" he adds, as if cracking a whip. But (cunningly!) I've thought about this, whiling away the hours of the previous night's watch, and have prepared a potential article to humor the stupid bastard.

I begin banging on the keyboard, pandering to the Capitan by starting with a quote from an old traditional Irish sailor's song "The Sea Rover," one of the Captain's favorites when maudlin and drunk: *I am an old sea rover and the blood through my veins is fresh and salty as the sea...*

I then go on to describe the attributes of the crew of the MV Suriname, how they are "confident of the sea" and other clichés, but claim that the romantic age is over and the salty sea does not flow through these people's blood—only the necessity to work for a living, a shitty living at that, locked up on a ship for months on end. I lament the loss of the Albatross as a symbol of the sailor—a creature who only lands to mate—and suggest a more appropriate symbol for the modern worker onboard would be a caged parrot. Maybe some of the old traditions are gallantly carried forth by the superannuated-licensed officer class (I have in mind the preposterous rank system and the tendency to resort to juvenile punishments for crew "misbehavior," but that remains inferred rather than stated). But this is a Leviathan task, to revive archaic practices. I entitle the piece "A Valediction to Imperial Hydrarchy," with a wink towards radical historian Peter Linebaugh.

The Captain looks a mite confused and then chuckles approvingly. "Yes, you can write! This is OK! Mourning the lost traditions, yes." And he leaves me there, not mentioning the outstanding rusting to be done, so I take the opportunity to write about the injustices of the global banana trade for the rest of the afternoon.

I bring the writing up for the Second Mate to peruse during the early morning watch. He reads and laughs sardonically. "It is good," he says, "but it is naive. There is no mystery to the sea, it is simply the ocean and we are a metal box floating on top of it. And it is dangerous, stupid even. We are all fools, and we do it only because we have to. It is about money, that's all."

The Inefficiency of Capitalist Globalization

The Captain invites me up to his quarters the following night and opens a bottle of Scotch whisky. "Let me tell you a story," he begins, "to explain what this business is all about."

It's like he is about to dictate his grand memoirs. It's like he is preparing his last confession. I fumble for my pencil, excited.

But his testimony is disappointing. It's just a straightforward story of the madness of globalization. "I was Captain of a schooner taking cargo from Cork, Ireland—yes, your shitty country—to Brazil, another shitty country, and back again. We would load a cargo of livestock at Cobh, and sail across the Atlantic, two weeks. There in Brazil, the cattle would be slaughtered and made into canned meat. That's a Brazilian specialty—slaughterhouse skills, you know. I would load up the ship again with canned meat, and sail back to Ireland. The canned meat was sold in Irish supermarkets."

Silence.

"Is that it, Captain?"

"Yes."

Like Falling Off the End of the World

Day by day the ocean gets darker and the clear blue sky becomes dotted with clouds. The temperature drops subtly. We find ourselves wearing more layers of clothes each night on watch. A great big whale bids us farewell from tropical waters with a spectacular fountain of water and a graceful leap, crashing dramatically back into the ocean. Right out in the middle of the Atlantic, six days from Europe, we pass bobbing fishing boats from the Spanish fleet. Fish stocks are so depleted that fishermen have to go to extraordinary lengths to fill their quota.

A day later we pass some discarded oil barrels bobbing about in the water—litter all over the world.

The excitement of heading towards the Caribbean and the exotic ports on that side of the Atlantic is inversely proportional to the depression of heading towards cold, wintry North Atlantic waters. Rotterdam in winter never has the same alluring appeal as, say, tropical Paramaribo. Work on the deck becomes more difficult with the rain and the cold, and the seas become choppier. Sure enough, a couple of days from port, just beyond the Azures, the ship begins rolling long and deep, ten second rolls, on big North Atlantic swells. Sleeping and eating become acrobatic chores, balancing acts against the forces of gravity. Traversing the passageways calls to mind a clown act, or the endeavors of a punch-drunk hobo in the park. And intermittently, the contents of one's stomach will take a leap. Some people's visages take on a startling shade of blue. "Everybody gets sick, don't worry," the Chief Engineer tells me. "I've been getting sick for 25 years. Here, hold this, you'll feel better." He places a potato in my hand. I feel better because I laugh for the first time all day.

The Captain has the deckhands out in the winter gale painting and rusting, just to spite them. There's plenty of indoor work they could be doing, but he's in a rage because he's gotten wind of a "party" that took place below deck the previous night. "Drinking is prohibited on the boat," he thunders. Except for the officers who drink brandy every night in their fine staterooms, the fucking hypocrites.

I bring the toiling workers coffee on the deck, spilling most in the process, slipping and sliding on the treacherous swaying surface. The six men are fuming to be out in the gale; despite oilskins and rubber boots they are soaked through and miserable, chipping at the interminable rust. Manuel thanks me for the coffee and finally exhibits some of the malevolent spirit of a seafaring motley crew. "That fucking Captain better watch his step or he will have an accident," he mutters bitterly.

The 4 to 8 a.m. watch is getting busy. As we approach Europe, our radar and the waters are becoming dotted with vessels—other cargo ships, fishing boats, coast guards, liners, and oil tankers. We are off autopilot and have to change course occasionally. The Second Mate doesn't trust the navigation of the small fishing vessels, nor does he trust the Satellite Navigator. Short of grabbing his sextant and shooting the stars, he prefers to keep a very close eye on the procedures before him with his keen eyes. "Ships go down every day and every night," he tells me. "Somewhere in the world right now a big ship is sinking. We hear SOSs all the time on the radio."

The Captain comes in drinking his morning coffee, and joins the conversation uninvited.

"Like that yahoo of a yachtsman we found in the middle of the Atlantic lying half dead in his little dinghy. We lost a whole afternoon rescuing that fool." The Captain would quite clearly have preferred to steam past the disabled vessel, but maritime etiquette implies that passing ships must come to the rescue of vessels in distress.

"But the Company received good press for that, Captain. We lost time, but as the Company Director said, it was good for public relations." This from the Second Mate.

"We should have left that arsehole in his tub, to teach the other foolish yachtsmen a lesson. They are all jackass yahoos, forever causing problems for the merchant marine!" He changes the subject. "What is the weather forecast for today, Second Mate?"

"Bad," says the Second Mate warily, "Strong winds, rain, the same as yesterday."

The Captain has gotten out on the wrong side of the bed. "A good day for chipping rust on the starboard boat deck," he murmurs nastily, and leaves the bridge.

Even the Second Mate is provoked. "He should have more respect for the crew…" he says, adroitly.

"It's true, but they just take it," I say, "They don't complain."

"No, they don't complain," says the Second Mate, peering intently out the bridge window.

We are approaching Rotterdam, and the weather is wretched but we have made good time. Twelve days and 21 hours. We have crossed six time zones, sailed 3,800 miles, used about

50 gallons of oil per mile, and got hundreds of thousands of bananas across the vast ocean, on time. The Second Mate calculates that the banana company makes a good half a million dollars of gross profit on the bananas. "What they pay for a small bunch of bananas off the shelf in Holland is about the same as a day's wages for the banana worker in Honduras." "Second Mate!" I exclaim, shocked that the normally demure man would make such an overtly political statement. "You should keep your head down, do your work and not consider these things that don't concern you!" I say sarcastically, mimicking his own words, his own mantra. "Yes, you are quite right," he says, and smiles for the first time with an endearing air of complicity.

It's all over. We have docked in Rotterdam, the icy wind whips around the port, and we are all wrapped tightly in many layers. The bananas are being unloaded with the latest state-of-the art cranes; in no time at all the nicely ripened fruit is frisking across Europe in articulated lorries. The port is cold, industrial and sparsely populated. Europe's primary port has long been mechanized and the longshoremen downsized. It's like sailing into a cemetery, a place haunted by the ghosts of the generations of workers who have vacated the space in place of great hulking machines and zippy conveyor belts. The teeming lucidity of the Caribbean ports contrasts bleakly with this depressing vista. The only contiguous element is the presence of armed guards.

I have to present myself to the Captain one final time in order to sign off the ship. "Ah! The Irish scholar!" he exclaims mockingly as I enter his cabin. "Don't desert us now! Surely there are many more stories to write here!"

And this is the thing about this stupid fuck of a Captain—it's like he can see through you. He misses the essential part, but he gets most of it. I have a begrudging respect for him, his seaward ways and his blunt, overwhelming presence. Nevertheless, he still has the capacity to undermine any goodwill I might feel towards him. He begins to get all maudlin and faux philosophical.

"We are simple people, sailors. We fight the oceans and we deliver the goods. But there is something that I want to say before you leave this ship, something you should never forget."

This is interesting. There's nothing better than a good epiphany at the end of a long voyage. I'm all ears. The Captain pulls at his beard, stares beyond, and tears might have welled up in his cold eyes.

"Always remember that there is someone, somewhere in the world, who loves you."

I look at him blankly, and try to comprehend his words. Is their some hidden wisdom in there somewhere? The Captain has a smug look on his face and holds out his meaty paw to shake my hand. What he has said is completely absurd. Why would he bring up love now? Is he truly mad? Love? This hulking metal monstrosity is possibly the most loveless, unhappy place I have ever had the misfortune of occupying in my whole life. Love and the MV Suriname is an unthinkable notion. Love and the transatlantic shipping industry do not go together. Love and bananas? No! I shake the Captain's meaty paw, and smile at him as one smiles at a cop who has handed you back your false ID.

"Yeah, thanks…"

The Ongoing Search for the Revolutionary Atlantic

I sauntered off the loveless MV Suriname a happy man, a free man, one who would not walk up this gangway again. I thought of the Captain and the European Officer Class and their sad superannuated ways and the antiquated maritime class structure. I thought about the endless slog of useless labor, the unromantic characters that populate the ship, the browbeaten crew, and the absence of resistance. I thought about prisons, about claustrophobia and about Camus's description of a hellish place, "*It's a world without women, and thus without air.*"

But the last word is with the motley crew. As we share a final clandestine beer approaching Rotterdam, my Filipino mate Manuel tells me a real secret of the deep sea. "You ask us why we don't react to all the shit the Captain gives us?" says Manuel. "I will tell you why we smile each time he orders us around. We smile because behind that bravado we know he is scared." Some time ago, on another ship of this line, there was an accident. Apparently there was a German Captain like ours, a bad man who mistreated his crew. And there was a Filipino crew, like this one, quiet, minding their own business. Far out in the Atlantic the Captain went for a stroll around the forward deck. The night was dark and the waves were pounding the ship. Nobody heard his screams and the body was never found.

NEW WORLD

Mexico
Belize
Cuba
Haiti
Dominican Republic
Honduras
Costa Rica
Guatemala
El Salvador
Nicaragua
Panama
Suriname
Guyana
Fr. Guyana
Venezuela
Colombia
Ecuador
Peru
Brazil
Bolivia
Paraguay
Chile
Argentina
Uruguay
N
W
E
S
New World

THE RESURRECTION OF VAMPIRO

POLI
POLICIA

Caracas, Venuzuela, 1992

People spoke of him in quite revered tones. "Wait until you meet Vampiro," they said, or, "things will be clearer when you speak with Vampiro."

Caracas University radicals seemed united in their high regard for this legendary anarchist. And there he is now, on stage, the lead singer of a ska band, *Autonomia.* He is tall, skinny and dark-skinned, wearing a red and black striped t-shirt and black drainpipes, de-rigueur punky-mod style—topped with short spiked hair. He fills the stage with his mischievous swagger and the audience sings along every song like an unruly choir.

"*Viva Anarquia*!" he screams, "*Viva!*" respond hundreds of young voices in return.

It is an afternoon memorial concert for a student leader shot down a few days ago during campus protests. She was popular and, needless to say, her death is totally unwarranted. The mood of the assembled students is grim. But that grief is transformed into rebel resilience and renewal prompted by the passionate, infectious performance by *Autonomia* and their fiery cheerleading singer. The infectious chant "*El pueblo unido jamas sera vencido*" transforms into a ska-ed up bop. And the show closes with people chanting and clapping and dancing as if they had just won all their demands and a holiday in Cuba to boot.

Venezuela in 1992 was in a state of turmoil. The Peres government was acting as handmaiden to IMF policies that are devastating to the economy. The cost of basic foods doubled overnight and riots broke out. The military was sent in and hundreds of citizens were shot down in the streets. Now the Peres regime is hanging on by tender hooks and revolt is palpable. The students are in the thick of it, and the campus is virtually a revolutionary autonomous zone. The police continually violate the traditional institutional autonomy of the university by entering and engaging in pitched battles with rebel students determined to drive them out. Casualties are rising. A dozen students have been killed since the uprising began. Military tanks are stationed permanently outside the front gates.

Inside the sprawling campus, all concrete and steel—that depressing modernist architecture—it is clear the students are in control. Every wall is draped with graffiti and banners proclaiming allegiance to this or that revolutionary organization. Tables are thrown up everywhere as the rainbow of movements and political party's hawk their line. Students of various faculties meet in assemblies and thrash out issues and strategy. There is a perceivable energy of revolt, as if everyone is down with the program. Music plays everywhere in the university, and it doesn't seem like much studying is going on. Students mill about and the cacophony of voices fill the air with clamor. Everyday life on the campus has become an ongoing rebellion.

Over at the auditorium, the crowd is chanting and demanding an encore, *Autonomia* return to the stage to much applause. Vampiro takes the mic and commands everybody to hush. Slowly and carefully, Vampiro picks his words. His eulogy for Claudia, the slain student, is suitably staunch and heroic. That she was "A burning inspiration," and "An unfaltering militant fighting for justice," these kinds of things.

Then strangely, Vampiro's voice breaks. He stops amidst the homology. His head sinks. His clenched fist moves to his nose. An uncommon silence grips the auditorium. "And," he says quietly, "...she was my lover, and I will never forget her."

There is a strange rumble in the crowd. Claudia's boyfriend, surrounded by a group of consoling mates, looks aghast. Vampiro launches into a slow song, like an Irish lament—a sorrow-filled, haunting ballad of love and desertio—most uncanny for a ska band.

The next day I meet him, the famous Vampiro, and he is back to his upbeat, charismatic self. He is delighted to meet a *companero* from Ireland and immediately presents me with one of the bundle of books he is carrying—*Campesino struggle in the Venezuelan Highlands.* I am bowled over by his warmth and openness, I feel embraced by his rich character. But such are the charms of

Vampiro that before we can really talk he is besieged by a horde of friends, well wishers, and admirers. We find enough time to talk politics and he warns of the authoritarian tendencies within the current rebellion. "This people's insurrection runs a very real risk of been hijacked by a populist demagogue..." he says, "We need to encourage and support the barrio assemblies."

And then he was off, caught up in the urgency of the moment that was the 1992 rebellion of Caracas. Sometimes a figure personifies a moment, or a movement. With Vampiro, it was his open spirit and sharp, immediate analysis of the situation. And he embodied all that is seductive about the rebel milieu—smart, vigorous, and passionately committed to some great, mysterious ideal.

A Friday Night in Blackout Books

Some years later, three Venezuelans walk into Blackout Books, New York City's Anarchist bookstore of the time. It is my Friday night shift and I am arranging the Latin America section. A conversation begins and it appears they are earnest Anarchists who seem to know everything regarding the South American revolutionary struggle. I think it is something in their total assuredness and the righteousness of their cause that reminds me of someone whom I had met in the past, someone who could also generate this esteemed self-confidence.

"*Companeros,*" I ask, although a shot in the dark: "Do you remember a *compa* called Vampiro who was active in Caracas in the early 90s?"

"Hmmm." A pause. The three look pensive.

"A fine comrade" says one. "He had a lot of guts and balls," says another.

"Almost a local legend, no?" says the third.

"What happened to him?" I ask, hoping not to hear the worst.

They confer amongst themselves.

"*Calle Insurgente*?" "Maybe *Calle Bolivar*?" "But they removed all the bodies, nobody was sure..."

One turned to me. "We believe he fell during the 1993 uprising. Was he a friend of yours?"

I feel a horrible chill, and my heart dropped.

"No, not really. I met him that was all..."

Chavez and the Punk Rockers

Hugo Chavez, was elected President of Venezuela in 1999. He was one of the conspiring military officers of the failed 1993 uprising. During the uprising Chavez was imprisoned, and subsequently released. He seemed a strange bedfellow on the summer streets with the likes of Vampiro and the anarchists. But such is revolt; it takes all sorts and all forms.

Chavez now leads a populist government that stridently stands up in the face of the US and snuggles up comfortably with Fidel, while at the same time accommodating the IMF and global capital. Anarchists like Vampiro are once again out in the streets protesting Chavez, but not with the pro-US bourgeois counter-revolutionaries.

Caracas has become an increasingly dangerous capital. The streets are teeming criminals and muggers. I returned in late 1999, after traveling in Brazil. Our hosts, a bunch of strung out anarchists put us up in their fortified apartment. Fortified because the area they live in, near the city centre, is plagued with anti-social problems. With its steel door, and inner security bars, the place resembles a jail. Inside there is nothing to rob, there is little by way of furniture, primarily just a record player from which Crass and other dirge emanate, extremely loud. The anarchists were exceptionally drunk this night, falling around the place, but also falling over themselves trying to make us feel welcome and at ease. They are sound people, but clearly the struggle is at a low ebb. A remarkable looking punk, dressed up in some quasi-Susie and the Banshees-Nazi look, speaks to me in a quite incoherent Caracas street vernacular. "*Echando vaina*" punctuates her every sentence, street talk for something—what, I have no idea. She passes over some inflammatory liquid and I feel its heat boil my insides. These punks, although political activists, are clearly, at this time, not very active.

The drink overwhelms my sense of returning to Caracas and makes me sentimental. "Is this what the rebellion of 1993 was fought for?" I ask, referring to the Chavez Populist regime and our drunken revelry.

"No, no, no!" they say most definitively, stumbling around.

"And speaking of 1993, do any of you remember a *companero* called Vampiro?"

A pause. "Hmmm," they say. "The singer from *Autonomia*!" says one. "A good street fighter," says another. "Disappeared. A long time ago, *echando vaina* ?" says the Banshee.

Gracias a la Vida

And I thought of Vampiro, and his spirit of resistance, his legend. C*ompaneros* whom we cherish and whom we miss. Why do all the best people perish?

Sometimes Latin America can be overwhelming, with its long history of courage cut down and valiant aspirations destroyed by brutish repression. Like a long opera falling inexorably towards a fatal finale, replenished with sufficient passion to sustain a sense of horror. We embrace the tragedy, because there is nothing else left, just horror.

"He must be dying of boredom up there in the mountains," says one.

"Years and years, doing nothing," says another.

"Fucking school teacher," says the third.

"*Echando Vaina*," says the Banshee, "all these years, Vampiro, a rural teacher."

I smile. Vampiro's resurrection. Not all Latin American resistance stories have a tragic ending.

LOOKING BACK ON THE SANDINISTA REVOLUTION

A Tale of Two Narratives—People's Power from below; Terror from Above

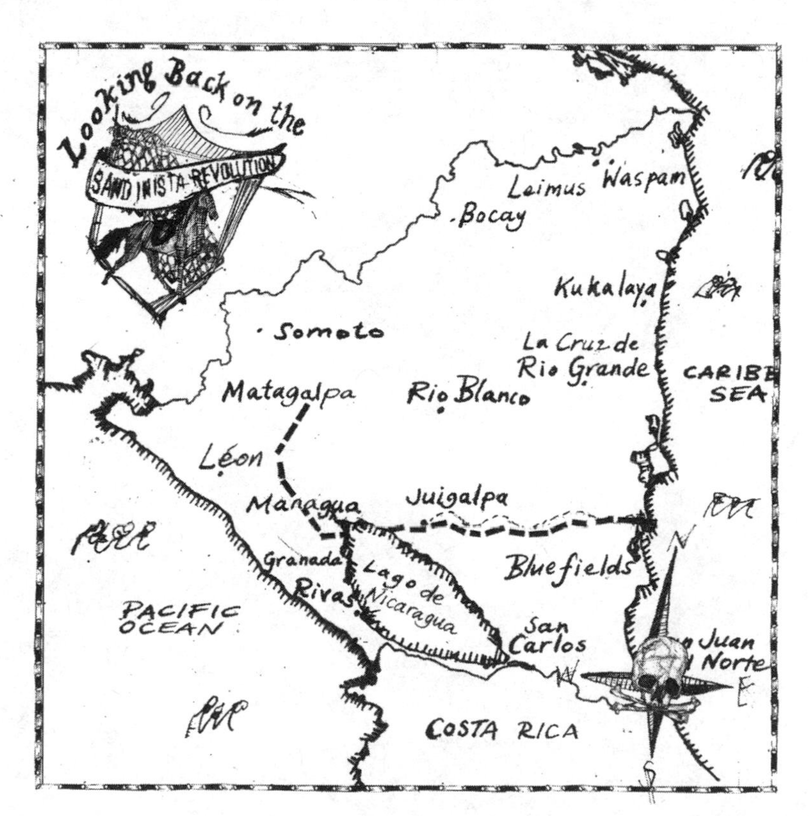

YANKEE HIJO DE PUTA
NO PASARAN
FSLN
YAMAHA

"I've gone to the mountain to be with the guerrilla, and if my return is not possible, don't look for me, because I will be there hidden amongst my people."—*Gravestone inscription of 19-year-old Tamara, a Sandinista insurgent from Condega who fell in combat on May 19, 1979—shortly before the Sandinista's triumphant entrance into Managua.*

"Nicaragua is my farm," boasted General Anastasio Somoza, the despised ruler of Nicaragua who continued his family's reign supported by US intervention in the 1930s. "Somoza is a son of a bitch, but he's our son of a bitch," responded US Secretary of State Henry Kissinger. When Somoza stole millions of dollars from the relief funds donated after the catastrophic 1972 earthquake, it was the beginning of his end. After 20 long years of bloody war for national liberation, the 1979 General Uprising finally deposed the dictator. The FSLN (Sandinista National Liberation Front), a politico-guerrilla organization inspired by the Cuban model (but not the Cuban ideology), created a new revolutionary space where radicals could begin to dream again and formulate a new society at the end of the twentieth century.

It was a youthful revolution, conceived of and led by a new generation of politicized militants. The armed rebellion became a people's insurrection, and like a great storm, served to cleanse and renew Nicaragua. Its was bloody, and it was brutal, but there was also something beautiful contained in the tale of the Nicaraguan revolution. The unimaginable happened—the dictator was overthrown by the insurrection of a united people, and this tiny Central American nation in the shadow of the US assumed the mantle of becoming the kernel of a new kind of revolutionary struggle. Not manipulated by Washington nor Moscow, but rather driven by a desire for genuine national self-determination and people's democracy.

The story of Sandinista Nicaragua is one of two main narratives. One is the story from below, where changes were made in society that allowed poor people access to land, education, health and a new sense of freedom. This narrative is a story of working people learning to take control of their lives, and the State attempting to help them. The other narrative comes from above, and that is the story of US-backed war of terror, as the counterrevolutionary forces—called Contras—waged ferocious and unceasing war on Nicaragua, thus sapping the resources of the newly-born nation, claiming the blood of tens of thousands of citizens and undermining the radical social program of the Sandinistas. This narrative is one of power reasserting the old order and not stopping until the emerging story from below is fully crushed.

The US-backed Contra (the Nicaraguan Resistance) was a good example of how terror works. The Contras were a proxy army made up of elements of Somoza's despised National Guard—mercenaries, anti-communists, and a variety of discontents. They were based in military camps along the borders of Honduras and Costa Rica, and the whole operation was directed and funded by the CIA. Their long campaign of terror was effective in rendering the Sandinista government program unworkable and making the border region a graveyard.

And finally, there is a sub-plot to the first narrative of people's power from below. This deals with the autonomy of the indigenous people living on the isolated Atlantic seaboard. Within this scenario lay both the seeds of the destruction of the Sandinista Revolution and the potential salvation of its revolutionary project.

Halcyon Days in a Sandinista Co-op

Of course beyond the historic revolution and the dramatic Cold War context of Sandinista Nicaragua, there remains the everyday struggle of the people to survive in a destroyed country. What is life like at the very grassroots? I decide to find out by joining the 1989 Irish Coffee Brigade. 21 years old, and never having traveled beyond Europe, I am filled with all kinds of exotic notions about this romantic revolution in tropical lands. Motivated by a touch of adventurism, and a desire to offer practical support to the Sandinistas, off I march to assume my place in the metaphorical trenches with Orwell's *Homage to Catalonia* tucked under my arm. Just as Chiapas would be the place to go for radical pilgrimage in the 1990s, Nicaragua was the popular destination of international solidarity activists in the 1980s.

The Brigade is comprised of 23 volunteers committing to six weeks picking coffee harvest with an agricultural collective in Matagalpa, on the frontline of the Contra war. We are an incongruous group made up of students, civil servants, farmers, artists, and even bank officials; an eclectic bunch of well-meaning people, aged twenty to sixty and from every walk of life, all drawn to this remote place about as far from Irish society as we can possibly imagine. We have been captured by the optimistic message sent about the globe by the Sandinista revolution in this tiny country, about 5,000 miles from ours. We're not unusual—the inspiration of the Nicaraguan struggle has attracted thousands upon thousands of international solidarity activists and spawned a generation of campaigners that would ultimately form the backbone to the NGOs and social forums of the 1990s and beyond.

The Bernardino Diaz Ochoa Co-op is a coffee plantation that was reappropriated after the triumph of the revolution in 1979. *Somocistas*—supporters of the dictatorship—had fled to Miami and their land was snapped up by the new revolutionary government. Private property of those who did not flee was respected, and a mixed economy was promoted. A program of land reform began immediately—with the sharing out of farms and land to the peasantry. Recuperated land was parceled out to be farmed cooperatively or collectively. Indeed, twenty percent of arable Nicaraguan land was quickly redistributed among the poorest of the rural poor—1.5 million hectares was distributed to 200,000 families.

The Diaz Ochoa Cooperative is a wretchedly poor place. About three hundred people live in dirt-floored wooden shacks scattered around picturesque hills. The kids are big-bellied and dress in rags. The women walk about shoeless and there is no electricity or running water. Nevertheless, these *campesinos* are clearly proud of their reappropriated plantation. They tell us stories contrasting their current satisfaction to the era before the revolution—when noone had good land; when they eked out a squalid living on the hillsides, working for the plantation owners for pathetic wages. They had joined the FSLN, fought the dictatorship, and ultimately reaped the benefits of the revolution. Of course, there are many social and political problems at the co-op, but all in all, the Irish Coffee Brigade gets a most favorable impression: The Diaz Cooperative is a quiet and industrious rural place where people go about their collective work enthusiastically, despite the shadow of war hanging over them.

The villagers embrace us right away. Early one Sunday morning (our only sleep-in day) I am woken by an amiable youth and militiaman, José. Some days before I had mentioned that I had never ridden a horse. So José saddled up his father's horse, which stands outside our door all bedecked with a Sandinista flag, and they are ready to show me the ropes. So I get to learn how to ride a horse in the mountains of northern Nicaragua with a young farm lad as a teacher, who is wearing a Sandinista combat hat and a red and black *paliacate*. He suggests that I am ready to face the Contras now on my horse, and I think that at this moment I might just be up for it—ready to fight for their little struggling co-op on the edge of the war.

There are endless tales of Contra terror. Many families have lost members to the war. In the night we hear mortars and gunfire from the hills. "Contra attacks," explain the locals grimly. An armed local is stationed outside of our sleeping quarters. "Where did the AK-47 come from?" we ask him. "The government," he says. Here is another extraordinary thing about their revolution: the Sandinistas armed the people. Most governments would live in fear of an armed populace.

Gaggles of Sandinista army soldiers pass by on the dirt road. Sometimes we stumble upon them bathing in the nearby river. These young men look worn out and terrorized. They jump at our sudden arrival. This interminable war is affecting the very heart of Nicaraguan life. A good night's sleep is impossible; violence is everywhere, real or imagined.

Despite the shadow of war, the coffee harvest has to be collected. It is tiring but not strenuous work, picking coffee. The whole community is out, from kids to old folks, and young girls seem to be the most skilled, the most dexterous; their fingers dart across the low, fruit-laden bushes. They've brought their radios, and blast the lively and idiosyncratic Radio Sandino all day long. The Bangles' "Eternal Flame" is interspersed with Sandinista marching anthems, and The Rolling Stones' "Angie" with Cuban *son*.

And then, one day, our pastoral tranquility is disturbed by the arrival of some Sandinista officials. They've come to talk to us about the political situation. They drive in on fine four-wheel drive vehicles, whose sleekness contrasts with the great lumbering East German truck that is the village's sole method of transport. They bring us pineapples and a variety of other fruit that nobody on the Diaz Ochoa Co-op has. It seems strange that these city people would come out so far into the countryside to talk to us, as the *campesinos* have told us plenty. These are young Sandinista officials, suave and sophisticated, the sort of striking revolutionaries you see in Oliver Stone movies. We are captivated, of course, by their presence and their ardent revolutionary discourse about the global anti-imperialist struggle and the need for implacable militancy. But they don't seem like *campesinos* or soldiers—they are preened, middle class professionals. The officials are here to talk ideology, and so, for the first time in Nicaragua, we are subjected to the word "Marxism." It reminds me of something I had heard at a lecture by Noam Chomsky. Marxism in the third world, he said, is largely the ideology of the radical intelligentsia who hope to take power riding the wave of popular struggles.

But, I think, better to have the radical intelligentsia talking up the workers, the peasants, and the revolutionary struggle than the benefits of neoliberal capitalism and the free market.

We took off from the co-op a few days later, teary-eyed and filled with ardor for the Sandinista Revolution. We have witnessed a wretchedly poor rural community building for the future with demure optimism, and delighting in the ability to run its own plantation. It has been a lesson of self-determination in action. Here in the Diaz Ochoa Co-operative, people are hopeful about the future. The Sandinistas, they tell us confidently, will win the upcoming elections and the US will be forced to concede to their power and stop funding the Contras. It is that straightforward. And a Nicaragua at peace, for these *campesinos*, would be a fine place to live.

Christmastime in Contra Country

The coffee harvest is completed and most of the Brigade heads home. Three of us from the Irish Brigade—Ian, Mags, and I—accept an invitation to visit a Contra village on Nicaragua's northern border with Honduras. There's an Irish priest involved, an outlying parish, a mass, and some sinners—Catholic things, and its Christmastime. The *padre* came here 10 years ago to support the base church, choosing the preferential option of the poor line popularized by liberation theology. Most of his vast rural parish encompasses pro-Sandinista communities, but a few of the isolated villages near the border support the Contras. And that's the area where we are headed. As we bounce along on the dusty back roads of the northern mountains in the *padre's* pickup, he fills us in on the latest local news.

"The Contras abducted four farmers from the outskirts of Condega. They disemboweled them and cut their throats. It's a message to the others—don't vote Sandinista."

We are two months away from the decisive February 1990 national elections. Canvassing for the opposition UNO coalition (National Opposition Union), the Contras seem somewhat eager. The *padre* attributes their enthusiasm to the largesse of their benefactors—US patrons are funding the Contra terrorists to the tune of ten million dollars a year. This canvassing and disemboweling is a highly profitable business.

The opposition UNO, a ten-party coalition made up of most everyone who is not Sandinista—conservatives, liberals, and even the communist party—are officially receiving $100,000 from US backers, and there's much more under the table. What UNO is offering the electorate is an end to the Contra war and the crippling economic sanctions imposed on the country by a

US embargo. Or to put it another way, if the UNO loses the war then the economic embargo will continue. Blackmail? Better to say the electorate is confronted with a deaththreat. Nicaraguans will go to the polls in February 1990 with a gun to their heads.

Predictably enough, the Contras are upping the ante before the big day. There are daily attacks on soft targets—clinics, agricultural collectives, isolated hamlets—and intense pitched battles between Contra raiders and Sandinista troops. Civilian deaths are mounting; the hills are strewn with the bodies of young Sandinista conscripts, local farmers fighting on either side, and dead mercenaries who have failed to make it back to their base in Honduras.

"Looks quite like Ireland, doesn't it?" says the *padre*, cheerfully.

We are winding along a dirt road off the paved highway, deep into the breathtaking, scenic mountains. This is Contra territory and our imaginations are filled with images of ambush and violent explosions. Four white guys in a pickup truck? Any clown lying on a hill could take us out with a Rocket Propelled Grenade (RPG—big favorite amongst the Contras). Our only hope, I'm speculating, is that they think we are US Armed Forces—oh perish the thought.

"Have you been out here before, Father?" I ask. "A couple of times. I've had a few difficulties. A while ago there was an attack during mass, and a youth got killed." "A Contra attack?" I prod, "Well, not exactly. Just some irate mass-goers had a go at me. I had to defend myself. A fight broke out. But they were Contras, yes."

Nothing to worry about, then, on this treacherous road—we're going to be killed during Holy Communion anyway.

Over a mountain path, down a horse trail, through a shallow river, and we have arrived. A bunch of sullen villagers wearing their Sunday best are gathered in a field. The village is a huddle of stick huts with dirt floors and grass roofs, like any poor rural community in Nicaragua. The *padre* is received courteously by the village leaders. They know he is a Sandinista sympathizer subscribing to liberation theology, "the communist gospel" according to its opponents. But it is understood that he is here on a mission of faith, and that supersedes politics, at least for most of them.

There's tension in the air. The *padre* has disappeared to prepare for mass, and we three *brigadistas* are left at the mercy of the unfriendly stares of the local youths. With some horror, we realize they are in an advanced state of inebriation. The *padre* has the sanctuary of being a holy man, but we have no such celestial protection: we are lambs for the slaughter. The *padre* has invited us along on the premise that it is good for the rebel community to see some international solidarity volunteers up close, to dispel myths in their ranks that we are all baby-devouring communist gargoyles, as the propaganda goes. At this moment, it seems that our presence is not dispelling those myths.

A gangly hillbilly sporting cowboy boots and a big Stetson hat stumbles over and begins a diatribe, shaking his fist angrily. Our saving grace is that none of us understands a single sentence of his slurring Spanish. We smile at him, nodding our heads sympathetically. Is he going to hack us to death with a machete?

We are saved by the bell (at least the church bell), summoning all to mass. We scurry to the sanctuary of the church. My fellow *brigadista* Ian laughs outloud—"What would your anarchist friends back home think, Ramor?—finding refuge in mass!"

Inside the dingy church the *padre*, bedecked in ceremonial white robes, leads the congregation through the "celebration" and I look around at the faces of the young drunken men at the back of the hall. They're Contras—farmers by day and terrorists by night. I focus on one teenaged *campesino*, who giggles to his mate and then gets embarrassed when his grandmother turns to scold him. Has he received counterinsurgency training from US handlers in the border camps in Honduras? Is he one of the Contras who burns down Sandinista schools in the dead of night? Has he killed farmers like himself, men who till their fields and work hard and get little in return? What is the nature of his community grievance with the Sandinistas?

The best I can ascertain from questioning the *padr*e later is that these villagers were loyal *Somocistas* before the revolution; they had enjoyed the patronage of the local boss, and feel aggrieved to have lost that small amount of favoritism. And so, as they had before supply troops to Somoza`s National Guard and Army, they now supplied youth to the Contras. The *padre*'s interpretation that they are not so much die-hard Contras, as they are potential Sandinistas in waiting, seems wise. The revolution is for them too. Of course, the problem is that the Sandinistas don't have the resources to build a school or a clinic here, or to make concrete gestures of support, because with their chronic lack of funds they have to prioritize their own bases of support and fight the war. An intractable situation—this community fights for the Contras because they have nothing, and they have nothing because they are fighting the war.

We just about make it out of the Contra community intact. There is an ugly moment leaving the church, as a brawl breaks out. The *padre* plays his part, showing he can just as easily be a street-fighting neighborhood toughguy as a messenger of Christ Almighty. In the end, it is the aura and charisma of this man of the cloth from the north of Ireland that pulls us through this most extraordinary of encounters. I doubt that any other pro-Sandinista foreign activists have passed or would pass through that isolated Contra-supporting hamlet deep in the mountains of northern Nicaragua.

The Atlantic Coast—Nicaragua's Third Front

The history of the Atlantic Coast region is one of migration and exile—a constant flux of people arriving and leaving—and of internecine strife. Even large sections of the indigenous population migrated from other regions. Buccaneers settled here in the sixteenth century, and the original inhabitants were wiped out by the Spanish, the British, and the Caribe, (a war-like indigenous group who migrated from the Yucatan Peninsula, some of whom ended up in the Lacandon jungle of Chiapas where they are known as Lacandones). The British brought slaves from the Jamaica plantations, and so the Creole culture was born. Escaped slaves, maroons, and pirates formed the Garifuna population and a variety of indigenous groups—the Sumo, Rama, and Caribe—formed the Miskito kingdom. It is said that the British united the indigenous groups into this kingdom, with their own king, aping the British monarchy model. Indeed, the Miskitos, who reigned from the 1600s through the end of the 1800's were described as Anglophile—they joined forces with the Brits against the Spaniards and even established themselves as slavetraders in the eighteenth century, finding their "commodities" by launching raids on other indigenous tribes. This unsavory history might go some way to explain why and how they've ended up joining forces with the Contra terrorists in the 1980s.

The Atlantic Coast region is like another country. People here refer to those on the Pacific coast (the rest of Nicaragua) as "Spaniards." There are no connecting roads with the Pacific Coast. With so little contact between the two sides of the country, the fact that they were constitutionally (and, arbitrarily) joined in 1894 is one of those absurd decrees of imperial history. The mistake of the Sandinistas has been to attempt to apply a Pacific Coast solution to an Atlantic Coast problem. Somoza was a ferocious dictator, but he had the sense (or laziness) to leave the Atlantic Coast to its own devices. It remained a forgotten backwater, an undeveloped territory mostly ignored, which has had both positive and negative results.

The Sandinistas came, lured by the rich biodiversity of the region, and in typically colonialist style began extracting valuable hard woods from the vast jungle stretching the length of the Atlantic Coast. They treated the inhabitants paternalistically (they were almost complete strangers—the Atlantic Coast region was by and large completely unaffected by the war of liberation against Somoza, and many locals in isolated villages had scant regard for the traumatic events that had occured across the country in 1979). The Sandinista idea was to nationalize the resource wealth of the region for the good of the country but the locals had other ideas. Unfortunately, the Miskitos fell into the orbit of the Contras. Suddenly the US government loved the Miskitos. President Ronald Reagan took a sudden interest in the human rights of the indigenous, claiming that the Sandinistas were conducting a campaign of virtual genocide against the Miskito Indians. The human rights group Americas Watch refuted that claim with the assertion that, "The most serious abuses of Miskitos' rights have been committed by the Contra groups."

The lies of the US administration regarding the Nicaraguan situation were quite astonishing. Ambassador to the UN Jeane Kirkpatrick, before a Senate Foreign Relations Committee in 1982, said that the Sandinista abuses against the Miskitos were "more massive than any other human rights violations that I'm aware of in Central America..." Such rank mendacity borders on the psychopathic. This came at a time when US clients in El Salvador had been responsible for 13,000 documented murders (in 1981 alone), and a veritable genocide of Guatemala's indigenous was being overseen by the US-supported Guatemalan military.

The basis of the charges against the Sandinistas was the relocation of 30,000 Miskitos from the war zone in northeast Nicaragua, which has been carried out in order to deprive the Contra terrorists of a civilian population to prey on. Some 300 Miskitos had been jailed, accused of Contra activities. Two-dozen deaths were attributed to excesses by Sandinista military operatives, some of whom were convicted by the Sandinista tribunals for war crimes. These were serious abuses, but they must be compared to the large-scale slaughter attributed to the Contras and the barbaric atrocities in Honduras, El Salvador, and Guatemala.

The road from Managua to the Atlantic Coast stops abruptly at Rama, and from there it is a five hour boat ride down the Rio Escondido to Bluefields, the main town on the southern Atlantic seaboard. It's a beautiful ride through rich rainforest until the coast area, which was completely flattened by the cruel Hurricane Gilbert of 1989. The once-dense jungle now resembles a denuded WWI battlefield. The damage is almost biblical in scale. The whole coast was pounded for days, leaving hundreds dead, thousands homeless, and the region's main industry—fishing—in tatters.

We debark at a rustic little dock at Bluefields as the sun is setting spectacularly over the port town, casting long, mysterious shadows. The pungent smell of rotting fish emanating from the numerous fishing nets scattered about the pier evokes nostalgic memories of the fishing villages of the western seaboard of Ireland.

"If you are Russian you are not welcome!" says a gristly old black man seated with a few mates on the docks.

"No!" we reply.

"If you're Cuban you are not welcome," said another in Creole English.

"No, we're not Cuban."

"Are you Sandinistas?" asks the third, suspiciously.

"We're here to relax and smoke weed…" we say, almost truthfully. We were also researching for a documentary on the Sandinista impact on the Atlantic Coast.

"That's all right, then," says the first old man with a great big smile. "You are welcome!"

Bluefields is a port with character, run down in a lazy and chaotic way. The typical British colonial architecture of the Caribbean—bright two-story wooden houses with shaded porches—contrast dramatically with the more familiar Pacific Coast architecture, all Spanish colonial arches and patios. There is a multiethnic feel to the streets, which are populated by Creoles, Garifuna, mestizos, and a few Indians. The cacophony of noise in the streets from the ubiquitous blasting reggae—Jimmy Cliff, Bob Marley and a variety of ragamuffin music—is interspersed with the cosmopolitan mix of languages—Creole English, Spanish and Indigenous languages, all spoken at the street stalls and open-air markets.

Our film shoot was based in Pearl Lagoon, an enchanting village eight hours, sailing time up the coast from Bluefields. Here the couple of thousand inhabitants, Creoles and Miskito, live in apparent pastoral simplicity, feeding off the sea and the fertile forest land situated in a beautiful enclave without roads or concrete cut out from the forest. The people live in ample wooden houses set out on grassy meadows without walls separating the commons. Animals roam freely and the mood is cheerful. There is no police station, and no formal government presence. It is an autonomous community, as much due to the desire of its inhabitants as to its geographic isolation.

Our hosts are some Rasta fishermen who claim to be Sandinistas, but I suspect that it is for the benefit of my companions, two English women filmmakers of whom the lads are most enamored. They do not seem too preoccupied by politics but do seem to have an endless supply of very fine sacred herb. Pearl Lagoon boasts a rustic reggae discothèque, populated by the black and mestizo youth (and-not-so-youthful) that is hopping every single night of the week until dawn. Daytime activities include leisurely fishing—shrimp a specialty—and a little farming. Everyday life in Pearl Lagoon has the illusion of being about as blissful as could be imagined in this day and age. The arrival of a bale of cocaine that has miraculously washed up on the peninsula (and whose appearance was explained by the locals as the result of the interception at sea of Colombian vessels by the US Coast Guard) is causing some social and health problems—everybody seems to be off their heads every night.

One day as we prepare to go off fishing, Rodney the Rasta man realizes that one of his nets is missing. He immediately attributes the deed to the "Indians." It seems any social problem in the town is attributed to the indigenous—be it robbery, molestation, or vandalism. Indeed, there appears to be almost no social interaction between the two groups, the indigenous and Creole, even in this small town—except trade. The indigenous, who dwell on the outskirts of the village, are no doubt second-class citizens in this micro-society.

And in this sense, there's no doubt that the indigenous have suffered racism in general and abuses in particular from the "Spaniards"—the Sandinista administration. This dispute emphasizes the contradictions of the Sandinista political strategy.

At the start of the revolution the indigenous demanded autonomy—"the aboriginal right of the Miskito, Sumo, and Rama Nations, as sovereign peoples, to freely determine their social, political, economic, religious, and cultural development, within their traditional territory and within the framework of Nicaraguan state." The 1985 Misurasata document challenged the Sandinista centralized state model. "An Indian self-government is the inalienable right of the Atlantic Coast Indian peoples to govern their lives and destiny and to administer their internal affairs within their traditional territory." This was revolutionary stuff, but not part of the Sandinista plan (Zapatista demands set out in the San Andrés Accords of 1996 are similar in aspiration). So the Sandinistas fucked up by not recognizing indigenous demands for autonomy during the first years of the revolution.

The problem, of course, was the fact that a sector of the Miskito community found common cause with the Contra terrorists in the early 80s, the period of the most intense Contra activity in the north-eastern region. The Miskitos were clearly aggrieved—this was yet another invasion of their lands that had been held since the sixteenth or seventeenth century—but was that reason enough to align themselves with the US-backed terror army? Was there no means to resolve the land conflict through negotiation with the Sandinista administration? The Miskitos made a very serious political blunder by siding with their enemy's enemy—the Contras.

The Nicaraguan conflict in the Sandinista era was actually fought on three fronts. Firstly, the Sandinistas fought to defend the revolution and consolidate their program of state socialism. Secondly, the Contras tried to destroy the Sandanista's social program and dislodge their government. Thirdly, the indigenous fought for autonomy.

In some ways the situation can be understood through comparison with the positions of the competing sides in the Spanish Civil War in the 1930s. The Sandinistas assuming the role of the Spanish Revolutionary Republican Government, the Contras the Franco-ist fascists, and the indigenous like the anarchists pursuing a project of *revolution within the revolution* beyond the parameters of fighting the war. The Sandinistas reacted like the Spanish Republican government in 1936, clamping down on the aspirations of those who called for autonomy (or in 1936, anarchy) instead of first fighting and winning the war against the Contras.

The question then becomes, what kind of revolutionary project were the Sandinistas pursuing? The repression against the Miskitos was carried out in the name of the war effort. The idea was that first the war should be won and then afterwards the social and political questions, like the demand for autonomy, should be addressed. The Sandinistas reversed this strategy and tried to appease the rebellious indigenous in 1987 by introducing the far-reaching autonomy legislation. Of course, the Miskitos did not help their own case by siding with the Contra reactionaries—nothing anarchist whatsoever about that—but this should not have undermined the legitimacy of their demand for autonomy.

The question of autonomy on the Atlantic Coast entangled the Sandinista government in another front of battle that they could scarce afford to fight. The early repression of the indigenous proved costly later on as they struggled in the Contra War. Why had they not addressed the problem from the start by granting a level of autonomy and thereby resolving the Atlantic Coast conflict? The answer to this lies in the authoritarian politics of the FSLN command. To understand the Nicaraguan Revolution we have to return to the Pacific coast and take a closer look at the Sandinista leadership.

Managua Highlife and the Comandantes

Tagging along with two Irish dignitaries—the socialist parliamentarian Michael D Higgins, and Irish Times journalist Michael McCaughan, I find myself at a barbeque in the Sandinista headquarters on a clement Managua evening in January, 1990. It's a classy affair; it's a long way from the front lines of the Contra War, a world apart from the rural poverty and pastoral simplicity of the Atlantic Coast, and a stone's throw from Managua slums.

They are all here, all the famous faces of the revolution. How small and insignificant they appear now, mingling amongst the party's hordes! There's the president, Daniel Ortega—you would almost miss him, he is so inconspicuous. He's just a small man with thick glasses and a bushy moustache and a very serious expression on his face, even as all those around him drink and make merry. I bump into Vice President Sergio Ramiro's ample belly as I raid the salad bar. He humbly apologizes, and gives me a very lovely, sincere smile. Tomas Borge, the Interior Minister and ultimate hero of the revolution—quite a tiny man with a lacerated face—wears a military uniform that seems out of place at such an informal gathering as this. The poet-priest Ernesto Cardenal is looking flamboyant in his beret and cape, and is surrounded by a bunch of foreign intellectuals. In fact, there are a lot of internationals present—there is singer Billy Bragg over there, chatting with the glamorous-looking Bianca Jagger. And this is the thing about the occasion: it's unlike any other social occasion I've attended in my several-months-long sojourn in Nicaragua. This has all the trappings of an outdoor cocktail party on the Upper East Side of New York.

The Sandinista administration cannot be judged by a cocktail party, although symbolically this might be reminiscent of the pigs feasting in Orwell's *Animal Farm*. Certainly the undignified post-election behavior of the party's leadership—stripping the state bare of anything they can get their hands on before the new administration took office—would give further testimony to the claim that the Sandinista leaders are capable of abusing their power.

Aside from corruption, the Sandinista leadership has also demonstrated authoritarian tendencies that alienated elements of the population, such as those on the Atlantic Coast demanding autonomy. The war for national liberation was fought by the authoritarian military organization the FSLN. The guerrilla struggle necessitated a clandestine and hierarchal structure with a disciplined cadre prepared to carry out the commands of the *comandantes*. After assuming institutional power the FSLN did not let go of the old power structures, and continued to run the country as if it were a clandestine guerrilla organization—top-down and premised in the discipline of the cadre. Fighting the Contra war kept the leadership in this mode. It seems probable that if they had not been confronted by the war, they would have weakened state power somewhat, allowing an element of workers' self-management, more independent agricultural collectives, and autonomy for the Atlantic Coast. Furthermore, it might be fair to say that measures towards these aims would have been enacted after the elections were won and the Contra War ended. The Sandinistas banked on the hope that an electoral victory would give them enough international legitimacy that the US would be forced to stop funding the Contras and end the economic embargo, and that international loans from the IMF and World Bank would become available to rebuild the country.

In retrospect, it seems a fanciful strategy. If anything can learned from the Nicaraguan war, it is that the US does not stop until its interests are appeased and its goals achieved. In Nicaragua, that goal was the total destruction of the Sandinistas, even if that meant devastating the country. As the NGO Oxfam has pointed out, what the Sandinistas offered the region was the "threat of a good example," and in order to protect US interests, this had to be eradicated.

I recall being in an El Salvadoran refugee center in November of 1989. The FMLN (*Frente Faribundi Marti de Liberacion Nacional*) was on the verge of taking San Salvador. Thousands of guerrillas held positions around the capital, the battle raged, and the government was—predictably enough—strafing the poor barrios from the air. Some young guerrilla leader called Specky Four-Eyes had led a commando team to take hostage a group of US Green Berets in the Sheraton Hotel. If El Salvador fell to the FMLN guerrillas, what would happen next? Guatemala? Honduras? The whole region was captivated by this spirit of rebellion, and it seemed we were on the brink of great change. Nicaragua and Cuba were on red alert, fearing imminent invasion from the US. Meanwhile in Europe, the Berlin Wall was beginning to come down and the USSR was continuing to disintegrate. "They will never tolerate it," says an ex-combatant of the FMLN, a man with a wooden leg, as we watch the TV at the Salvadoran refugee center. "The US will kill us all rather that allow this to happen."

And I think he was right. The Sandinista triumph in 1979 was an anomaly allowed by the counter-position of the USSR. Nothing of its kind would be allowed to occur again. The US, the lone superpower, with its colossal military and seemingly endless counterinsurgency budget, would not tolerate such miscreant behavior again.

The Last Dawn of the FSLN

Nevertheless, the Sandinistas persisted in their hope that

a clear democratic mandate, through elections sanctioned on US terms, would improve the national situation. The UNO opposition—despite its US support, financial and otherwise—was floundering in the polls. It seemed an almost certain victory for the Sandinistas. The final election rally of the UNO in front of the old Cathedral was lackluster, attended by maybe 50,000 supporters. The final FSLN rally held in the Plaza de la Revolucíon by the banks of Lake Managua was attended by a half-million flag-waving, cheering, red-and-black bedecked Sandinista supporters. It seemed nothing could stop them.

Managua on Election Day—February 25, 1990—is on edge. Election turnout has been extremely high. Few irregularities have been reported by the army of international election monitors. FSLN functionaries have begun setting the stage for their victory celebrations. As the first results came in that night, they show UNO gains. "Probably just some pro-Contra towns in the North," says Michael D. Higgins, Irish parliamentarian with plenty of experience pollstering. But as the night grows older the counts keep coming in, Michael D's optomism wanes and it's clear that the UNO are winning. A certain feeling of dread and disbelief comes over us. Jumping into Michael D's suburban—supplied by the Sandinista leadership—we drive down to the Olaf Palme Center, the election headquarters where Daniel Ortega is to appear at dawn. Will he accept the results? Will he call the FSLN out onto the streets, denouncing the polls?

As we drive through the night we pass little gaggles of UNO supporters, gathered around bonfires celebrating. The mood is tense, the atmosphere confrontational. It seems impossible that the FSLN has lost the election. There is going to be war over this. Michael D orders the car stopped and picks up a young Sandinista militant on his way to the bus station. "The war has begun again; I'm going to the mountains," he says with some conviction. His only weapon appears to be his guitar. He sings us a song, and off he goes.

At the Olaf Palme Center, hundreds of journalists and internationals mill around. There is a sense of absolute disbelief and shock. Most are sympathetic to the Sandinistas and appalled at the results they are hearing. Everyone waits for the official Sandinista word. Will they declare martial law and send the troops into the streets? Will they call for a general strike, or people's insurrection?

Daniel Ortega walks out slowly around 6 a.m., and reads the statement from the FSLN with profound gravity. "The FSLN recognizes and honors today's election results," says the *comandante*, as the whole world watches. Incredibly, the FSLN is accepting defeat. The UNO victory is incontrovertible: 55 percent to the Sandinistas' 41 percent. The unimaginable has occurred.

Ortega continues to read out the long FSLN statement—thanking the martyrs, the militants, the mothers, and everyone else who has made the revolution possible. "We leave victorious," he says, "because we Sandinistas have spilled blood and sweat not to cling to government posts, but to bring Latin America a little dignity, a little social justice." And even more than the dignity of the actual words, what is striking is the *comandante's* heavy tone; his voice is cracking like a dead man walking, like a man with his heart broken in two.

The hundreds of assembled journalists, internationals, election officials, and government functionaries interrupt his speech, spontaneously breaking out into song—*"Adelante marchemos compañeros, avancemos a la revolución."* This is the Sandinista anthem, a stirring marching song; but now, sung in the Managua dawn, it takes on a haunting, melancholic tone.

Photographers put down their cameras, journalists stop scribbling on their pads, and the whole theater is overwhelmed by a strange passion. People raise their clenched fists and sing louder and everybody has tears in their eyes. Daniel, overwhelmed by emotion, leaves the room. The song ends and people look at each other, distraught. Strangers embrace and all that is left is the sound of stifled cries from Sandinista supporters mourning their loss.

Over at the Intercontinental Hotel—the headquarters of the international observers, corporate media, and those who can afford several hundred dollars a night—we go in search of the Irish politicians who have come as observers. By chance I share an elevator with Jimmy Carter, head of the observation mission.

He looks crestfallen and in need of a good night's sleep. I smile at him, somewhat shamefully, realizing full well that I have let down the tradition of the propaganda-by-deed anarchists—because, of all the US presidents, Carter is the only one I ever had a soft spot for.

Some Irish politicians, sleazy right-wingers who are using the junket paid for by the state to booze and whore, are at the Intercontinental bar with some Irish military officers, also election observers. They were all drunk, despite it being only 8 a.m. Some (sober) US officials have joined them, military advisors or some sort of operatives. They are very friendly with the Irish, and the group makes toasts to "the return of democracy to Nicaragua," and to "UNO and the clean election process"; they stop short of toasting the success of the Contras and the US intervention, but that is in the air, that smug sense of satisfaction with a job well done.

Too disgusted to spend one more minute in the company of these scumbags, I take off and find myself downtown in the vast, empty *Carlos Fonseca Plaza de la Revolución*. Some construction workers are dismantling the stage from the cancelled Sandinista victory celebration. Black and red flags blow forlornly from the empty bleachers. Just a few days earlier this very plaza was filled by the biggest political demonstration in Nicaraguan history. How could half a million people be wrong?

The pundits say that many wore the red and black but voted UNO. Some say they were Sandinista at heart but voted UNO to end the war, to stop the economic embargo. Others say that the Sandinistas 41 percent of the vote was a fine achievement, despite governing a crippled country at war, but that the silent majority came out to vote UNO. The mainstream media presents it as if these were free and fair elections and the opposition won, and it is a victory for democracy winning over—if not Communism—some kind of undemocratic socialism.

A victory for a democracy, delivered from the barrel of terrorist guns and by election extortion. That's capitalist democracy for you.

End of the Revolution

Nicaragua has returned to a different kind of nightmare in the 1990s: the dictatorship of the market. Sure enough, the war has ended, as the US stopped funding the Contras, and the embargo has ended—the IMF and World Bank have finally released funds for reconstruction projects. But Nicaragua has not prospered. Consecutive governments have implemented neoliberal policies that have returned the indices of poverty to Somoza times. The rich are now much richer and the poor are poorer. The rate of literacy has declined, health and education programs have been starved of funding, and the infant mortality rate has risen dramatically. All the social gains of the Sandinista revolution have been rolled back. The country has returned to being the poorest in the hemisphere, alongside Haiti and Bolivia.

The Diaz Ochoa Co-op in Matagalpa—that little plantation of hope—has been evicted by the *Somocista* landlord who returned from Miami. The seventy-five families have returned to scratching out a bare living on the rocky hillsides. Their sons and daughters might have been lucky enough to find a low-paid job in any of the *maquiladoras* sprouting in the new free trade zone. Or maybe they've tried their luck on the long road to the US.

Up north, the Contra communities found that they gained nothing with the new administration. In an absurd and cruel irony, the ex-Contras joined up with the ex-Sandinista soldiers to form the *Revueltos*, an armed group that for a while militantly protested the failure of the new government to award them land.

On the Atlantic Coast, the neoliberal government attempted to privatize the forests that the Sandinistas failed to nationalize. The indigenous resisted once more, but their dream of autonomy remains further from realization than ever before. More landless mestizos have migrated to the Atlantic Coast, encouraged by an administration that had no plan in place to deal with this demographic nightmare. Relations between the new settlers and the locals have deteriorated and a balkanization of the region is a real threat.

Predictably enough, and much to the satisfaction of the US administration, the FSLN has disintegrated under the intense pressure. A primary aim of the US policy in Nicaragua was not only to depose the Sandinistas from power, but also to destroy the organization completely. This they achieved in the post-election period with some help from the Sandinistas themselves. The *piñata*, or the free-for-all grab for everything in sight, reflected badly on the outgoing government. Ministries were left without a vehicle or a telephone. Property appropriated by the revolutionary organization was privatized into the hands of individual Sandinistas. Splits appeared in the ranks, and a whole swathe of the old revolutionary leadership formed a new party, the Sandinista Renovation. But the base stayed with Daniel Ortega and the FSLN. In subsequent years, as the opposition party, the FSLN has dropped any radical pretenses and embraced neoliberal policies, privatization, and a reformist social program. Party leaders have being besieged by scandals of corruption and improper behavior. The whole glorious moment in history which was the Sandinista revolution sank into the grotesque and obscene.

The Sandinistas have even lost the battle against forgetting—the revolution is over, and it is almost as if it never occurred.

Postscript.

Would it have been any different if the FSLN had chose a different form of government? If they had relinquished more power and allowed workers' to self-manage in the factories and independent co-ops to flourish on nationalized land? If they had granted autonomy to the peoples on the Atlantic Coast from the start? Can truly revolutionary social programs be carried through when the people are confronted by an unrelenting war waged by a colossus, the world superpower?

One lesson we can learn from the Sandinista experiment is that in a world with only one superpower, there is no space for seizing control of the state and maintaining a careful, dangerous balancing act against the wishes of the ultimate powerbroker. With the US as the sole superpower, it seems futile to seize the state against its' wishes, or to even attempt it. From the total defeat of the Sandinistas have arisen new ideas of struggle, new formulations of revolutionary organization. Change will now come from below and remain there, building alternative structures of power without seizing the state. Another world is possible, despite failed revolutionary programs like the Sandinistas'.

Among the thousands of international volunteers learning in Nicaragua during the 1980s was a young, bearded, pipe-smoking Mexican radical called Rafael Guillén. He would emerge a decade later in Chiapas using the *nom-de-guerre* Marcos. Revolutionary Nicaragua created a space to formulate new forms of revolutionary discourse, namely anti-authoritarian and autonomous. These other forms took shape in the Communal Movements of Central America and further afield with the *Sem Terra* in Brazil. Seen in this light—as mid-wife to a new radical political discourse—perhaps the Nicaraguan revolution was not in vain.

THREE CUBAN TALES

Havana, 2000

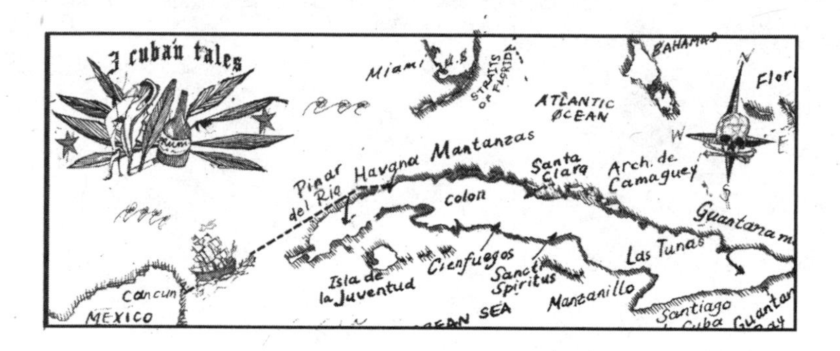

ANTIMPERIALISTAS

The Exile

Before even arriving on Cuban shores, the intrigue has begun. I received an email from an acquaintance, requesting that I contact a Cuban exile in Cancun, my port of departure in Mexico. They want me to bring a "package" to another unknown character, a "brother," in Havana. People tell me Cuba is a country in a state of war. But I've never being there, and I don't know anything.

A few days later, I'm sitting in a bar in downtown Cancun and a dodgy man sporting lots of gold jewelry, a Hollywood shirt, and a little manicured moustache is shouting at me in quite incoherent Cuban Spanish. He is brash, loud, confident, and full of wise-guy stories. I quickly understand he is no fan of Fidel, and notice that he has some prison tattoos. Most striking is the fact that this young-ish man has only a short stump left of one arm, and the other is a mangled mess of skin grafts and gristly veins. He deftly lights his Marlboro's by holding a matchbox under the short stump and cracking a match with his working limb. It's a neat operation. He performs this and other agile tasks with panache.

"Do you know my brother?" he asks.

"No."

"He is a better man than me," he continues.

"Really?"

"He is a musician, a poet, and very intelligent," he informs me.

He lights another cigarette and looks around somewhat suspiciously. "I liked the rum and the women too much. Not Antonio. He studied, worked hard. Whenever I got in trouble, Antonio came to my rescue. He's my older brother, but he's more like a father." He finishes his drink and clicks his fingers to beckon the waiter for another round. The Mexican waiter is clearly unenamoured by this crippled Cuban with attitude, but he is cautious. Maybe the Cuban is not someone to fuck with. "Antonio was the only person I told I was leaving," he says conspiratorially. "I trust him that much."

"Yeah, yeah, trust," I murmur. I am beginning to greatly mistrust my decision to become involved in this operation. What fucking package am I to carry into Cuba? They are harsh with counterrevolutionary activities, that much I know.

"You know what happened to me?" he asks, throwing back his beer. "No, no, I know nothing. I don't even know why I'm here. Something about taking a package to a brother…"

"They locked me up for a year!" he shouts suddenly. "You know why? Do you?"

Maybe this character is deaf as well as crippled. "No. I know absolutely nothing. Nothing."

"They stole a year of my life for selling t-shirts! For selling t-shirts for dollars when the dollar economy was illegal. And do you know what happened? Do you?!" I feel weary. "No, I don't."

"They legalized the dollar economy while I was in prison! When they let me out, every dog in the street was selling t-shirts for dollars!"

"That's fucked up," I concede.

"And most of the other prisoners were inside for even more absurd crimes." He begins getting visibly excited, emotional and angry and I'm beginning to warm to him. Maybe it's the drink.

"You know what's going to happen to poor little Elian?" He suddenly changes subject to the shipwrecked six-year-old Elian Gonzalez who was kidnapped by the Miami Mafia before the US Authorities snatched him back in a dawn raid and returned him to his Cuban-based father.

"He will probably suffer some post-traumatic hell after his Miami ordeal."

"No, no!" he laughs. "He will grow up hating Fidel and will try to escape Cuba as soon as he can. Cuba is a prison; Fidel is a dictator…" "Is he?" My sympathy towards him cools again. I've always admired Cuban resistance to gringo Imperialism.

"Have you ever been to Cuba?" he asks.

"No."

"You'll see! You'll see! Police on every street corner! If you talk to a Cuban, he'll be arrested! And there's nothing there: the people live miserable lives, miserable. No money, nothing to do, nothing in the shops, nothing to eat…"

"So why don't they revolt?" I ask. "If life is so bad, why don't they rise up like they did in 1959?"

"They want to, but they can't! If you complain, you lose your job. If you organize a meeting, your neighbors will inform to the police. If you protest in the street, they put you in prison!" I have heard this before. It wearies me. I want to hear something different.

"Is there nothing good in Cuba? Do you not miss your country, your home? Is life better here in Mexico?"

He stops suddenly, lights another cigarette with the stump of his arm, and throws back his beer. He grips me strongly with the mangled arm.

"I'll tell you something," he says softly. He looks like he might cry. "When I left prison, I realized I had to escape Cuba. Of course I couldn't tell anyone. Not my wife, nor my child, nor my family, nor my buddies. If I had been found out, they would have put me in jail again, 5 years, minimum…"

"Wife and child!" I exclaim, by mistake.

"I couldn't even tell them," He says sadly. "My wife had her suspicions when I started swimming a couple of hours every day. We lived in Guantanamo, near the US military base there. If you reach the shore of the base, you are granted automatic US citizenship."

"That's quite a provocation!" I interrupt.

"Better to risk your life than live like a prisoner in your own country!" he replies, clearly delighted by his own wit. I suspect this was prompted by the slogan on my t-shirt. It shows a portrait of Emiliano Zapata with his immortal words—" Better to die on your feet than live on your knees." I'm a big supporter of the Zapatistas, and Cuba was the antecedent. I'm hoping for a positive story, but it's not sounding too good.

"I swam for two hours every day for a year, until I was strong enough to swim past the coast guards and around the bay into Guantanamo. So many people have drowned attempting this! If the tide turns, if the wind changes, you're finished. I was taking a big risk."

Clearly he must have had his arms then. I'm intrigued. Prison, death, or exile—it's a brave decision to make.

"The day arrived. It was calm and still. I immediately knew I had to leave. I went to Antonio, my brother, and told him I was going away, that I might not come back but to tell my wife and child that it'll be OK and that I will return for them. And to forgive me."

He finished his beer, and angrily demanded more from a passing waiter. "Antonio pleaded that I stay. No, I told him, life is intolerable here in Cuba, I'm going…"

"I swam out in my shorts, and nothing else. I swam for hours until night fell, and passed the coast guard boats. I was exhausted, but I made it to the shore. My arms got me there. I was strong. Strong." I look inadvertently at his sad stump and his mangled good arm. My stare begs the question. "They held me like a prisoner for a few months at the military base," he continues. "The gringos were fed up by then with Cubans. They were reluctant to greet us, but they had to. Because of the Cuban Adjustment Bill any Cuban who washes up on US soil is automatically granted citizenship. But they don't like us. We are treated like shit. Nevertheless, I was happy to be alive, and to be out of Cuba. I couldn't contact my family for months, and they thought I was dead. It was hard for them, not knowing. Eventually I made it to Miami. They looked after me there. Soon I got work; the dollars flowed in. It was the good life; I was living it up. I was saving, too, to bring my wife and child over, Antonio too, even though he's still a communist, and still believes in Fidel…"

This latest twist comes as a surprise. This character before me would clearly be considered a Miami counterrevolutionary bandit by the Cuban authorities, and now it turns out his very brother—the clever one, the musician, the poet—is a loyal communist! A die-hard communist, in this day and age! The plot thickens.

"I fell in love with a Mexican woman in Miami. I was confused. What do I do about my wife who thinks she will join me soon? My child? But I was in love. I was blind."

He's quite drunk now, and maudlin. He knocks back another beer. "She was beside me in the car when I had my crash. The wheel fell off, we slammed into a wall. As you can see, I lost an arm, almost both. They saved this one by taking veins and skin from my leg. Anywhere else I would have lost both arms, but do you know something? The US is more communist than Cuba! They did everything possible to save my arm! And me, a new émigré!" He chuckles at the idea.

"You asked me what I like about Cuba, what I miss. I'll tell you." He grows animated. "The education system in Cuba is better than in the US. And the health system, despite there being no money, is really for the people. And I tell you what, I miss my buddies. Cubans stick together. I had a great bunch of pals. We had a great time, drinking and dancing! There wasn't any money, but still we partied every night. Because in Cuba there is nothing, but people invent ways to live well. If something is missing, a Cuban will invent it!"

At last, something positive. I will carry this grain of hope with me to Cuba. People of invention. And if there is no good story in Cuba, I will have to invent one! It's almost time for me to board the boat to Havana. We're both drunk now, but he more so than I. He suddenly becomes overwrought with emotion. Tears well in his eyes as he tells me to embrace his brother for him, and to "tell him to come to Mexico, where life is better than both Cuba and the United States."

There was still one more question that needed to be asked. "So how did you end up in Mexico?"

"Life is hard in the US. You're on your own, nobody gives a shit about anybody. I got tired. Money, that's all. Nobody cares about anything but money. After the accident, after I lost my arm, I had nothing left—only my Mexican girlfriend. She stood by me, she cared for me. So we came here to her home in Cancun. I get a pension from the US; it's not much, but with a little business here, we get by. I'm hoping my daughter can come over soon. It has been six years since I saw her."

He is in floods of tears as he attempts to embrace me Cuban style. His arm stump prods me in the chest, and it feels strange. He hands me a black holdall bag—"for Antonio," he chokes, "and tell him I'm OK..."

I glance back one last time and see the initially cocky wiseguy, decked out in Tommy Hilfiger and gold, reduced to a damaged, broken man weeping his heart out for lost life and the pain of permanent exile.

Havana in a Time of Its Own

Havana is fucking mad. I'm careening wildly at ridiculous speeds along the famous Malecon on a yellow taxi-scooter called a *Co-co* (coconut—because it resembles one) and the night air is warm and humid and full of strange smells. Pungent aromas of burning kerosene or butane gas or unrefined gasoline or... who-knows-what, but strange fuel is burning everywhere—in houses, in the streets, in the weird variety of vehicles bombing along the dimly lit Malecon. There are infamous old American cars from the 40s and 50s, Soviet style trucks, old motorbikes with sidecars, and Fiat Bambis. Lots of Eastern-Bloc Trabants scurry along, tiny beside the mammoth articulated lorry buses called *Camelo*'s (Camels) and the occasional big fancy foreign Jeeps. And everywhere are the wasp-like little yellow coconut taxi's with their Italian scooter engines going at terrifying speeds on fucked-up darkened roads.

The *taxista* has the audacity to ask me for $30 for the fifteen-minute joyride from the port and I give him $2, which is still over the odds. He drops me off in Central Havana, the wrong side. It's evening and the tight-knit old crumbling streets of this once-magnificent colonial *barrio* are teeming with life. Ill-lit and in ruins, the streets are filled with mystery and possible danger. Figures linger in shadows, street girls beckon from numerous darkened doorways, young hustlers hiss at me, children run alongside, and old men drink rum while playing dominoes noisily under lonely street lamps. On every block stands a dandy looking man in a leather jacket and black beret: a cop. The police resemble Parisian students at the barricades circa 1968—*tres chic.* Still the crowded streets, more like alleys, are full of hookers and hustlers and all kinds of potential miscreants. The enormous old tenement buildings sit languid and menacingly over the alleys, edifices bursting to the seams with bustle and banging and blaring music and loud voices and children's screaming games and televisions and general mad clamor. Havana is overflowing with life. Suddenly my fear leaves me and I realize there are no dangers; this overwhelming bustle is normality, and suddenly I feel relaxed and happy, welcome here in the gutter and heart of the old battered city.

But I am still lost. My directions to Antonio's house make no sense. Every helpful citizen sends me off in another hapless direction. I am wandering a maze of labyrinthine, dark and dank alleyways (the plumbing system has completely disintegrated in this part of town and it conjures up medieval images at moments, as streams of piss and shit flow into the street). I clamber up and down broken staircases in pitch darkness, knocking on musty old doors falling off their hinges, crossing decrepit back patios into hellish basements, or arriving on the roofs of the high tenements where chaotic cement rooms have been built randomly. Yet everywhere in these overcrowded slums the people help me along, direct me, accompany me, laugh with me, smile, and invite me for coffee or rum. I meet the whole lovely neighborhood in a few fumbling lost hours. There is something quite enchanting here, despite the ruins, and I realize it might have something to do with the solid community structure here—people living in each others shadow and looking out for one another. Or perhaps my good fortune is the strange luck of a hopelessly lost tourist in an extraordinary city.

Tired and bewildered, but exultant and emboldened by the numerous strong sugary coffee shots and the powerful homemade rum proffered in every doorway, I decide to venture into a bar on one of the bigger streets. It's a dodgy looking place, crawling with devastatingly beautiful young girls dressed to the nines in all the finest street girl fashions and suave, designer-label young hustler dudes all gangstered up. I push my way to the crowded bar and find a stool in the corner. A salsa/merengue band starts playing and everybody starts to dance—magnificently, sexily, and with tremendous grace. Everybody dances; the whole place erupts violently with thrusting and gyrating and wriggling hips. A waiter with his thick, dark hair greased back lavishly, attends to me.

"You wanna girl? Lotta beautiful girls! You ask me, eh?" he says in slick American English. "No thank you, but a Bucanero beer would be lovely," I respond graciously.

"Bucanero?" he sneers. "We have Heineken, Carlsberg, and Crystal." Bucanero is a cheap local beer. He is obviously not impressed by my lack of sophistication.

The Bucanero is great, and I am besieged by hordes of soliciting *jineteras*, asking if I am alone, and informing me they would like mojitos. Impossibly tight clothes, sporty stripes, and huge platform shoes are all the rage in Havana in 2000. For the fashion connoisseurs, I can add that this same style was all the rage in Zambia in 1999 and Brazil in 1998. Such is globalization.

But it's tiresome, the constant harassment by these *jineteras*, women who would deny voraciously being prostitutes but would expect financial remuneration for time spent with "boyfriends." I notice that there are other foreigners here, paunchy older European men accompanying pretty young girls. It's not a pleasant sight.

"Where are you from?" I am asked for the umpteenth time by an impudent stranger, and I'm getting wearier as the night evolves, my response has gone from an honest, chatty Ireland to a less warm Iceland, to a more obscure Guyana and now to a distinctly menacing Kosovo. It's all hustle here—men and women, girls and boys; all hustle with an unwavering confidence. It's reminiscent of Havana of another era, of the 1950s Hollywood films, of stool pigeons, gangsters and molls. Where's the much feted fucking revolution that brought an end to all that? But then I remember that Fidel and the bearded ones were no Islamic fundamentalists.

"Love is free in Havana!" laughs someone behind the bar, as I fend off yet another mojito-desiring *jinetera*. I turn to look at the woman with this loud infectious laugh.

"Love is free in Havana, they tell you, but these young girls will leave you naked in the street!" She almost collapses laughing at her own words. "Honey, you are so innocent I think you will be lucky to make it out the door tonight!" Again she nearly falls over with the force of her own raucous laughter. "I am quite in control of the situation," I reply defensively. Innocent! I just told the last hustler I was a war veteran on rest and recreation in Havana!

Nevertheless, it's a relief to talk to someone who is not asking for a mojito and describing possible lewd acts that could be performed immediately with some urgency. Victoria and I chat over the bar while she washes glasses. She is a cheery nurse in her late thirties who, she says with a sigh, needs the extra money. She's one of these very familiar people, but I can't place her. I'm thinking she looks a bit like a smaller Angela Davis, what with her intellectual-looking glasses and lips pursed in an entrenched way. But with that laugh, she is also reminiscent of Whoopi Goldberg. This Bucanero has my mind lopsided. We chat merrily and suddenly it strikes me that is my first night in Havana, it's late, and I have not found my contact Antonio. I have nowhere to stay.

"Victoria, are there any hotels near here? "Honey!" she guffaws, "It's four in the morning, nowhere is open at this time! Maybe *La Inglaterra* up in Capitolia."

"How much is that?"

"About $150 a night."

Fuck it. "Are there no *Casas Particulares*? Guest houses? $10 a night places?"

She almost pisses herself laughing. Victoria finds everything I say hilarious.

She first tries to ply me off to one of the lingering *jineteras* in the bar—"She's a nice girl, clean. She won't rob you," says Victoria. A very young girl claiming to be eighteen sits beside me at the bar. She says her name is Ludmila. She is bright and cheerful and laughs easily. I think we are getting on like a house on fire until she says she would like seventy dollars from me. "What?!" I say innocently. Ludmila then looks me straight in the eye with her huge Bambi eyes, and pulls her tight, tight top down a little until the taut shape of her nipple peeks over the material. In a movie, it might be considered an alluring cinematic moment; here in this late-night, dismal, beer-stinking bar, it comes across as it really is—the saddest moment, a young teenage girl selling her flesh to a drunk foreign man whose name she hasn't even asked.

Victoria takes me under her wing. "Honey, you come with me. I'll keep you out of trouble." And she laughs like a tickled child. So I am stumbling up a dark crumbling staircase after Victoria clutching a bottle of rum at 5 a.m. She has kindly offered me a roof when it becomes clear I was doomed to wandering the streets until dawn.

There's a ferocious smell of piss in the corridor outside Victoria's apartment. The whole rambling tenement smells of piss and that strong butane gas from the cookers. She pushes in the creaking old door and steps into the claustrophobic darkness of her single room. She turns on a dim strip of light in the corner, which throws up eerie shadows across the decrepit little space. I immediately notice there is only one bed, and not enough space to swing a panther, but Victoria is nonplused. "It's not much, but it's my own place," she says defiantly. We sit down on the side of the moldy old bed and drink straight rum from the bottle. She likes her rum, I notice, and it loosens her tongue.

She tells me she was with a man for ten years and then he ran off with a younger girl. At least she was left with the apartment. She works in the hospital for over forty hours a week for 240 pesos a month—about twelve dollars. She has her ration card that guarantees her all the basics, but anything beyond that—like soap, fancy clothes, or her favorite, an apple—is only for sale in dollars, so she has to work in the shitty bar to earn a few dollars. Still she is lucky, she says—most people have no access to dollars. The *jineteros* and *jineteras* make the most money, she says, much more than doctors or anybody else. Victoria then jumps up playfully, and pulls her tracksuit bottom down, and squats over a bucket in a corner, and pisses merrily while chuckling about something. There are no flush toilets in the whole tenement.

"Would you like to eat?" she asks.

"Yes, please."

She pulls open the huge old fridge. Inside I can see, by the shadows of the dim light, that there is only emptiness—a water container and a few bits of vegetable. And vacant shelves, and darkness. She fries some garlic in a pool of strange smelling oil and dips some bread-like substance in it. She serves it on a tin plate. "Yum, thanks," I say, and I'm embarrassingly nauseous eating the food.

The rum is good: it cost two dollars in the local 24-hour dollar shop. Victoria munches away on a dollar apple as she drinks—a delight, a delight. Around dawn we fall upon the bed and sleep in each other's arms.

I wake from deliriously sweet dreams to a maddening, rowdy clamor outside. It's a little after dawn and the neighbors are creating havoc just feet away, the other side of light walls. Babies scream, people holler at each other, things bash and crash, and the din is intolerable.

"What is going on?!" I ask Victoria, who is crouched over the bucket pissing voraciously.

"The neighbors," she says, "they rise early." Her voice turns grave. "They have put a hex on me," she continues. She squats down again to piss.

"The neighbors have hexed me and I have to urinate all the time. They want my apartment. They have four children in one room. They want my room. They hexed me."

She pulls up her clothes again and approaches a strange doll on the floor by the side of the bed. It is an odd-looking simple black doll surrounded by a variety of eclectic objects: plastic flowers, matches, coins, some cards, bric-a-brac. It's a little altar.

"I don't have money to go to a *Santero.* I need to go to a *Santero,*" Victoria says with some distress as she kneels before the doll. She blesses herself gently and rises. She begin to laugh to herself, the moment of introspection passed. Then she attends to me, her nursing qualities coming out. She sticks her long fingernail into my ear and digs out some wax as she lectures me on Cuban behavioral physics.

"Don't you think your urination might have to do with a kidney infection?" I suggest, appealing to her professional nursing capacity.

"Of course not," she chides winsomely. "The lady next door wants my room; there is little I can do until I see the *Santero*."

Victoria has little money for anything, and worries unceasingly about that fact. She spends an enormous amount of time mopping her little floor and cleaning everything. The room is a dingy, depressing, dilapidated hole, but a clean one. She sings as she cleans, sad songs of heartbreak and melancholia.

And she also worries about me. Every day I go out on my errands or search for Antonio, and return a little late. She sniffs at me and says, "you have been with a girl!" "No," I would say, "Don't be ridiculous!" But she is absolutely convinced that I go out and have sex with every *jinetera* in the street all day, then come back for dinner. I insist that I do nothing of the sort, but she is convinced and unerring in her suspicion. Then she laughs and talks of all the foreign men coming to Cuba to fuck girls. It is true. Cuba is becoming the brothel of the Caribbean once again, forty-two years after the start of the Revolution that aspired to change all that.

I invite her out the last night before leaving, in an attempt to cheer her up and allow her to forget about her problematic hex. She hands me her identity card and says that if I don't carry it the cops would bust her for *peligrosidad*—"dangerousness," a catch-all Cuban law used to keep locals away from foreigners. We eat and drink and go to the club of her choice, oddly enough a dancing-girls club full of feathered girls in dental floss bikinis doing ballerina-style exotic dance. After the *Espectacular*, the disco pumps into action. Victoria and I start to dance. Young girls, dressed to kill, begin to dance rudely in front of me, pushing Victoria to the side. Before I can say anything, she pulls them aside and threatens them. It is clearly time to sit down and converse, before a brawl breaks out.

"Do you like Fidel?" I ask.

"Yes," she says without hesitation. This comes as a surprise, as she's spent most of her time complaining with great articulation about everything. "I love him! He is my hero. And Che."

"But you have so many criticisms of the system here!" I point out.

"Yes, but Fidel is fighting for us. We're a poor country, but look at all we have achieved!" she says vigorously. Victoria, child of the Revolution, goes on to outline the whole scenario—the economic blockade, the Helms-Burton Law, the collapse of the Soviet bloc. "Are you a communist?" I ask provocatively.

"No!" she says, and laughs raucously at the suggestion. By way of explanation she proceeds to tell me the story of how a white dove landed on the shoulder of Fidel during an early rally, and this was a sign among the spiritual element of the Cuban population that He was chosen as a leader to lead the people out of misery. I have read this story in the *Rough Guide*, but it's a little different to have a believer relate it in a dancing-girls' club, late at night in Havana, over strong rum and with eyes ablaze. I am relieved. I don't have to invent any stories; Cuba invents them.

The next morning I leave because I can no longer stand the intolerable racket of the tenement, the unceasing noise pollution, the pungent gas and oil smells that poison the building day and night, the constant peering eyes of the nosy neighbors (will they hex me? I wonder, alarmed), and the grinding misery of Victoria's life—in which, despite our fond reveries, I have no right to be a tourist.

Caribbean Nights

Antonio is finally located. Returning to the vicinity of the address, I encounter a random man loitering suspiciously at the corner. He's a shifty character who sniffles a lot. We go for a drink in a gritty local bar. It's a dodgy place and we drink La Tropica, an unusually malty tasting beer. "Antonio is living with a *gringa* girlfriend in Miramar," he informs me, looking about nervously. "He's pretending that he still lives here to hold onto the apartment, but only his son stays here now. He's living with his fancy woman in Miramar." Miramar is the posh district, I ascertain, where all the mansions and embassies are located. The shifty guy changes the subject.

"You like cocaine? You want some?" He gives me a sniff of good cocaine then offers to sell five dollars' worth. Turns out he has spent several years in jail for attempting to flee the country. He exhibits a collection of appalling prison tattoos, all proclaiming great love for his mama. A cop wearing a stylish leather jacket and a cool French beret appears on the scene, and without doubt it's time to bid my coke-fiend informant farewell.

The bus to Miramar is a veritable nightmare. The people are crushed in, door to door, and more people push on at every stop, through both the front and back doors. It is unbearable. It's hard to believe people have to travel daily in this bedlam. I just about squeeze off the bus intact, only two or three stops past my intended drop-off point. (I began my push to the door far too late.) The overloaded vehicle pulls off, groaning, as the people trapped inside shout and argue vehemently. Miramar, in Havana's suburbs, is fancy. Boulevards are lined with splendid colonial mansions in bad need of repair. I pass the Libyan, Palestinian, and Iranian Embassies before I chance upon a lovely, simple John Lennon statue sitting on a bench. Paradoxically, Lennon's music was banned here in the sixties, and so today they have a 24-hour guard watching over him—perhaps to make sure he doesn't cause any trouble or to ward off would-be assassins. The mind boggles. The guard is kindly taking tourists' photos as they perch themselves on the bench.

It's such a relief to be away from the noise and bustle of central Havana! Like any leafy, posh suburb, it is silent and cloistered and the scent of privilege lingers. Antonio's residence is part of a relatively swanky modern block. I approach with caution, clutching the black hold-all, this bag of mystery.

Antonio opens the door. He smiles warmly. "We have been expecting you."

He looks like his brother, dark and handsome, only a few years older. The apartment is spacious and nicely furnished. Silvio Rodriguez, a Cuban loyalist, serenades from the stereo. There's a middle-aged American woman sitting on the sofa, engulfed in a fog of cigarette smoke. A half-empty bottle of rum sits on the table.

"Would you like some rum?" she asks in English. "Tonio, get him a glass." Antonio returns with ice in a glass and speaks in good English.

"Did you have any trouble bringing the bag into the county?" "No," I say, "They were checking my other bags so long they got bored and let me through." "Cuba is a country at war," points out Amy, the Californian. "People don't realize that." "I noticed. There's a cop on every corner."

"There are counter-revolutionaries on every block," she continues. "Need to root them out. That's what the Neighborhood Defense Committees are there for, too."

"Do you like Johnny Cash?" asks Antonio with a smile. He puts on a CD and the rogue folk voice of Cash fills the room. I'm beginning to like this Antonio. "How is my brother?" he asks in almost a whisper. I'm not sure how to answer. Should I say he's a bitter, broken counter-revolutionary with missing limbs and a drinking problem?

"When did you last see him?" I ask. "Six years ago," replies Antonio. "He came to me one morning and announced he was leaving. He didn't tell anyone else, not even his wife. We were very close. I miss him very much."

"Are you in contact much?"

"No, the phone costs too much. We talk briefly maybe once a year." I don't know what to say.

"He's doing very well in Cancun," I offer.

There's a silence. Amy throws back her rum and inhales her heavy filterless *Popular* cigarettes. Antonio empties his glass too; these people like their drink. "Still friends with the Miami Mafia, is he?" interjects Amy. "Telling you lies about Cuba, about Fidel? He left his wife and kids here, and went to Miami to screw around." "My brother suffered here in Cuba," says Antonio quietly.

"He said," I respond, "that Cuba spends all its time fighting wars on other continents, yet the plumbing system in Havana has never worked. He said, 'who should you help first, your brother or your neighbor?'"

"Cuba has its priorities—education, health and international solidarity," says the Californian, irritated by my words. "There are no spare parts for the plumbing because of the US embargo."

"I fought for two years in Angola," says Antonio, without fanfare. "We beat the South African Army."

That quiets me. Cuba routed the South African apartheid army and their mercenary allies in Angola. Cuba helped the FSLN in Nicaragua overthrow the Somoza dictatorship, helped the FMLN combat the El Salvadorian dictatorship, supported Allende in Chile—the list goes on. Wherever there is a hurricane or disaster in Latin America, Cuban doctors are always the first internationals on the scene. I even recall two Cuban pilots in Prague in the 1980s promising to come to the aid of the Irish against the British army if the need ever arose (there was rum involved).

"Your brother said you should come to Mexico, that Mexico is better than Cuba or the USA."

"That is his message?" asks Antonio.

"Yes." I remember that I'm holding the black bag, "What's in the bag?"

"It is everything I need to go to Mexico," says Antonio. There is another silence. "What?!" says Amy, aghast.

"My brother wants me to join him in Mexico, my sweetheart. He says there are opportunities for me there. He says there is work, money."

"Antonio," she says slowly, "You are almost fifty years old; you have a good job, your children, your family, your life-long friends here. You have me, Antonio, you have me…" she trails off.

"Yes, my sweetheart. I have you, and I have all this, and I love Cuba. But I have no money; I am dependant on you. I am dependant on you or I am dependant on Cuba. You have chosen to come here. I have no choice. I want to be free to travel."

A horrible silence comes over the room. The music finishes. The only sound is of rum being thrown back. Someone has to break the hard silence.

I make an attempt, "Your brother says you are a Communist, Antonio." "Yes, I am," he says. "But now I want to be a communist somewhere else."

"I'll go get more rum," I say, taking my leave, as the couple stares at each other in uncomfortable silence with tears in their eyes. The night air is humid and oppressive, but I am relieved to escape outdoors.

It's a beautiful Caribbean night with a clear sky, a full-moon, and streets humming with activity. Clustered around occasional streetlights, the young people play baseball. How healthy and athletic they seem, and I am reminded that Cuba really has the healthiest population I have ever seen. Friendly and helpful, too, I think as the youths directed me to the nearest 24-hour dollar store. It is a shabby imitation of a US franchise, with a wide range of goods not available in the peso stores. I glance around and see it is filled with rubbish—candies and cookies and chocolates and hot dogs and all kinds of unhealthy, processed food. A bourgeois family eats hamburgers and drinks cola, no doubt dreaming of McDonalds. I purchase a twenty-year old bottle of Havana Club for five dollars and can understand why the lady is so hostile—maybe that's the dollar store attitude.

I get lost on the way back, wandering the darkened streets, and chance upon the ocean. It is vast and restless, and a soft breeze blows in from the infinite darkness. The dilapidated seafront reveals evidence of a once-fine promenade.

At the edge of a crumbling pier, a fisherman and his son are sharing the quietude and the meager pickings. We share some rum and lament the depleted Caribbean fish stock. He is a gristly old man with an easy laugh and few teeth—and tales to tell, I suspect. "I knew Don Ernesto," he starts. Ah, a Hemingway character. I am intrigued, but he does not reveal the mysteries of the seven seas to me.

"Give me $5 dollars and I will tell you about Hemmingway and the fishermen," he offers. I give him another swig of rum and move on.

I don't want to intrude on Antonio and Amy and their drama. The bag is delivered.

I have concluded my mission. Poignant, heartrending scenes are not my forte.

A gleaming red 1950s Cadillac pulls up and the driver offers me a ride to the center of town. It is a stunningly fine old vehicle, a labor of love; even the leather seats have been polished to a T. The couple, newlyweds, have been cruising the streets looking for passengers. "There's nothing else to do," explains the woman monotonously. The uptight guy gestures that

I should lower myself down in the regal seat. "It's illegal to pick up tourists," he says hissing at me as if it is my fault. They seem disappointed I am not from the United States and am so fond of Cuba.

"Life is profoundly boring in Cuba," says the young woman with some finality. I look at her husband, an older man wearing a tie, and I can't help chortling. He is polishing the dashboard as he drives. Tedious old fart, indeed. "Why do you laugh?" he growls.

The famous Malecon is lively. Clusters of people gather on the dimly lit seafront. Waves crash over the sea wall, lending an unpredictable mood to the proceedings. I sit on the wall and gaze out to sea. The night is filled with spirits and I'm not sure if it is melancholy or sinister. Various *jiniteros* and *jiniteras* approach, hawking oil paintings, cigarettes, drugs, and their bodies. "No, *gracia*s," I repeated, respectfully.

"Victoria is looking for you," says a voice in the darkness. I peer into the distance and suddenly a smiling young girl emerges into view.

"Excuse me?"

Then I remember—it is the girl from the club on the first night, the girl who called herself Ludmila, who claimed she was 18 and exhibited her breasts to me as if they were some artisan's craftwork.

"Victoria is looking for you. She wants to take you out dancing," she giggles. Ludmila looks completely a girl now, wearing shorts and a t-shirt in place of her tight *jinitera* gear, and sniggering like a fifteen-year-old and hanging out on the Malecon with a gang of similar teenage tricksters.

They sit around, and ask me questions about the world beyond Cuba, these inquisitive youth. Jennifer Lopez is a big hit with the girls, and the boys are all about Puff Daddy. "Manu Chao?" I offer, but nobody knows the name. Their joy and mirth is infectious, and soon I am clapping along to their quite brilliant Michael Jackson impressions. Nearby, there's a sculpture of a metal spiral staircase leading up high to a brick wall. A boy runs up the stairs and stops. "Let's go to the United States!" he shouts in English, banging his fists on the brickwall.

They all laugh. A huge tourist cruiser sails into the harbor, and begins hooting its loud whistle. Everybody on the Malecon waves at the ship, and the tourists thronging its decks don't even wave back, they just flash away at them with fancy cameras. This crew of rich, fat whitey's coming in like a bunch of conquistadors coming back to claim "the jewel of the Caribbean."

It is the saddest moment. The long dark seafront seems to become engulfed in a wave of melancholy and longing. The sea ebbs and flows out.

TALES FROM THE VANQUISHED PIER

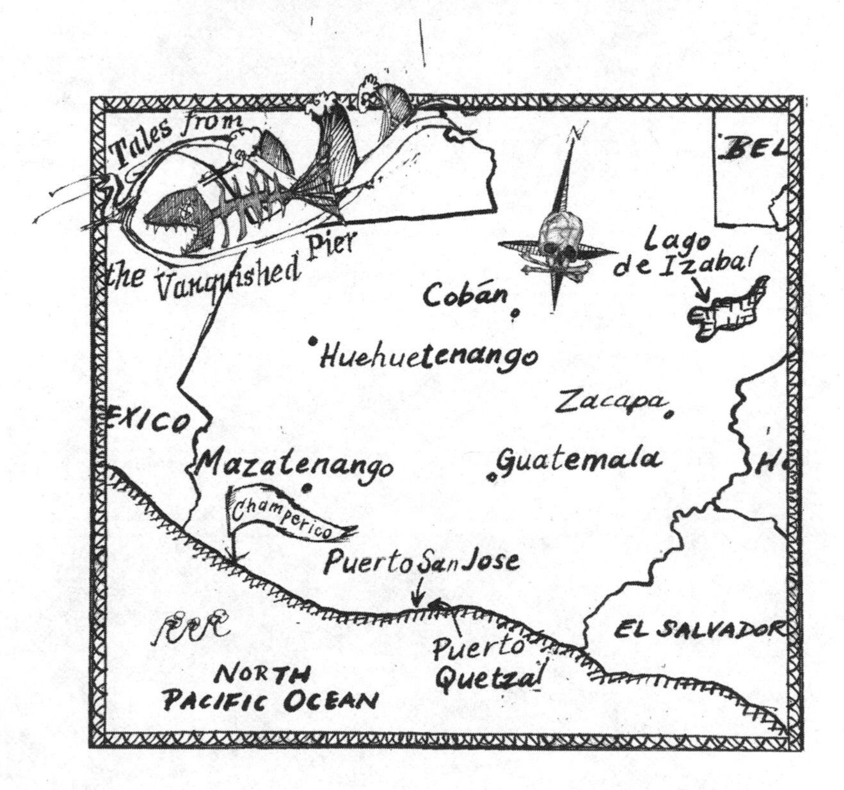

POLICIA

"The unspeakable boredom of life at Champerico..." Aldous Huxley, 1934.

I met some bored young housewives at a bus stop in Guatemala. Having fled Mexico—due to a problem with immigration, and nothing better to do, I decide to accompany them back to their seaside town. We chat away on the long journey over the mountains—in Spanish, in English, and in light intimacy. It appears that their absentee husbands work as peons in New Jersey, part of the clandestine workforce, undocumented and vagrant. They send their cash back home while their wives swan around with their mobile phones, wearing the latest fashions, bored and listless with life in the abyss; this mad little port town, their community, and their families being destroyed by the demands of the new labor market.

They are all delighted to talk a bit of *Ingles* with a dandy maestro—"a professor of English" my hat for this episode, as good a cover as any, with all the wives so thrilled to have such a distinguished guest in their not-often-visited seaside town. Champerico gets one line in the tourist guidebook—"a tawdry, sweltering, dilapidated place—dangerous and unfriendly." My kinda town. It was the hub of Pacific coast commerce and seatrade until the end of the pier fell into the sea and all the ships went elsewhere. Now the town has become convulsed with criminality, the cocaine trade and all its unsavory spin-off industries.

"I am interested in the psycho-geography of places quite off the map," I explain somewhat mysteriously to my eager, newly-initiated students. One takes out a pen and scribbles the new word down on her pad.

"Psycho-geography—a useful word, *maestro*," she says enthusiastically.

"Yes," I say, getting into the swing of this *maestro* business, "next time you write to your husband, impress him by asking in English about the psycho-geography of New Jersey."

"I will, maestro, *sí*!" she says, delighted, and I feel a little cruel as I chuckle to myself.

The wives bicker over whose house I should stay in as we finally pull into Champerico. It is dusk, the town is dusty and lazy, and we witness quite a dramatic hit-and-run outside the bus station. A man lies in a pile on the road as a large old American car drives away at high speed.

"Turf wars," says Veronica, by way of explanation, dismissing the violence petulantly. "You will, of course stay, in my house—OK, *maestro*?"

I decline the offer diplomatically, preferring instead to find my own hotel room. This falls well with all of the wives, and I am ushered to the deserted but atmospheric Neptune Hotel, which overlooks the ocean. The ocean is dark and vast. Great waves roll in interminably from the deep Pacific, crashing uneventfully upon the black volcanic sands of the deserted, unkempt beach.

A quaint, rustic circus haunts the beachfront. The large old tent is stitched together in a patchwork of many different materials giving it a vaudeville-like appearance. Amongst the junkyard of vehicles scattered around, I spot some monkeys swinging about and a group of alluring transvestites smoking in the shadows. Beyond the circus tent, the beach is lined by a long row of eerie, decrepit, wooden restaurants. The wives have warned me of these establishments—places where apparently men get gunned down in their hammocks. Here, they say, congregate gangsters, whores, bad cops, and drunken old soldiers—all consolidating useless lives. They leave their guns at the bar, drink for two or three days and nights, fight each other, and then stumble off with unsavory hookers.

A suspicious character joins me as I enjoy a quiet beer before the exotic sunset, seated under a tired old palm tree in front of the Neptune Hotel. "Lovely ladies," he says, referring to the departed housewives. "But they don't like to, you know, enjoy life. I can introduce you to some girls who like to have fun."

A pimp, I suspect.

"I am a *maestro de Ingles...*" I begin, hoping to discourage any further hustling. But this slim, twitchy young-ish man sporting dark glasses and a fancy beach shirt has his own agenda. He claims he's Mexican, but judging by his accent I suspect he's South American, probably Colombian—a suspicion further validated by the wads of foreign currency he is carrying in his fat wallet, which he exhibits as he insists on buying me a cocktail and *Caldo de Marisco*, a seafood plate, at a nearby seafront restaurant.

I am proven wrong—he is not a pimp. As the night evolves, and he keeps buying me cocktails and telling his wild stories, it becomes clear he is not trying to sell me anything, although he is definitely some variety of hustler. Despite the fancy clothes and fat wallet that suggests a businessman on vacation, he has that haunted look of a hunted man carrying many secrets. His particularly scurried demeanor is augmented by his continual glances over his shoulder, as if he expects to be grabbed at any moment.

But nevertheless, he is a sympathetic character, in need of nothing more than a friend upon whom to unload his horror stories before the night is through. He brings me on a wide roam of all the bars and brothels of this wretched place and introduces me to a whole variety of guttersnipes dressed in Tommy Hilfiger—the typical desperadoes and degenerates found in any criminal location beyond the global mall. Drinks flow, my glass is kept full, and the inevitable pandemonium ensues.

Why is this lovely old lady trying to sell me her pretty teenage daughter for $20? Why is the bar suddenly in a state of uproar? Has the Colombian drugged me, or is it the tremendously strong rum? How did I end up in the back of this police pickup truck? Why am I now running down backstreets pursued by my "pal" the Colombian? Why is the Neptune Hotel owner carrying a large pistol in his underpants as he holds me, naked and deranged, vomiting all over his patio?

I wake up late and find it was not a dream. The owner's daughter mops my room with a smirk on her face. I notice I am still naked, and the remnants of *Caldo de Marisco* littering my chest do not add to my charm.

"My papa is upset with you, *maestro*," she says. "He told me to tell you that you must not vomit on the patio." "Yes, yes, of course," I mutter, quite confused. She steps out with a coquettish smile and I pull the sheet over me.

My confusion is further compounded when the Colombian comes in with an armful of beers. "Ah, *maestro*! Not the owner's daughter!" he says, with a conspiratorial smirk.

I thought that I had fallen out with this guy. I recall, in my groggy hung-over state, having fled from him at some moment last night. A police pick-up truck?—it's all a blur.

"Here," he says jovially, "you gave me your wallet to mind last night." He hands it over and I glance in, noticing that all the money there within remains untouched. The Colombian cracks open a beer and begins to relate some of the previous night's adventures, and I can hardly believe him. Having an urgent need to vomit, I take my leave and escape his monstrous company one more time.

The early afternoon beach is populated by cheerful strollers, most of whom are indigenous families dressed in wildly colourful traditional weaves. Some are paddling about in the calm sea, still wearing all their clothes. It is a strange juxtaposition of modesty beside the other beach-dwellers, mestizos sporting the latest Miami bikinis.

My stroll along the sea-shore is rudely interrupted by a very drunk man in ripped underpants throwing himself pathetically into the ocean, in what I perceive is a feeble attempt to drown himself. Feeling guilty after last night's excesses, I do my good deed for the day by dragging him out of the water. His wife runs over in tears (I can tell by the piss dripping down her leg that she too has had a few drinks), screaming and ranting, and the two of us drag him up by his heels, leaving a trail in the sand. The elegant wife, the owner of one of these beach-front restaurants, is apoplectic with gratefulness and explains that she is an Argentinean and this terrible Guatemalan drunkard is her once-fine husband who, ever since the war ended, has been listless and despairing. Nobody calls him Colonel anymore, and he keeps trying to commit suicide. Indeed, I nod sympathetically and take my leave, for I am a *maestro* and I have a date with the forlorn and lovely Veronica for an English class.

Veronica has being waiting two years to join her beloved husband in New Jersey, which she dreams of while packing export shrimp fifty hours a week at the only factory in town. She waits patiently, dotes on their son, and wears all the latest New York fashions. She keeps respectable, eating ice cream in the afternoon with the other marooned wives. Despite living in a Caligulan town of unfathomable depravity, she and her cohorts manage to uphold their uncommon virtue and bourgeois morality. "I am faithful to my husband because I know he is faithful to me, and working hard to bring me up there," she explains.

She blushes very prettily when I invite her for a beer—oh horror! But still she comes, this Cinderella, only pulling herself away at sundown to retire to her shanty house, satisfied that the gringo *maestro* does indeed desire her.

When night comes in the port, strange men approach me and ask about my "friend, the Colombian" and invite me into darkened doorways. I desist and sure enough find the Colombian in one of the more relatively upscale brothels cavorting with criminals. He greets me like a brother and immediately orders me a most magnificent *Caldo de Marisco* with a giant lobster and a ridiculously strong rum cocktail, though I decline the large-breasted lady he proffers later as dessert.

A sinister police pickup truck (which looks strangely familiar) pulls up slowly outside the door. Suddenly I notice I am alone at the table, and all my cronies have disappeared into the shadows. A dodgy character claiming to be some kind of "Intelligence" Officer beckons me to the darkened window of the truck and asks me where my "Colombian friend" has gone.

"I am a humble *maestro* of *Ingles*, Officer," I reply, "and I know nothing except letters and the poetry of Pablo Neruda, so I am afraid I can be of no assistance to you..."

A lonely-looking transvestite blows me a kiss as I wait for a hotdog from a little food stand by the deserted circus, run by a kindly mute and his sad-eyed mute son. A woman with a Prada handbag talking on a mobile phone is explaining to someone that the circus was cancelled because the tent collapsed, but that nobody had turned up for the show anyhow. And the little tiger died, she continues, after getting kicked in the head by an irate horse.

Nobody turns up for the Saturday night disco on the beachfront either, so, drenched by a sudden violent tropical rainstorm, I retire to the quiet Neptune Hotel. The evangelical owner, still carrying a large pistol in his pants, is in a chatty mood.

"I used to be a police officer, but now I want to go work in the United States." He is wondering if maybe I know someone who can help him get a visa. "Maybe the Colombian," I suggest. "No, the cops got him tonight," he says with a sigh.

It's midnight in Champerico. The hotel owner has gone to bed and his daughter is mopping the patio, dressed in a towel. "Do you need anything, *maestro*?" she asks.

I consider barricading my door with the desk to make sure I don't land myself in any more trouble tonight. The evangelical's pistol predominates my unsettled dreams.

The elegant Argentinean restaurant owner treats me to a marvelous *Caldo de Marisco* with huge shrimps for breakfast. The beachfront is deceptively calm and the sun shines on the Sunday strollers. The Argentinean suggests I should come live with her and her husband. "He needs the company, *maestro*," she says. The husband appears, looking sheepish but respectable now that he is clothed. He thanks me humbly for rescuing him from the sea the day before. His wife insists that he join me as I eat the complimentary *Caldo*. He is a philosophical ex-soldier-turned-fisherman whose conversation turns from "Are you enjoying your visit to Champerico, *maestro*?" to "there is no joy, no happiness, no love in this life..." He turns away and looks to the infinite ocean, sighs, and probably hates me for having dragged him out of the sea.

His wife turns out not to be Argentinean at all, but Salvadorian. All is explained to me by Veronica, the innocent, as we lick ice creams in the afternoon sun. "She is a consummate liar and a drunkard and is driving her good husband to suicide," she says. However, the real problem, it appears, is that she is Salvadorian, which, for Veronica the Guatemalan, is her worst sin. The conversation turns, as usual, to New Jersey. "I would like to work as a beautician there," she says wistfully.

We are interrupted by yet another character sporting cartel sun-shades asking after my "friend the Colombian." And then, in a potentially embarrassing moment, a scantily-dressed teenage prostitute, one of the Colombian's pals, greets me cordially. "You know her?!," asks Veronica incredulously. "No, not really," I say, "but I have met her mother."

It's almost time to leave Champerico. I stroll the vanquished pier, watching fisherman haul in their catches. Where the pier ends, dramatically falling off into the sea, the fishermen have with some ingenuity rigged the old loading cranes with harnesses to lower their boats into the water sixty-five below. They are hard men burnt by the sun, who speak in a harsh colloquial Spanish that I can't understand. They work boisterously in collective gangs, sharing the burden of lifting and portering. A one-legged prostitute, of quite startling Asian beauty, guffaws with the men. A soldier, his rifle slung over his shoulder, jots down notes on a pad. A passing young lady sporting Gucci shoes explains to me, in between conversations on her mobile phone, that the soldier is there to check that all the fishermen return—"He documents the drowned."

I return to say goodbye to the phony Argentinean and her suicidal husband. Now she is wearing an *Arena* t-shirt—the Salvadorian death-squad party, so I'm not so sure about living with her after all. An unemployed, ex-circus transvestite is sitting with her and they offer me a *Caldo de Marisco*. At another table the ex-Colonel sits alone, swigging heavily from a bottle of rum.

Veronica walks me to the bus station. She blushes as I kiss her farewell and she grips my hand a moment too long. She offers her house for when I return. Of course, I say, and we can continue our studies. "I will be fluent when I go to New Jersey!" she enthuses. "And, *maestro*, how was the psycho-geography of Champerico?" she asks cheerfully.

"Certainly not boring, anyhow," I say.

The chicken bus is filled with all kinds of farm livestock, and the people are crushed on top of each other. A pal of Veronica's chats with me, as she licks ice cream and answers her mobile phone. "Poor Veronica," she says, "Nobody has the heart to tell her that her husband is living with some *gringa* up there, and they've just had a kid."

A molester is loudly denounced by a young, fashionable, woman and the culprit, a shaven head soldier, scurries away pleading innocent. The bus has a mechanical fault and cannot exceed 10 mph on the rugged road, so the journey takes all day. I feel very strange. I'm still convinced that the Colombian drugged me, but I'm not sure at all.

A CARNIVAL OF DREAMS

The Passion of the Brazilian Left

Once there was a black El Dorado in Brazil
It was there, it lived, fought, fell, died and rose again
It rose again, a peacock of all colors, the carnival of my dreams
And was born again, Quilombo, now it's you and me.
Quilombo

—*Gilberto Gil*

When Latin America was visited by hell—the military dictatorships of the late sixties and the seventies—resistance was crushed like a flower under a boot. In Brazil, even the wonderful, melancholic pop songs of the era—sung by Gilberto Gil, Caetano Veloso, Maria Bethania, or Nazare Pereira—became victims of the repression. The flowering of culture was incarcerated or forced into exile. As Pelé and the Brazilian soccer stars mesmerized the world, the military dictatorship murdered and tortured hundreds of thousands. Such is Brazil—characterized by aching beauty and startling cruelty.

Amazon Adventures

The journey begins in a British Army Armored Personnel Truck. How can that be? How can a journey to the heart of the Amazon, into Brazil—the most beautiful and precious country imaginable—begin in a fucking British colonial war vehicle?

Because, it seems, everything is connected. Maybe if the British Army hadn't occupied Ireland and they hadn't murdered the three IRA volunteers in Gibraltar and I hadn't attended their funeral and a British agent hadn't thrown grenades at the mourners and shot three more dead, then perhaps I wouldn't be here years later on my way to a meeting of international rebels and revolutionaries and people who want to change the world.

So this British Army truck is the only possible way of crossing through Guyana (for a while referred to as "British" Guyana) to Brazil by land. It is a thrity-six-hour haul over a dirt track through the understated Demerara Woods—understated because this is part of the Amazon Rainforest, and to call it a "wood" is the equivalent of calling a tiger a "pussy." It is dense, rich, fertile jungle and there is one single dirt track that traverses it from Géorgetown, the Capital of Guyana, to Lethem in Brazil—a journey of about five hundred miles.

We board at a market in Tigers Bay. The decommissioned British Army truck is being filled with sacks of grain, drums of gasoline and a variety of building materials. On top of all that, we are squeezed in—all 11 of us. Most are traders, involved in cross-border trade, while others are Brazilian workers returning home.

We, the two foreigners, are delighted to find ourselves positioned at the rear of the open-backed truck. What a wonderful view, we think, as we bounce off down the dirt track, a panorama of trees and mountains disappearing behind us. Two hours later we are caked in mud and being attacked by an army of insects. The rest of the passengers snuggled deep inside the truck smile at us politely—tourists! It was exciting for those first few hours—the lush, fertile rainbow of green colors, a kaleidoscope of nature, huge beautiful butterflies, the rich aroma of the forest, a world further and further from civilization.

And when the excitement ebbs, when the panorama becomes enclosed into one single frame—a receding dirt path framed by a wall of forest on either side—that doesn't change for hours and hours, when the world becomes an insular passage of numbing boredom and bumpy discomfort, then the romanticism flies away, leaving an innate desire for creature comforts and for the journey to end.

But it has barely begun. Night falls, and the air is dense and moist, and the shrill sound of the forest remains a dark secret: out there beyond the wall of trees exist all kinds of life. Only we can't see anything, and all we hear is the cacophony of night sounds and the tormented rumble of the army vehicle struggling over rougher and rougher track. Soon we are being thrown around in the pitch dark. The truck tumbles down gullies, clambers back up near-vertical hills, crashes through streams, and rumbles over delicate tree trunk bridges. The truck groans and creaks and tilts dramatically; we are gripping the metal frame with all our strength, and the tarpaulin covering allows overhanging branches to smash through occasionally. It is like being on a rollercoaster or a ghost train in a demolition derby, only it doesn't end, there's no finish. Time lumbers by torturously, and we don't ever stop; we flail heavily into the endless night and there is only infinite discomfort.

Beyond daydreaming, in that fevered underworld of sleep-denied delirium, and beyond pain, when ones muscles should still ache from gripping the metal bars so long and ones arms should have been ripped from their sockets long ago—it is then that the legions of Brazilians tortured by the Dictatorship come to mind. Suddenly the world turns upside down.

Down a craggy ravine tumbles the bulky British Army truck, overturning in the pitch darkness. In slow motion, I fall on top of the body that had been positioned horizontally beside me, but is now vertically below me. Then a fifty-gallon barrel of oil rolls on top of me. It is one of those excruciating moments between life and death that remains imprinted on one's consciousness like a rapturous vision. And then to emerge on the other end—I am unexpectedly still alive and flailing around in the chaotic darkness, and all around figures move frantically about, in a dissonance of screams and grunts. Indeed, surprisingly we are all alive and, although bruised, share cigarettes and laugh nervously in the deep Amazonian night, uneasily relieved still to be here.

Our truck is pulled out of the ravine by another British Army truck and I'm beginning to have more than a little grudging respect for British military engineering. We all climb back on board and, with heroic resignation, continue our pilgrimage.

As dawn light seeps through the forest canopy and day returns like a resurrection, we pilgrims are rewarded with our first beautification. The forest miraculously opens up into a small clearing, and there in the shadows, is a peaceful clump of little grass-roofed dwellings. We blink our eyes, startled, and then, figures appear from the sublime to the ridiculous, running out of the huts while pulling on trousers and shirts. Suddenly young Rastamen are hanging from the back of the truck offering handfuls of marijuana for sale. The truck slowed almost to a halt, and the deals are made; the herb costs mere centavos. And just as suddenly we pull away and return to the enclosed passage through the forest, the surreal clearing receding in sight and memory. Did it really exist at all, and are we imagining these powerful joints?

I would discover later that it was a Maroon settlement; its occupants are the descendents of runaway slaves who set up shop here in the sixteenth century. Maroon settlements are Guyana's version of Brazilian Quilombos—or like pirate utopias and Freetowns. Today's inhabitants are a bedraggled residue of that feisty, clandestine world, now struggling to survive in a forest encroached upon by loggers and a government wanting to control the land. Maroons are employed, it is said, as assassins and hired guns for rich farmers in their internecine wars, with their contemporaries and the landless peasants searching for plots of land to claim. Looked down upon by both the East Indian and the Afro-Guyanese sections of Guyana's society, the Maroons—about 2% of the population—remain isolated, discriminated against, and despised.

Ah! Brazil

By early afternoon, we have left the forest and traveled through a vast savanna; for as far as the eye can see, the burnt earth undulates gently in hills littered with low shrubs and bare trees. This dramatic change in environment marks the unspecific frontier between Guyana and Brazil. Some hours later, we pull into a small town—Lethem, population a few hundred—with tumbleweeds blowing up and down the sandy roads.

Finding the immigration office is a problem. "Take a canoe across a river, walk a trail for a half an hour, and you will find an office on the side of a road," we are told.

We walk for forty-five minutes under the boiling sun where we finally stumble upon what appears to be an immigration office. A figure appears, dramatically silhouetted by the sun. As we get closer, we perceive the uniformed figure of a woman. She is tall and striking, sporting tight Ray-Bans, her hair held up in her peaked hat, her military uniform an iniquitous challenge. Throughout my travels, I have had untold trouble with immigration. As with cops and soldiers, no situation on earth is ever made better by the arrival of a immigration official. But she is the exception to the rule. She breaks into a huge, welcoming smile and starts chatting to us in a most marvelously musical tongue, of which we do not understand a single word. We slump down, and this magnificent border official fetches a couple glasses of water; she removes her sunglasses and her eyes blaze with intrigue and wonder.

Seduced by her august approach (and her devastating charm), Timo, the photographer, and I have both fallen for her. We melt as she takes our passports, stamps the pages with petulant grace, and hands them back with a warm smile. Fleetingly lovelorn, we depart, with reluctance. We lean out the window of the dusty bus, waving tragically as the old vehicle pulls away. One couldn't make it up—Brazil is already a land of unmitigated passion.

Passion and cruelty. We arrive in Boa Vista, a dusty frontier town populated by cowboys, shysters, criminals, and the usual dodgy border crew. Boa Vista is the bastion of a particularly vicious band of *latifundistas*, large estate owners, with a penchant for killing Indians. Massacres are common, the most recent being a slaughter of eight indigenous men from the Yanonami tribe. Better to move on than lose another moment in cemeterial towns like this one, with its endless lines of concrete warehouses and car repair workshops. We board a jungle bus to Manaus, and into the Amazon proper—no Demerara Woods nonsense, this is the real thing.

And it's the same view, a wall of trees; we are enclosed in a uniform corridor of forest until we debark to cross the Amazon (or one of its tributaries) by motorized raft. The vast body of water is muddy brown and warm to the touch. It is more that a half-mile wide at this stretch. We putt-putt across on an archaic low-slung raft, the bus almost tilting into the waters, and I imagine the brown liquid full of man-eating piranha and fish the size of crocodiles and crocodiles the size of boats. The imagination can run riot, because all this is beyond the imagination.

But the ride through the jungle is monotonous; we are in a regular bus and on a basic road, most of it paved. We pull into Manaus around dawn. Manaus is the place where the mad German-Irishman Fitzgeraldo, in all his hubris, built a grand opera house in the middle of what was then almost pure jungle. He dragged ships over hills to get the materials here. Lots of workers got killed—a good example of the kind of mental disease that affected the ruling classes of the nineteenth century high colonial period.

Anyhow, Manaus is today an Amazonian metropolis of over a million inhabitants, and it is baking hot and sweaty. Nobody bothers to wear much in the way of clothes, and even in the bus station, or now in the airport, people are clad mostly in what would be considered underwear in other places. Older people in Ireland would consider this to be going around "naked." We are in the airport because we have just discovered that the ferry to Belem, upriver to the Caribbean, would take five days sailing, and the *Encontro* is beginning tomorrow. So we find an affordable flight.

This ten-seater motor vehicle with wings is implausibly called an airplane. My disbelief is further validated by the fact that we never fly higher than the tip of the jungle during the entire six-hour flight; real airplanes touch the clouds. At one point, crossing the Amazon where the muddy Rio Negro joins with the clear Rio Amazonia, we can see water as far as the horizon; there is no land in sight anywhere. The Amazon River is that immense.

The hours of endless green rainforest end suddenly half an hour from Belem, as if someone has taken a ruler and just cut away all the forest in a straight line. Suddenly the forest is a field; suddenly the jungle gives way to agriculture. This brutal incision welcomes us back to civilization. Then the forlorn skyscrapers of Belem appear on the horizon, and a pall of smoke lingers over the city.

Encontros sin fin

We are here to attend the third *Encontro* (Gathering) For Humanity and Against Neoliberalism, in Belem, capital of the Amazon, on the cusp of the new millennium. It follows the First *Encuentro,* convoked by the Zapatistas in Chiapas in 1996—a great success, which drew six thousand participants from all over the world and marked itself historically by (in)formally bringing together the new political constituency that was forming into a global movement. The majority of the attendees were from social movements (as apposed to political parties), activist groups (as apposed to politico's or academics), NGOs (not—yet—government or UN representatives) and church groups (from the preferential option of the poor faction, not Rome). The term "Civil Society" was ostensibly used to describe the crowd, although the hordes of anarcho-punks, ex-guerrillas, Maoists, and militant feminists present could hardly be considered "civil." "Multitudes" was another word used to describe the horde because they were representative of the majority of people worldwide who were not part of the ruling class. Representative of, not representing—that is an important distinction.

The Second *Encuentro* took place in Spain in September of 1997, again attended by thousands from a similar range of groups. This gathering further consolidated the idea of the growing Movement, and contributed towards further development of tactics, strategy and philosophy. I avoid the word "ideology," because the movement remains studiously post-ideological as a means not to be pigeonholed as Marxist/Anarchist/Autonomist—a Movement in which all movements fit, was the guiding philosophy. Strategically, the Movement is directed against neoliberal (global) Capitalism, and fights for government from below—decentralized and premised in self-determination and autonomy. It employs tactics of direct action mandated by participatory democracy (*Mandar obedeciendo*—To command obediently). It is a humanist philosophy, based on solidarity, participation, and respect (*Para todos todo, para nosotros nada*—Everything for everybody, nothing for ourselves).

The third *Encontro* in Brasil was proposed by the *Sem Terra*

(Brazilian Landless Movement) and endorsed by the Zapatistas. But somewhere it all went horribly wrong.

How we lost the Encontro

Let's start with the Opening Ceremony. We are gathered in a sweltering tropical park in the center of this lush breathtaking city, being mesmerized by an array of liberating cultural performances—musicians, dancers, singers, artists. Aching beauty, accompanied by frustrating brutishness. There's insipid political maneuvering going on. The same crowd that was clapping with delight at the sensual dancers is now booing the ignoble speakers from the organizing group.

The *Sem Terra* (Landless Movement) who was to host the event, has been shoved aside from the organizational mechanics by the Belem City Council, a left faction of the PT (The Workers Party, Brazil's main opposition party at the time). *Sem Terra has* pulled out because they've accused the Belem City Council of abusing the *Encontro* for their own gains, using the Zapatistas' popular image to make themselves look good before the upcoming Elections. Remarkably and unbelievably, the venerable third *Encontro* for Humanity and Against Neo-liberalism has been hijacked by the Workers' Party faction to become, for all intents and purposes, a showcase for their electoral hopes. Using the public funds at their disposal, the PT council has gained control and is using all the city's facilities to host the *Encontro*. Welcome to the Belem City Council *Encontro*!

Nevertheless, this night is not one for the tricky politicians; it is a social gathering to celebrate the coming together of thousands of radicals and our culture of resistance. Eddinho of Sao Paulo is typical of the spirit of the night, and indeed of the whole *Encontro*. He is warm and friendly and shares whatever there is to share with anyone. Part of an anarchist group that has traveled far to be here, he is appalled by the Machiavellian behavior of the politicians from the PT—"We must take back the *Encontro*!" Sharing and passion and openness and solidarity are in abundance; the celebration is great, people's hearts are wide open.

The next day it is clear that the setup for the Gathering is all wrong. In a university setting, the PT has created a conference center with large auditoriums facing central podiums. The speakers on top of the podiums have microphones, while the audience has earphones.

The Movement does not gather in conference halls to listen to specialized speakers and select representatives—this Movement meets in open assemblies where all can speak, and participatory democracy can be exercised. This conference center setup is more reminiscent of the old left—centralized and hierarchical, dominated by educated white men. (In this case, men a lighter shade of tan). We find ourselves in circumstances more like a Communist Party meeting or a political party convention. This is not in the spirit of Zapatismo!

This Movement would not allow the Zapatista delegation to be spirited around as VIPs, as they are here, hidden from view and overly protected by handlers. Nor does this Movement have guards at the entrances making sure people have paid their dues—this Movement does not exclude poor people! And this Movement is not patrolled by cops walking around with their hands on their batons, as is happening here. So this is the crux: we've come here to build a movement to change the world and we find that the prefigurative politics of the proceedings replicate the dominant discourse. The scourge of organizers thinking and acting like the State!

Unsurprisingly, some of the NGOs (the "nice" faction), falling into step with the political party, are trying to negotiate a compromise solution. "We must respect our hosts," they say, and focus on "getting work done." But the stirrings of a rebellion rumble among the multitude.

Another Encontro is possible!

Word gets around, and people seep away from the boring lectures in the large auditoriums. In the open-air cafeteria, a mass of people—indigenous and women's groups, representatives from the Quilombo movement, internationals, radicals, youth, students, and punks have gathered and are engaging in lively debate. They are constructing an Alternative *Encontro* and unlike the staid, controlled, official *Encontro*, here the energy and passion is palpable. Under a light *palapa*, a gathering of people of every class, color, and subculture spontaneously takes control of the proceedings and says !*Ya Basta*! A mutiny! Quilombo!

Critics would understand this as the typical decomposition of the fragmented left, unable to hold a meeting without a plethora of splits and defections. No, this is something else. We are constituting a new movement. This is not an argument over ideology or the correct line; this is fundamentally about methodology—for political participation, not political representation. This Movement is not about politics, it's about political action.

And this is why the Landless Movement, *Sem Terra* was wise to pull out. The Belem *Encontro* has turned into a gathering about fomenting party politics and consolidating political power, not building a social movement and strengthening popular power.

A Carnival of Dreams

We are off again, out to a *favela* to dance and drink and sing. There is something unique about how Brazilians celebrate; the whole community is in the street, from two-year-old kids to eighty-year-old grannies. The music is a wonderful, uplifting samba that inexplicably commands me to enjoy myself. The mood is happy and impulsive. It reminds me of the wild nights during the West Belfast *Feile* (Festival) when all the woes of poverty and hardship find wings and soar, if only for a few hours, and people celebrate life. We are invited to join a bunch of revelers at their table. Don Josheu and his extended family—daughters, sons, grandkids, friends, and friends' parents—welcome us like long lost family members.

Timo, the photographer, snaps away merrily. Later, perusing these same shots, one gets the feeling that it is an epic reunion of great friends. The Brazilians look joy-filled and ecstatic, while we, the visitors, appear somewhat bemused and overwhelmed. The huge smiles all around are not put on for the camera.

Don Josheu and his extended family are impressed that

we have traveled so far and wish to reciprocate our solidarity endeavor. Beers keep appearing miraculously on the table and conversations are attempted enthusiastically by all and sundry through a variety of mediums, due to lack of common tongues. Again it must be noted that people are predominantly clothed in their underwear, and these dance-forms would be banned in most "respectable" countries. There is no youth or beauty barrier—this is an unpretentious utopia for all. The separation between children's space, youth culture, and adulthood is diminished—a healthy fusion. Everyone dances and makes merry, from mischievous kids to audacious retirees; openness, sharing and solidarity are again the enduring characteristics of this long night of revelry.

Occupy! Resist! Produce!—Sem Terra Uncovered

We are lodging in a Jesuit seminary. It has all the trappings of the usual seminary enclosure—high walls, monastic silence, and pious simplicity. The unique thing here is the seminarians are fiery radicals whose eyes fill with passion when they talk about the social movements or the *Sem Terra* landless movement. At the beachfront of Icoraci, the mouth of the Amazon, we learn about the *Sem Terra* from these devoted young seminarians.

A workshop is in session. Seminarians are spelling out the facts to a group of visiting delegates. Forty-six percent of the land is owned by one percent of the population. People are driven from the land, dispossessed, pushed into the slums at the edge of the cities.

"Nobody is going to give you land if you're poor and powerless, so what is to be done?" begins a Seminarian. "Vote for political change? Pray and beg for land? Emigrate? The *Sem Terra*, just went out and took land. Direct action gets the goods. They saw a piece of unused land, joined together, and occupied it *en mass*. Solidarity is strength. And they did it in the hundreds of thousands..."

After the dictatorship ended in 1984, space opened for old forms of resistance with new forms of organizing under the umbrella *Movimento dos Trabalhadores Rurais Sem Terra* (The

Movement of Rural Workers Without Land). The idea was an old, and simple one—to reoccupy idle land and work it. The land would belong to those who work it, and with land comes dignity and liberty.

In fifteen or so years, *Sem Terra* grew from a few thousand disparate land squats to its current status as the biggest radical popular movement in the world, with a support base of millions and 150,000 camps around Brazil (each a growing community on occupied land, and 50,000 settlements, "legalized" communities). How did they become so strong? The answer seems to lie in their strategy of mass mobilization, their commitment to participatory democracy and the tactical use of nonviolent direct action. They are not a political party, but a social movement. They are not a trade union, although they struggle collectively. They are not communist, but they are communal.

Power lies in the camps; each camp is an autonomous unit, and decisions at camp-level are made by an assembly—direct participatory democracy. Each camp networks with other camps on an interstate level. In order to put emphasis on decentralization, the national organization is very small—only a few offices, a newspaper, a press office, and a rotating council committee (somewhat like the Zapatista Clandestine Council) that oversees implementation of policy. (Indeed, the *Sem Terra* are now looking at the Zapatista Autonomous Councils as a model for larger, regional organization.)

This all sounds similar to the Zapatistas, yet they developed completely separately, continents apart. One common factor has been the influence of Liberation Theology; both movements grew rapidly in turf already set up by the Catholic church of the poor. This brings us back to the seminary. The young seminarian, Gilmar, is a devotee of the movement and spends most of his time organizing in the camps around Belem. I suspect his Lord must wonder where his wayward seminarian has wandered; there is a conspicuous absence of God as Gilmar decries capitalism in the name of the people.

Gilmar and I visit the *Sem Terra* office in Belem. It is a nondescript little house in a poor suburb. Inside there are about ten volunteers who are busy as bees, and people come and go constantly. A song, the "*Hino do MST*" blasts away from a stereo—it is a rousing marching cry that immediately brings to mind CNT and FAI songs of the 1936 Spanish Revolution. On the wall—beside numerous posters about local demonstrations, strikes, occupations, and more global (or Anti-Globalization) themes, hangs a prominent portrait of Carlos Marighela. Marighela was a guerrilla leader assassinated by the Dictatorship in Sao Paulo in 1969. His famous work, *Mini-Manual of the Urban Guerrilla* (1969), became standard text for many armed struggle groups in the 70s—the IRA, the Red Brigades, FMLN, Red Army Fraction, and so on. What is this renowned figure of the armed solution doing on the wall in the local headquarters of a totally unarmed mass movement? A volunteer explains that Marighela is a hero and a martyr and a national symbol of resistance. And his theory of clandestine armed struggle? "We have only our scythes and sticks, we do not use arms."

Back at the seminary, Gilmar explains his irritation at the movements failure to protect itself sufficiently. The systematic state repression aimed at *Sem Terra* has resulted in dozens of extrajudiciary executions and many imprisonments. "The people have no defense! The suicidal pacifism of the organization will get us all killed!" The seminarian was all for setting up armed self-defense militias to face the private armies of the *latifundistas* and the paramilitary police, who operate without impunity.

And this is a real problem: it is clear that *Sem Terra* have not been pacifist, but that the organization stops short of using arms for fear of engaging in an armed struggle with an enemy who holds all the power and military apparatus. So the question is how to protect the militants, the spokespeople, and the people engaged in direct action, without entering into clandestinity?

Nineteen *Sem Terra* members were killed in 1996 in a land invasion at El Dorado de Carajas by the paramilitary police. Nobody was charged. *Sem Terra* activists continue to be murdered, imprisoned, beaten, and tortured. But *Sem Terra* remains hesitant to use weapons as self-defense or become clandestine. "Our only chance of victory is to get everyone aware and participating, using whatever arms they are able to use. In our occupations women, children, and old people use what they have: wooden sticks, stones, knives. Another has a .38 revolver. We don't recommend using firearms. This tactic is certain to frighten..." And it would be sure to bring the full wrath of the military state upon them. Armed self-defense in Brazil would be suicidal. Yet still one must wonder, how to defend the people at the mercy of paramilitary death squads and murderous police?

Tale of Two Encontros

Back at the *Encontro* the next day, both the official and the alternative forums continue with gusto. At the conference center representatives from Colombia's guerrilla—the ELN (National Liberation Army)—warn of US interference in their country in a strongly anti-imperialist presentation. The FARC (Revolutionary Armed Forces of Colombia) representative had already being expelled from Brazil. Under a thatched *Capella* by the seafront, impassioned speakers at the alternative *Encontro* engage in participatory democracy with such gusto that they almost come to blows—I don't know why, it's all in Portuguese. In the conference center I can understand, since every speech is simultaneously translated, but it's increasingly academic and I keep drifting off into siestas. As the Situationists used to say—they are speaking with corpses in their mouths. Back at one of the alternative assemblies, a group of hip-hoppers are demonstrating their craft and it's clear to everyone why hip-hop is such a huge and important form of expression in the urban *favelas* (slums). The alternative *Encontro* invades the official *Encontro* in the form of a nude protest by some anarcha-punks and, at this burlesque juncture, all chaos is unleashed.

Two Distinct Movements

It's fortunate we are not an armed movement because otherwise tonight's finale of the third *Encontro* for Humanity and Against Neoliberalism would be a bloody mess. As it is there are different factions screaming, pushing, and—at one appalling moment—individuals are resorting to fisticuffs. Several thousand people from both *Encontros* had contrived to gather in the main conference center to thrash out a final Joint Declaration. In the spirit of Zapatismo it has been decided that we should "work it out." But what common ground is there?

The debate is between those who wish to reform and those who wish to radicalize the state of affairs. Is it enough to have a representative at local or state level, or is it more conceivable to build non-representative power from below? To attempt to win elections, or to take control at the grassroots through popular power? Is the movement lobbyist or activist? Is the goal to reform or to revolutionize? Clearly there is little common ground. The night air fills with clamor and tempers are unraveled. The representatives from Belem City Council tries to read out an unacceptable declaration, the stage front becomes a mess and resembles a cattle market on a Sunday afternoon. Eddinho, the generous and impassioned Anarchist from Sao Paulo is at the front of the stage engaged intense debate with some pro-PT Trotskyites, and it seems pointless when there is so much to be gained with the rest of the crowd.

Elsewhere, the music begins and people drift there. As has been the case the whole time of the *Encontro*, people informally make their own meetings, alliances blossom, and common cause is found. And, this being Brazil, everybody dances quite ecstatically—the Afro-Brazilians, the indigenous, the youth, the landless, the locals, the hip-hoppers, and the punks. A noteworthy moment of unity is achieved—not a political unity, but a social and cultural unity as we come together in common refusal of the formal *Encontro*, and rejection of political maneuvering and party politics. We begin to organize in a new space.

A Life Worth Living

Belem in the sordid heat. The *Encontro* is over. I wander down to the seafront, to the Ver-O-Peso market. Although antiquated and dilapidated, it feels consoling. The fishermen laze about on their vaudeville boats, small old sloops tenderly worn from innumerable sea journeys. The echo of samba music drifts easily over the docks. A sudden tropical downpour engulfs the waterfront and the rain falls fresh and ferocious, cleaning away everything except the pungent aroma of rotting fish and vegetables. More sloops sail in and the robust fishermen, burnt raw from the unrelenting sun, unload their catches—fish the size of humans, humans the size of characters from Jorge Amado novels. Scantily dressed prostitutes saunter out and lie familiarly on the hulls, chatting. These are hard, muscular women, like the men. Children and wives embrace their returning husbands and fathers, relieved that there have been no drownings this time. There's a taciturn kind of happiness here, an intangible strength of presence, of contented working men and working women. It is a nostalgic scene, and life has probably not changed for a hundred years in Ver-O-Peso. When capitalist globalization has finally ruined and blasted its way off the world stage, this kind of fisherman's globalization will remain.

I wander over to a kiosk overlooking the sea. A young mulata tends her little *palapa* like a rose garden. I order a coffee and she smiles and remembers me from a visit a few days previous. For the millionth time, a stranger engages me with this fond, intrigued openness.

"And where is your friend, the photographer?" she asks, enquiringly. Timo would have loved this, but he's already taken off. The woman, who introduces herself as Janaina, chats away in the enchanting music of her tongue, spitting through the gaps in her teeth and it reminds me of the initial encounter with the migration official at the border, and I realize this is not an exception, but the norm. A carnival of dreams. I swoon in this wonderful culture that is unsullied and sociable. This absence of cynicism and an abundance of simple trust have somehow turned my world upside down. We may have lost the *Encontro*, but we have gained the Brazilian spirit.

Nearby, a gang of young girls strip a young boy down to his lurid boxer shorts with much mirth. He is mortified, and too proud to cry. The girls return to finish the job and, playfully yet brutally, strip him naked. Now he cries, and everyone laughs. Janaina laughs too with an uncharacteristic nasty edge, mocking the forlorn boy.

Such is life in Brazil, this aching beauty, this startling cruelty.

DIEZ DE ABRIL

Stories from the Zapatista Autonomous Zone

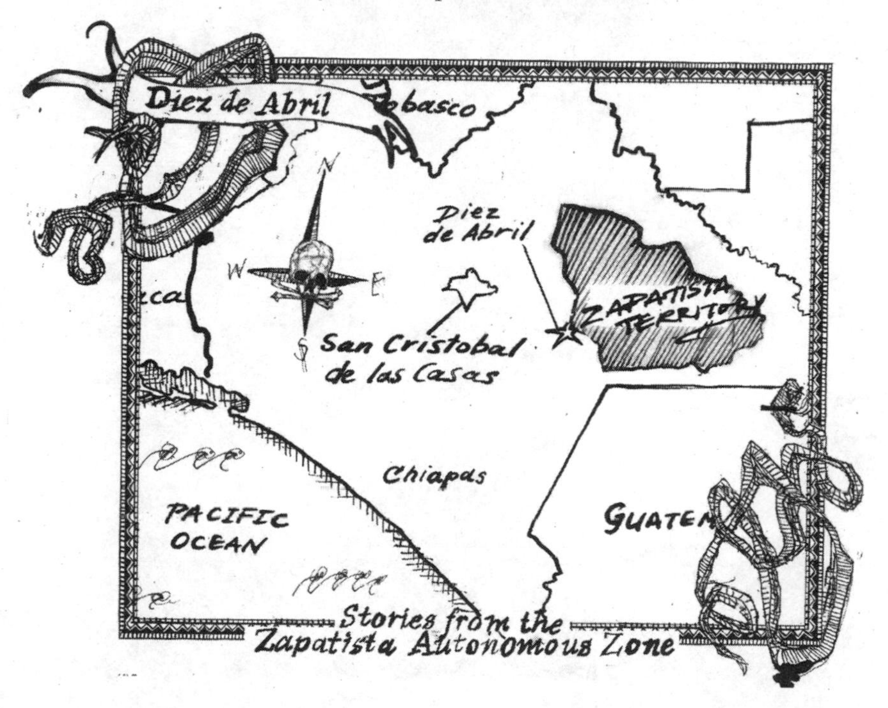

A little child, big-bellied and mucky, stumbles out of her dirt-floored house into the sun and smiles radiantly. This is seven-year-old Rosa, a child of Diez de Abril born of Cristina and Manuel, two Zapatista Militia volunteers. It is January 2003 and, despite much adversity, Rosa is alive and well. She lives where she was born—in a fertile valley near Altamirano, Chiapas, which was occupied by the EZLN in 1994 and populated by a Zapatista support base community in 1995. Her short life encompasses the life span of this rebel community and her tumulteous history, like that of Diez de Abril, has been one of struggle, hardship, uncertainty, and ultimately hope.

Land and Freedom: A Reality

The village of Diez de Abril is a product of insurrection and resistance. It is an inspiring example of how a dispossessed people, united by necessity and will, can organize themselves and satisfy the demand for land and freedom by employing radical direct action. So it was that landless Tzeltal and Tojolabal indigenous farmers joined with the EZLN in the early 1990s, participated in the armed insurrection of 1994, and seized this land by force. They drove the *finquero* (land estate owner) away and defended the gains of this local revolution from subsequent police, military, and paramilitary threats with their bodies and their political guile.

Three hours of highway and twisty mountain roads from the town of San Cristobal, this young village sprawls across the floor of a lush green valley. What was once a massive cattle ranch owned by one man was converted by seventy five rebel families into a thriving self-sufficient community supporting some six hundred people. Located at the gateway to the Lacandon rainforest, the village lies on the frontline between Zapatista territory and government-controlled space. There is a military base two miles away, and army convoys constantly patrol the road less than a mile from the community. In light of this threat, the community made a request for an international presence through Human Rights groups to monitor the increasingly fragile situation and support the community by acting as a deterrent to military intervention or any violations of the San Andrés Peace Accords which prohibit military presence in Zapatista space.

How the Irish Arrived in Diez de Abril

In early 1997, I arrived as a representative of the Irish Mexico Group and met with community representatives about the proposed Irish involvement to assist the community by monitoring human rights abuses, military incursions, and paramilitary threats. The group back home was to act as a voice beyond, using the media in Ireland and internationally to raise awareness and provide information. The volunteers based in Diez were to work alongside the community in development projects or day-to-day labor, and in the process of accompaniment, hopefully ideas of global struggle and resistance cross pollinate.

The leaders—elected *responsables* from the community assembly—welcomed our idea and the project was presented at the next assembly. Before about a hundred adults, questions were answered and a consensus was reached on our initial six-month presence—they invited us to stay.

As the first Irish volunteer, I set up camp in our new residence. An international camp had already been established in the village, but *campamentistas* were random and inconsistent, sent by the central human rights group in San Cristobal de las Casas. The Irish Solidarity Encampment is to be located in one of the abandoned and rundown ranches, the *Casa Grande*—formerly the farm manager's house, but the luxury is relative. Unlike the houses in the village, it has cement floors—not earth—in the kitchen and sleeping quarters that make up our "camp." But like everyone else we fetch our water from the river almost a mile away, cook over the open fire, see by candlelight when the village's DIY electricity, tapped from the high tension cables, fails (often), and trek to the latrine down the field. From the *Casa Grande* perched on top of a hill, I can see the whole village. That first night I sat, with my rucksack unpacked, staring out over a dark and quiet glen. There's not a concrete structure in site, nor is there a single car. The muddy lanes are filled with horses chomping on the grass. Is this primitivist heaven or the depths of depraved poverty? I'm not sure at all.

Early Years of the Community

"Before we worked for the landowners we lived in poverty, members of my family died from hunger," explains the young Tseltal farmer Manuel, cradling the little baby Rosa in his arms. Of all the families, it is with Manuel, Cristina, and their children Rosa and Marcos that I spend most of my time in the community. "But now with the Zapatistas," he continues, "we have land and control over our lives; we can make our own decisions."

During the first couple of years, the community thrived, the crop was good, there was coffee and fruit, and materials were bought to make decent homes. Latrines were built, a basketball court was laid down, electricity was pirated from the road, and a community store was set up. The village was designed to give the people space and social areas.

Meanwhile the political context within which the Zapatista communities existed was hopeful. The first round of agreements between the EZLN and government delegates at the San Andrés talks were signed, and a political solution to the indigenous communities' demands seemed to be moving forward. For communities on re-appropriated land like Diez de Abril this meant less of a threat from the Mexican military and paramilitary forces.

As 1996 moved into 1997 the political context began to change, and so shifted the mood in Diez de Abril. On New Year's Eve the village celebrated the third anniversary of the uprising and looked towards further consolidating the gains of the three years. Projects were in the works with NGOs—an education program for the children, a health initiative, and a commercial proposition. But there was a shadow over the community.

Everything had changed, but nothing had changed. Nothing had changed with the government, with the military, with the system of injustice they confronted, or with the power structure. The government had entered into talks and signed agreements, but it soon became clear they had no intention of honoring the San Andrés Accords. The military promised to return to their bases but were instead preparing for war.

"The government, deaf and blind, are getting ready to hit and kill those they don't see or hear," warned *Sub-comandante* Marcos in a communiqué, January 1997. "The pre-emptive military campaign of the government has begun...The order to attack is already on the tables of the commanders of the Federal Mexican Army." It was an anxious time for Diez de Abril. The people were tense, making preparations for the inevitable. Would they flee to the mountains like they did during the last military offensive in February 1995, or would they stay and fight and die in their homes?

Daily Life in the Community

The day begins before dawn.

"Wake up," says Manuel cheerfully, entering the solidarity camp. "Its time for work." I look at my alarm clock. Is he mad? It's 5:30 a.m.

"Come on, let's go to the milpa (cornfield)."

"Ok, let me get a coffee first," I mutter.

The walk to the collective *milpa* takes an hour. We cross two rivers, pass through a verdant forest and climb around the side of a mountain. I need a rest even before beginning work. Half the community is here already, spread about the vast *milpa*—fertile land by the riverbank stretching for about a square mile. Men, women and children plant seeds on land that has been cleared and burnt. Walking in lines, they plunge pointed stakes into the hard soil and then drop three or four kernels of corn into the four-inch-deep holes. It's intensive labor and by the time the mid morning sun is climbing high in the sky I'm ready to drop. Manuel indicates it's time for *matz*, or the eleven o'clock lunch break. We all sit down in a circle on the ground, and Cristina prepares the corn mix with water and sugar for us and the little kids.

"Where were you on January 1, 1994? "I ask Manuel.

Manuel tells the story of how he was in Mexico City working as a laborer around Christmas in 1993. With much surprise, he received word from Cristina that the insurrection was planned for New Year's Eve. He rushed back to Chiapas just in time to join the mustering troops. *Compas* from this municipality attacked the town of Altamirano, taking control of the town hall with relative ease and running out the few cops and soldiers in town. As it was New Years Eve, most of the garrison was on leave or at home with their families. The Zapatistas held the town, recruited locals and spoke to the press. A couple of days later they successfully retreated from Altamirano without a single loss, as the government was drawn into talks with the rebels.

Manuel and Cristina are very proud of their participation in the Uprising. It was a year later when their unit, made up of some seventy local men and women, organized to invade and occupy this farm. The armed Zapatistas arrived in the dead of night, and the *Finca* manager and his lieutenants were dispatched. The *Casa Grande*, a symbol of the hated old regime, was burnt and destroyed. Many of the occupying Zapatista insurgents had worked on this very *finca* as low paid *peons*. Seizing control of the farm was for them even more satisfying then for the rest. "In truth," says Manuel, "I never thought we would succeed. I thought we would all be killed."

Cristina serves lunch, and the *matz* is delicious. Too soon we resume toiling on the land beneath the hot midday sun, and we continue until two or three in the afternoon. By the end of the workday, we have still only planted seed in about an acre of the *milpa*. There's lots more planting work to be done over the next few weeks.

Droughts, Floods and the Threat of Military Invasion

If 1997 was a hard year for the community, 1998 was a cruel one. The state Governor, a rabid *PRI-ista* (Institutional Revolutionary Party, the governing party), intensified the low-intensity warfare against the rebels. The arming and training of pro-government paramilitaries cumulated in the massacre of forty-five people, mostly children and women, at Acteal in December.

The first few months of 1998 brought constant tension in Diez de Abril. Reports came in weekly of other Zapatista villages being attacked and invaded by the police and military. Several times, convoys of military vehicles amassed near the entrance to the community. The women would mobilize to block the entrance, armed with sharpened sticks; the men would retreat further, ready to repel the attack with arms if the troops passed a certain point. The international volunteers waited fretfully, with camera's ready to record the whole debacle.

"There's so much worry that the children feel it and become sick," says Cristina one day, passing the international camp carrying a sickly looking Rosa to the community health advisor.

Military and police helicopters and occasional warplanes fly low over the glen. Every day they swoop in—sometimes taking photos, sometimes following people in the fields, and sometimes just lingering. In other communities the people drive long pointed stakes into the ground to stop the helicopters from landing, but here there's just too much open ground to do that, and so the people try to ignore it as much as possible and not let themselves become frightened. Nevertheless, when we give crayons to the children, helicopters and warplanes figure in all the drawings.

The community keeps us busy. The sun is splitting the stones and Nicolas and I are sweating up on the roof of the collective store putting the finishing touches on the very impressive *Tierra y Libertad.* "Paint it bigger so the helicopters can see it clearly!" shout the *compas* from the ground. News comes in of the military entering the community of Nueva Esperanza. This is a nearby community, smaller and more vulnerable than Diez, who the army has been bullying. Earlier in the year, the twenty-five or so families were forced to flee to the mountains as a battallion of troops occupied the village, burning houses and killing livestock. In light of the threat, Diez de Abril mobilizes on red alert once more. Old folks and children are packed off to the mountains, women sharpen their sticks, and men take up defensive positions around the valley. Often when this happens we remain the whole day on alert, until word comes through that the threat has passed.

Of course, if it's not the army or the helicopters or the myriad other social, political, and economic problems the communities have to contend with, then there is always nature. 'El Niño' has been causing problems in Chiapas—there has been hardly any rain for months; the ground is rock hard, and the fields and mountains are dry and thirsty. Forest fires are running rampant and the sky is heavy with smog. On May third, Day of Santa Cruz (the saint of water), there's a twenty-four hour pilgrimage by the village elders to ask God to send rain. All day and all night, the procession moves around the valley from water spring to water spring, beating drums and playing the flute until the participants arrive at a state of deep spiritual reverie. Out at the *milpa* plain, the ground is hard and scorched from the extraordinary dryness. "We're all going to die of hunger if the rains don't come soon," says old Don Anselmo in dismay, overlooking the famished land during the worst drought in living memory.

In the village center, we are ringed at night by the sublime sight of the surrounding mountains burning radiantly and ferociously. The cornfields are being razed and the forests destroyed. Night after night the community mobilizes to fight the fires. It's an impressive feat, as hundreds of *campesinos* stream up the black mountainsides whooping and shouting and carrying buckets of water and an assortment of leafy branches to beat out the flames. Little Rosa could be seen these long nights, carried on her mothers back *rebozo* style among the dancing flames. The firefighters work hard all night to bring the blaze under control and eventually, near dawn, they succeed.

Here is a true fighting spirit—the whole community mobilizes to combat the fire. Here is autonomy in action—in the absence of any state fire services (there are fire brigades in the nearby town of Altamirano, but they don't serve the indigenous communities) the people organize effectively and efficiently.

As the development of the community is put on hold, preparations for the worst continue. A tentative tranquility hangs over the lush, picturesque valley cradling the village. "War comes closer," observes Manuel, as he shows me his hunting rifle, a .22. This really is no match for the semi-automatic rifles of the military. Women pass by the international camp with huge containers of water balanced magically on their heads. Men go over the hills, buckled under the burden of heavy sacks of coffee beans on the way to the market town. Children collect firewood and shoot catapults at hapless dogs with deadly accuracy. Life continues, under the shadow.

April 13, 1998

The nightmare began around 5 p.m. when hundreds of men from the paramilitary police and federal army invaded Diez de Abril. The village, caught unaware, had no time for organized resistance. The invaders hurled CS gas and beat heads as they entered, breaking up the villagers' attempt to block their passage and creating a state of chaos and confusion. Children choked on the poisonous gas and shots rang out as the soldiers fired into the air. Three Norwegian international observers were violently apprehended and thrown into the back of a truck with hoods over their heads. Alfredo, a 17-year-old villager, ran to help the Norwegians and for his trouble, he was beaten, stripped, and kicked into the truck. The security forces then began sacking houses and stores and taking work tools, provisions, and anything of value they can lay their hands on.

While her mother and father get beaten on the front line resisting the invasion, little Rosa was carried into the hills by her grandmother Petrona. As she protected Rosa in her arms, the soldiers burned Petrona's humble house to the ground. This event would no doubt quicken Patrona's death the next year from cancer.

As fate would have it, the other Irish volunteer and I had left the previous day for San Cristobal, leaving *campamentista* duties to four Norwegian anti-fascist comrades. So it is them and not us who are abducted and beaten with guns to their heads.

Within twenty-four hours, they would be summarily deported and put on a plane back to their country.

News filters through to San Cristobal about the sacking of Diez de Abril, the disappearance of young Alfredo, the deportation of the Norwegians, and a child drowning in the river while fleeing the military. The next day, some human rights people drive to the community and return with testimonies and denouncements. The missing child is called Rosa. The community fears she has drowned. We organize a group to go out to Diez as soon as possible.

A somber mood hangs over the community. People are picking up the pieces—so many houses have been sacked, so many possessions have been stolen, Dona Petrona's house was burnt, everybody is sick from the gas, and people are tending wounds. As ever, the villagers are resilient, showing spirited resistance. "We won't go one step backwards," says Don Anselmo, a sixty-five-year-old patriarch, limping from a rifle-butt whack in the leg. All that remains of the invasion are the empty CS Gas canisters (made in the USA), the charred remains of Dona Petrona's house and the one Norwegian observer who got away. "They shot over my head," she explains, "but the *compas* hid me under a table in one of the houses."

To my utter relief, Manuel and Cristina appear with little Rosa. She had indeed fallen out of her grandmother's arms and off of a tree trunk bridge spanning a small river, but someone rescued her soon enough. And the reports of her drowing? "*Chisme*," says Manuel, "it's all gossip. Word gets around and things get blown out of proportion."

The attack on Diez was part of a broader military strategy to punish the Zapatista communities. There were many notable military incursions into Zapatista communities during the spring of 1998. One was the April 11 attack on the Flores Magón Autonomous Municipality in Taniperla, in which a thousand troops swooped in at dawn, detaining nine people and deporting twelve international observers. On May 1, troops invaded the Tierra y Libertad Autonomous Municipality at Amparo Aguatinta—fifty-three detained, eight Guatemalans were deported. On June 3, the rebel town of Nicolas Ruiz sustained 167 arrests. There was the June 10 the military attack against the San Juan de la Libertad Autonomous Municipality in El Bosque where the troops—some carrying bazookas—opened fire, mortared the surrounding hills, and pursued the fleeing villagers into the mountains, killing nine.

The Zapatistas remain silent, their guns hidden, and the eloquent literary spokesman *Sub-Comandante* Marcos' pen is idle. The military has pounded the Zapatista support base, but like a lithe boxer, they've taken the hits and are awaiting their moment to strike back.

The Struggle Continues, Through Floods and Migration

The poor harvest of 1998 means the men have to migrate in search of work in order to feed their families. Most of the Diez men end up working in construction in the mega-tourist resort of Cancun. They are paid eight dollars for a ten hour day's labor.

The torrential rains of '99 cause the river to rise, breaking its banks and flooding a large portion of the *milpa*. Life in the village becomes miserable as the paths and dirt roads become mud swamps. The small wooden homes leak and the wood for the kitchen fires is damp.

I return with Cristina and Manuel to the *milpa* to assess the flood damage. Half the harvest is submerged in water and ruined. Looking over the water-logged plantation, Manuel shook his head and says "The drought, the fires, the floods, the destroyed harvests—it's not right. The heavens are really screwed up." They've heard of global warming in Diez de Abril, but for them such things come from the heavens, from the pantheon of Gods.

Despite such apocalyptic overtones, a group of enthusiastic young villagers defied, or perhaps with the tactic support of the Gods, founded a new community nearby on expropriated land. Calling it Cauahtemoc in honor of the legendary Aztec Chief who resisted the *Conquistadors* to death 450 years ago, the new village represents how the struggle has continued, and how it grows.

Little Rosa is now almost 4 years old, and a mischievous sprite is she, with a lovely spirit. On Valentine's Day, I am alone in the solidarity encampment in Diez on a return visit, feeling a little under the weather. She comes to me in the kitchen with a shy smile and, without a word, hands me a bunch of yellow flowers.

The solidarity encampment closed in the year 2000. The political environment had changed for the better—the PRI had been deposed and the newly-elected governor of Chiapas, Pablo Salazar was interested in political rather than military solutions. Diez de Abril no longer faced threats of military or paramilitary aggression. Happily, an international presence was not needed. Long term volunteers like Oscar, Katja, and Nicolas could take their rich experiences of a rebel community home with them, and see if zapatismo could find root elsewhere. Not forgetting the allegience we had built up with the community during the heavy years, a group of veteran solidarity activists return a couple of years later to install a gravity fed potable water system. The village offered some of us plots of land to live and work on—solidarity swings both ways.

Ni un Paso Atras!

Diez de Abril continues and thrives, against all odds, into the twenty-first century. This small village represents a successful manifestation of Zapatista revolutionary praxis. Where once there was a huge cattle farm, there now exists a thriving self-sufficient community supporting six hundred people. Through military invasion, paramilitary threats, droughts, floods, and fire, the community has suffered and consolidated. Families have left, individuals have gone over to the other side, and internal disputes have pulverized the consensus procedure, but still the village grows. Community decisions are made through an assembly process, and leaders are elected by the assembly on a short-term basis ensuring a kind of rotating democracy. And crucially, leaders are accountable to the community. Diez is part of the greater autonomous municipality network, hooking into a revolutionary grassroots Zapatista program that counts on the participation of as many as a hundred thousand people.

There is an autonomous school in the community with local teachers, trained at the Zapatista municipal headquarters. Unlike at the State schools, the children are taught the proud history of indigenous struggle in Tseltal and other indigenous languages. There are health promoters who not only dispense medicine, but also impart traditional medicinal knowledge using herbs, natural potions, and natural healing. The bakery cooperative and the women's organic horticultural plantation are working well, and the children are eating a good variety of vegetables, from the new community organic vegetable garden, increasing the general health of the community. And now there is a potable water, with clean piped water from an underground spring deep in the mountains. The community of Diez de Abril is looking to the future with determination and hope. Not one step backwards, as Don Anselmo likes to say.

Child of the Low-Intensity War

The first seven years of little Rosa's life have been tumultuous, dramatic, and occasionally traumatic, but like the community, here she is, young, healthy, and confident of the future. I can see her standing in the sun playing with the new water tap in the front patio of the rough wooden house, smiling radiantly. Why is she so happy? Because her favorite international solidarity activist came to visit?! No, most likely she is happy because of the arrival of a new sister in her home. The newly-born baby will be called Petrona, in honor of the grandmother whom Rosa never knew, but who carried her to the safety of the mountains five years ago when the military invaded. OK, Petrona dropped her into the river by mistake, but such was Rosa's baptism of fire.

And from that trauma Rosa moves ahead, carrying in her heart—like Diez de Abril—a new world.

CHICKEN BUS DIARIES

Mara Salvatrucha, Social War, and the Decline of the Revolutionary Movements of the 1980s. A Journey through the Central American Remittance Republics and the New Social War, December 2004

People in Guatemala, Honduras, and Nicaragua have always had to travel like this. One hundred people crush into generic American school buses, which have earned the moniker because of the propensity of the people to bring their livestock onboard. Sometimes the animals are tied up in boxes on the roof. In other Latin American countries the passengers cram on the roof too, but not here in Central America—the way the drivers swing the buses around the mountain curves will pitch anything off the roof that is not tied down. But the bus service is cheap and abundant, catering to the poorest passenger, and it must be said the buses are painted in the most exquisite manner—each one a blaze of color and a work of art.

I'm on the road, on my way from my home in Chiapas, Mexico to Nicaragua. I have a mere two weeks, but a full port of calls and no pressing engagements. I will just flow along and in good time arrive in Nicaragua, returning to that wonderful country for the first time since the end of the Sandinista revolution. It's a challenging mission—my six month stint in Sandinista Nicaragua in 1990 turned my world upside-down and resulted in my intermittent but ongoing presence in Latin America for the ensuing fourteen years working in international solidarity.

Things have changed a lot, and the Central American countries are no longer spaces of insurrectional revolutionary struggle. Each country is in political, economic, and social crisis, wrought by fifteen years of a harsh neoliberalism that has increased the level of poverty and hopelessness for the majority, the poor. I'm interested to discover what has happened to the revolutionary movements—not only the Sandinistas, but also the URNG (Guatemalan National Revolutionary Unity) in Guatemala, the FMLN (Farabundo Marti National Liberation) in El

Salvador, and the progressive movements in Honduras. Where has that radical spirit gone, and how is rebellion expressed in this new situation? In light of living amongst the Zapatistas in Chiapas and witnessing an inspiring struggle to create an autonomous space where people can control their own lives, how does the situation in the neighboring countries compare?

I leave Chiapas early one morning in December and cross the border into Guatemala. The border zone is typically hectic, and all the traffic is going one way—north—on the long road to the USA. It is disconcerting to enter a country that everybody else seems to be in a hurry to abandon. This river of Central Americans, some with the most paltry of luggage, is migrating with some urgency to the belly of the beast. Most will not make it; they will fall victim to robbers, Mexican immigration, tricksters, *polleros*, or the US border patrol. Some will perish in the Arizona desert, some will drown crossing the Rio Grande. It's a grim testimony to the desperate state of the homes they are departing, that they are facing such risks for the joy of some temporary menial job in a hostile, racist environment within a nation of curiously inward-looking and psychologically damaged people—half of whom actually voted for the dark prince of empire himself, Bush Junior.

Guatemala, Remittance Republic

I squeeze myself aboard the awaiting chicken bus leaving the border zone, quietly satisfied that the corrupt border official has only charged me a one dollar to enter the country. It shouldn't cost anything, but that's his little bribe. There are three people squashed into the short bench seat designed for little children. My long legs are painfully pushed up against the back of the next seat. But here is the first curious thing about chicken buses: the bodily and spatial intimacy with strangers is poignant. It's hard to think of any other situation that could result in an ancient indigenous grandmother—dressed in a beautiful huipile, with her long black hair held up majestically by a multicolored pompom—sitting on top of me. I can feel her breath on my cheek. On my other side a tubby drunk is asleep, his head resting on my shoulder and his hand—comically enough—gripping his balls. It's about as uncomfortable as can be imagined, but such is public transport in Guatemala, and without owning a car, there is no other way to traverse the country.

It's a democratic space. All but the rich are onboard—indigenous families, students, workers, farmers, middle class housewives, and even some men who, from their conversation appear to be government officials. Among the twenty or so unfortunates squashed against each other in the aisle are a soldier, a security guard (carrying his shotgun), and a stallholder with her basket balanced on her head. We bounce along the rough but paved mountain road through a lush, steep valley for a couple of hours towards Huehuetenango. There we all pile off the bus and onto an awaiting one to Xela, another two grinding hours away. This time I have the window seat and two young girls are pushed in beside me on the aisle seat. These buses are hardest of all for young women, because they get endlessly groped and prodded by licentious males.

Conversely, the enforced intimacy leads to many accidental conversations. Being a foreigner allows me the privilege of being a curiosity for the locals, and conversation inevitably flows, beginning with the ubiquitous "Where do you come from?" and leading to sometimes wonderful and often turgidly dull chats with strangers in the cramped space.

Conversation begins with a chatty fifty-year-old man who is heading off to seek work in the gold mines near Huehuetenango. I didn't know there were gold mines in Guatemala. It turned out he lived in Miami for twenty years but has returned to Guatemala without misgivings.

"Why don't you go back to the US?" I ask.

"There's no money here in Guatemala, but life is shit in the USA. I am happy to be near my family and friends, even if I'm poor."

The young Mayan lad sitting on the other side of the bus joins in the conversation. He is about seventeen years old, and while sympathetic to the older man's position, he obviously can't wait to get on the road to the US.

"Have you no land here?" I ask.

"No land, no work, and all my friends have gone to work up North," he replies.

"What do they say?"

"It's good."

He is headed towards North Carolina, yet explains that a *pollero* will take him over the frontier at Tijuana. I pull out a map to show him that it would be better to cross the Texan border, but I put the map away when I realize he can't read—neither words, nor maps. It's going to be a long haul for him. We pull into Xela terminal, and the rush to exit the bus begins in earnest.

It is here that the news comes through that a chicken bus has ploughed off the road outside Xela, and the terminal workers are talking of about twenty dead. The listeners register quiet but not extraordinary shock, and proceed to pile onto the incoming chicken buses. I decide to change my plans and go the other direction, towards Guatemala City. It strikes me as a bad omen to follow the same route as the fated bus to Retalhuleu—like walking a minefield full of craters.

The same mountains that we traverse once offered refuge for the URNG guerrilla army in their heroic but doomed attempt to overthrow the state. The vicious counterinsurgency war, characterized by the endless atrocities committed by the administration against the indigenous people (claiming some one hundred thousand lives) has calmed, since the signing of the 1996 peace accords. The guerrilla coordination URNG has not fared well in electoral politics, holding down a paltry five percent of the vote—but then again most of their constituency, the rural indigenous, remain disenfranchised. Maybe it's the high indices of illiteracy or the fear of registering that causes the high rate of abstention, but it is calculated that a full fifty percent of the adult population, predominantly rural indigenous, doesn't vote.

Estela Maldonado, one of few URNG parliamentarians, is interviewed in the newspaper *Siglo Nuevo*. She paints a bleak picture. Few of the reforms promised during the 1996 peace accords have been implemented. There has been little improvement in education, particularly for indigenous communities; the health service has seen scant investment; land has not been redistributed to ex-combatants; and no justice has been seen for the victims of state violence during the war. Basically, laments the ex-guerrilla, ten years later, nothing has changed; the peace dividend for the majority poor has been desultory.

Not much has changed in appearance in the years since I first visited this part of the country—the houses are wretched and there are no signs, despite the end of the war, of development or economic prosperity. Each of the small towns we pass through has a prominent Western Union franchise, though, the remittance office. The level of migration is such that the government is unable to keep track of it, although they welcome the millions and millions of dollars flowing in from mostly clandestine labor abroad. Its clear that the Guatemalan statistics are approaching those of El Salvador, where half of the gross national product is garnered from remittances—money sent back from the US, Mexico, and Europe. This is a theme that will remain consistent throughout the journey—the historical Banana Republics have been superseded by the rise of the Remittance Republics.

Entering Guatemala City is quite disturbing. As cities go, it rates up near the top of the list of disaster zones. The infrastructure of the city has not dealt with the massive influx of migrants from the countryside over the last twenty-five years—a result of the widespread dispossession of land from the rural indigenous—creating a social and ecological catastrophe. The main economic activities of city-dwellers seems to be hawking goods on the sidewalk, working low paying service industry jobs, or slaving away in suburban *maquiladoras.*

I'm sure the city has its own special spirit and attractions that make it bearable to live in, but after several visits I've never found any indication of what it could be. There is a special darkness to the streets of Guatemala City. There are few shiny lights or spectacles of the kind that one comes to expect illuminating urban metropolises. A typical street seems to be a depressing row of windowless caves with merchandise falling out into the rubbish-strewn street. The pungent smells of gas fumes and food cooking from sidewalk stalls mingle frenetically with the claustrophobic heat of the sun. In the mad bustle, concerned citizens will actually pull aside a foreigner and warn him or her not to continue along the street, as it's "too dangerous."

It's getting late in the afternoon and despite the notorious danger of traveling after sunset (due to the threat of bandits on the highways) I catch the last bus to Puerto Barrios, the Caribbean port five hours away.

The sunset is gorgeous and the temperature rises as we cross the Montagua valley, a remarkably fertile region that produces many of Guatemala's cash crops and, closer to the Caribbean, hosts the country's important banana plantations. The land becomes more lushly tropical and the extravagant scenery is composed of an astonishing pastiche of fertile green colors.

From urban jungle to real jungle; here is the complete antithesis of Guatemala City, a beautiful rugged sweltering forest of fantastic regeneration. But I have to temper my visual delight. This is not global commons, a rich natural resource shared for the good of all; it is company land, once owned by the United Fruit Company and now in the hands of Del Monte. All the people are crushed into the inhospitable city because there is no room, economically speaking, here in this relatively depopulated region. The history of Guatemala is predicated in peoples' dispossession to make way for bananas, coffee plantations, and other agribusiness.

I peruse the day's newspapers, and the news is suitably distressing. The tabloid *El Diario* is all bikinis and gore. Across the page from a swimsuited beauty queen there is a picture of three young women lying murdered in an alley in a poor district of the city. One of the corpses sports a Miami tank top, with an image of a bikini-clad shadow emblazoned across her chest. It's the juxtaposition of too many women's chests—living, dead and illusionary—that is further cause for my revulsion. The triple murder of the young girls is nothing unusual for the tabloid; they are just three more victims of the veritable femicide occurring in Guatemala. Almost five hundred women have been murdered in 2004—fifteen hundred since 2001. A gangland killing, concludes the report, because one of the corpses has a few tattoos—an apparent sign of guilt. The fourteen-year-old, one Claudia Rodriguez Mendez, lies awkwardly with her torso twisted, and her jeans pulled down.

The other papers are filled with similar despairing reports. *El Nuevo Siglo*, a more social newsspread, has a poll of various citizens asking if they think 2005 holds more promise for the nation than 2004. The five candidates interviewed—regular street people—have given responses that range from profoundly hopeless to apocalyptically bad. The only light note comes from some bloke, a self-described Bible vendor, who predicts the arrival of "The Savior" next Christmas.

In *Prensa Libre*, there is a full-page glossy advertisement for trucks. Each truck is pictured with a flashy price tag in a star as if it were a great giveaway bargain. The perverse thing about it is that they are all totaled vehicles, fresh from terrible accidents. They're ravaged wrecks ready for the scrapyard, like the pickup with its front cabin completely flattened. *Damaged Vehicle Sale!* runs the headline excitedly. It strikes me as some kind of dismal metaphor for all that I am witnessing around me.

My hopes aren't high as we pull into the dark port town of Puerto Barrios. I love ports—the special energy of maritime zones in the constant flux of arrival and departure; the standard geography of the local space designed for the movement of goods and services; the freight trains, cranes, and mad bars. But I have been warned beforehand of the special delinquency and degeneracy associated with Puerto Barrios, a town convulsed by gangs and drugs. The infamous Mara Salvatrucha and associated street gangs have made their presence felt on the rough streets. The *Traveler's Guide* recommends that it be avoided, and feels that it is "particularly dangerous"—my kinda town.

I check myself into the shabby five dollar *Atlantico* hotel by the market. It's wise to take certain precautions in this class of hotel. My wisdom leads me to hide my money and passport by taping them to obscure parts of whatever furniture resides in the dank room. After twelve hours on chicken buses I need a drink and Guatemala's national beer, *Gallo* "Cock" is a lovely brew. I set off somewhat ambivalently down the main street, stepping in and out of muddy puddles, and most of the establishments seem to be populated by dodgy young Mafioso types and women of the night. Paty's, however has children running around it, suggesting a safer environment. A charming black woman with a Caribbean accent serves me beer and we chat lightly. "What ship did you come in on?" she asks, and I respond that I've come on the MV Chicken bus. She doesn't laugh, and gives me some more nuts.

I enjoy my *Gallo* at the bar and fall into conversation with the bartender's friend. She is named Isabel and hails from Nicaragua. It turns out that I have visited her hometown—the Pacific coast port Corinto—many years ago (when Isabel was about ten years old), as I was first discovering the beauty of Sandinista Nicaragua. She knows some of the people I had visited, like the Liverpudlian socialist Tommy who, she informs me, has since settled there and had a kid with some local woman. I cherish this kind of random connection on the road, whereupon one inevitably makes links across disparate territory. Why is she in Puerto Barrios? She responds vaguely—working. I notice her various messy tattoos and mention the three girls murdered in today's papers. She is not perturbed. Life is short and violent here, is all she says.

Isabel suggests we go to another bar. I follow her down the block to a rough dive. She disappears to a back room with a none-too-salubrious man and comes back in a chirpier mood, eyes aflame. I wonder if she is going to try to hustle me. But she seems more content to talk; the topic of conversation turns to the ravages of life in the port, the omnipresence of the Mara Salvatrucha, and the heavy police response to delinquency. I like Isabel, she is warm and engaging, and although she speaks a kind of rough Nicaraguan Spanish, she is graceful enough to temper her accent so that I can understand her better.

Her mother was a Sandinista, but she herself is not interested in politics. Now it's all corrupt, dirty, and fucked-up, she says. She goes on to describe her life, a sad story of a poverty-stricken childhood, a violent husband, her migratory flight to Guatemala, and her life of selling pirate CDs in the plaza in Xela and falling in with the gangs. She has a couple of kids, but they are in Corinto with her mother. She isn't a Marero—a Mara Salvatrucha—she assures me, although her boyfriend is. Many of her homies are in prison, she says, resignedly, and some are dead. She asks me for ten Quetzals—one dollar—and returns to the back room. I look around the bar and all the clientele, young gangsters who wouldn't look out of place in East New York, appear to be in an advanced state of alteration. Isabel reemerges a few minutes later, fried off her head.

"Give me some of that," I say, somewhat innocently, thinking it is marijuana.

"What?

"What ever you're taking...."

"No." She says, "It's bad, you don't want that."

"What is it?" I ask.

"It's bad," she says, and proceeds to slump against the table.

People come and go, whispering in Isabel's ear. They ignore me. In they go to the back room and out they come, furtively. Clearly I've fallen in with a bad crowd, so I should be on my way.

"I'm off," I say.

"Where are you going?"

I explain I have to make my way over the border early the next day, to the Honduran Port of Puerto Cortes. She gives me the names of a few friends of hers there, and I leave her in her crack-induced stupor.

Social War in Honduras

The road across the border to Honduras is unfinished, and the chicken bus trundles through muddy lanes and splashes across streams. We pass through endless banana plantations and I remember hanging out with the banana workers in this region about twelve years ago. They were trying to organize a union, and the local bosses responded by firing anyone who joined the nascent union and employing a security firm whose guards included ex-British army soldiers. These mercenaries patrolled the workers' villages in pickup trucks armed with shotguns and electric cattle prods—which they deployed on the workers, not the livestock. An Irish multinational company, Fyffes, imported the bananas to Europe, and although they weren't responsible for the regime on the ground—that was in the hands of local entrepreneurs—they were reaping the eventual profits. Now I plan to go to the Fyffes office in nearby Puerto Cortes, the main Honduran Caribbean port, and see how things have developed.

Puerto Cortes has changed dramatically in the past twelve years. Apart from the typical tropical port hustle, major US franchises dominate the town—McDonald's, Burger King, Pizza Hut, and of course Western Union. The streets are full of big SUVs and suburban vehicles, many sporting intimidating black tinted windshields. Clearly there has been a big injection of fast money—from reading the local papers I conclude it was drug money—but still most of the people live in squalor. Beyond the spruced-up town center the streets are motley, the pavement is in disrepair and the drainage is a disaster. This is usually a good indication of how equally the wealth is distributed.

I booked into a shabby five dollar hotel, the *Colon*, and set off towards the docks seeking the banana company headquarters. I'm disappointed to discover that Fyffes shut down five years ago. The operation has been taken over by Del Monte. The operative in their office tells me that he used to work for Fyffes. He laments their departure and intimates that things were better under Irish ownership.

"Mister David, a great man," he reminisces. I once met David McCann, one of the sons of the Irish banana dynasty, across a table in the company's headquarters in Dublin as we, a workers' solidarity group, accompanied a woman representative of the banana workers to argue the case for legalizing the union. The Fyffe's men promised they would take the idea onboard and talk to local bosses. Years later, under Del Monte, things don't seem to have changed.

"Is there a Union?" I ask the man in the Del Monte office.

"No," he says. "The workers are happy."

"Can I go visit the plantations?"

"No."

"Hmmm. Can I go talk to the workers in their village?"

"Well, you can try, but there is a company guard and he

probably won't let you enter. You need a special pass."

"Can you give me one?"

"No."

I go to a workers' compound, a small settlement on the edge of town where the tiny block houses are all cramped on top of each other like a miniature suburbia. It is enclosed by a metal fence, and the sole entrance and exit is guarded by a private security firm. Sure enough, they refuse to let me in.

You need a pass, they tell me.

"Where can I get a pass?"

"At the office in Puerto Cortes."

There is a street festival in the port that evening and I reckon I can ask around and find some banana workers there. But the street festival is so fucking brilliant that I get caught up in the revelries instead. Thousands of townspeople are out—everybody, from families with their children and old folks to ultra-hip teenagers. A half-dozen hot local outfits performed—salsa, reggae, hip hop. Everyone dances outrageously all night, the numerous street marquee bars are jammed, and the warm Caribbean night is filled with an ecstatic spirit of celebration.

The highlight of the night's performers was the Punta reggae group from Livingstone and the Garifuna coast. They have taken reggae music with Caribbean roots and mixed it with American hip-hop. The result is an explosive blast of rhythmic gangsta rap that is both viscerally erotic and explicitly socially conscious in content. It's the soundtrack to the crack cocaine Mara Salvatrucha generation, beats from the street—angry, violent, sexual, and lyrically moving. It's also the worst of American hip-hop—gun-totting, misogynist, amoral, and sectarian.

Late at night, when the families have retired to their homes and only the youth and drunks remain out in force, I meet Kenia and El Sordo, friends of Isabel's. Kenia is a black woman from Livingstone, and El Sordo a mestizo from the nearby industrial city of San Pedro Sula. They are glad to hear that their *homie* Isabel is keeping out of trouble, or at least alive and not in prison. They are in their mid-twenties, clad in gangster gear, and obviously Maras. El Sordo has "18" tattooed on his cheek, referring to Mara 18, one faction of the gang underworld.

"Everybody here is a *Marero*," says Kenia. She herself has a mangled tattoo on her arm. A few months ago she painfully and fruitlessly poured battery acid over it and completely botched the job. "I could get arrested for that tattoo," she says. "They hunt us down."

Apparently El Sordo doesn't come out in the daytime for fear of being arrested for gang membership. Some 1300 youth have been locked up in the San Pedro Sula region this year for "illicit association," an undefined crime that carries an automatic eight year sentence. It's an undisguised state war against poor youth. Similar to Giuliani's zero-tolerance policy in New York, the government has embarked on a *mano dura* (iron fist) strategy in dealing with delinquency. The implementation of that policy led to the murder of 108 Maras in prison, when the authorities locked the exits and set fire to the overpopulated prison wards.

This is the new war in Central America—the social war against youth delinquency. The same tools used against the guerrillas in the 80s are employed against the youth gangs today.

Mara Salvatrucha was born in the 90s on the streets of Los Angeles, as a self-defense outfit amongst the Salvadoran refugee community. Police reports claim that young exiled members of the Salvadoran guerrilla FMLN were instrumental in training and organizing the street gang in its initial years. The Maras came to El Salvador when, starting in 1998, more than twelve thousand gang members were deported from California. The return of hardened street gangsters from the mean streets of Los Angeles to the social disaster of a war-traumatized, poverty-ridden quagmire like El Salvador produced the ruthless gang subculture built around well-armed, rap-obsessed, deracinated males (and, to a lesser extent, females). It spread like a weed, clandestine and autonomous throughout the other Central American republics, offering not only identity and meaning for abjectly alienated youth, but also a source of income through organized crime in the forms of drug dealing, extortion, and robbery.

The papers quote numbers like a hundred thousand-plus gang members in Honduras. The media presents them as some kind of appallingly strung-out, violent Frankenstein beast mired in an underworld of ultra-delinquency and hardcore crime, and the facts on the ground go some way to support that analysis. There are an average of ten homicides daily in Honduras. The crime level is extraordinary. But the other side of the equation is that gangs are a product of an incredibly violent society, where police and military atrocities are commonplace and state-sponsored death squads—formed in the 1980s to eliminate the guerrilla—roam the streets with impunity, gunning down Maras and street kids. The Mara phenomenon is like a pre-apocalyptic manifestation of neoliberal social and economic catastrophe.

The bigger picture is framed by this part of Honduras being pulverized by the global drugs industry. The Atlantic coast of Honduras is a significant corridor in the transportation of hard drugs from Colombia to the USA. Millions of dollars' worth of contraband flows through this region every month, and the devastating spin-off is a flood of cheap gear and a flourishing clandestine economy overseen by *narcotraficantes*, warlords, and their private armies. The trickle-down effect of this rancid form of pirate neoliberal economy is turf war on the barrio level.

Kenia and El Sordo, strung-out Maras—"Would you like some rock?" they offer—don't seem to me the personification of evil. They seem more like people caught in an unremittingly hopeless position. Theirs is an all-consuming kind of economic and social dispossession—they have lost even the possibility of imagining a normal life. They are children of the barrio born into an unforgiving, despairing scenario, where the choices for those who don't want to work in *maquiladoras* or sell shit in the market are to emigrate, or hustle a living on the margins. But when a government deals with this kind of social malaise by declaring all-out war, as the Honduran state has done, it creates a dangerously volatile situation. Things spin out of control. It comes as no surprise, then, the monstrous attack carried out by some mad Maras in San Pedro Sula a week later. A chicken bus weaving through a poor neighborhood is held up and gangsters open up with machine gun fire, randomly killing twenty-eight passengers.

I spend most of the long bus journey out of Puerto Cortes, crossing Honduras to Nicaragua, perusing the newspapers. The Honduran press is a good read, with a lot of critical analysis of

President Maduro's *mano dura* policy and his lick-spittle bowing to the US (like his dispatching of troops to Iraq without having the cash to maintain them). *La Prensa* has a three page interview with the "guerrilla of congress," Doris Gutierrez, one of only four left wing Democratic Union deputies. She points out that the government's *mano dura* policy against crime only captures the "chicken thieves," while the massive corruption of government and big business continues unhindered. This outspoken activist, who has risen from the ranks of the decimated social movements of the 80s, faces constant death threats. The army has offered her protection and she has refused—these are the same people who murdered her *companeros* in the 80s.

I meet a young doctor on the bus. She has spent some years in New Jersey, but couldn't handle life there—she has come home to San Pedro Sula to work amongst her people for change. She could earn a fortune in the US, but has chosen to return to this desperate corner of the world because it is clear that she still believes that things can be better. She has spent a lot of her time stitching up people's gun wounds. "Better than doing plastic surgery and boob jobs," she says. Hers is a nationalist rather than a radical position, but it strikes me that she is the first positive voice I have heard in Honduras. The young doctor who fixes up the victims of the social war holds hope for the future.

At dusk, we approach the border. For the final stretch I am thrilled to have the company of an incoherent and remarkably chatty drunk bloke who works in the local mayor's office. He insists on showing me his official credentials and even those of his drunken mate, another fatso, who's lurching around on the aisle, jammed in with twenty other passengers. We trundle through border territory, through the mountains where the Contra mercenary camps were located during the anti-Sandinista counterinsurgency war. I ask the old drunk about the Contra War.

"We beat them. Communists. Sandinistas. Cubans. Hic!" he says somewhat proudly. This part of Honduras was the "unsinkable aircraft carrier" for the US military in the 1980s, a launching pad for covert military operations against the Sandinistas. I remember traveling around these same mountains, on the Nicaraguan side, in 1989. The region is littered with bombed-out schools and clinics and Sandinista agricultural cooperatives burnt to the ground.

The dusty border town of Guasaule is like a museum piece. Nothing has changed in fifteen years. People lived in wooden shacks and there is a creepy, suspicious, atmosphere, as if the war is still raging and nobody can be trusted. Strangely, there is no sign of a Western Union office. At dawn I fight my way up to the immigration window, where a throng of local traders scramble to have their documents stamped. I pay my bribe, and walk as fast as I can to get out of Honduras. The intractable problems of this condemned land lead me to conclude that if the end of the world begins somewhere on earth, Honduras will be the place.

Nicaragua: The Revolution Revisited

I am heading back to Nicaragua for the first time since the fall of the Sandinistas in the 1990 elections. It's hard to describe or even imagine the significance of the Sandinistas to the global radical left in the 1980s. They filled a similar space in the imagination as the Cuban Revolution in the 60s and the Zapatistas in the 1990s. The violent overthrowing of the Somoza dictatorship in 1979 imposed a revolutionary junta in charge of government, and a radical social program was implemented that had profound impact in terms of health, education, and land redistribution. There was a palpable feeling of hope, and as commentators pointed out, it was not so much the Sandinistas' communist tendencies as it was the threat of a good example that upset the US and its capital interests. The US launched the Contra War and finally deposed the Sandinistas in the 1990 elections, in which the population voted under the threat of continued war, sanctions, and the ire of the world's sole superpower. The fall of the Sandinistas and the rolling back of the revolution's gains represented a terrible setback for the worldwide progressive left. The US broke the back of the Revolution, the revolutionary Sandinista organization and the morale of the guerrilla movements in El Salvador and Guatemala. The post-Sandinista economic aid promised by the US was soon forgotten, and the economy has never recovered. By all accounts things are worse for the majority now than they were fifteen years ago.

I picked coffee here in 1989 at a co-op in La Dalia, Matagalpa. It was re-appropriated land, and the hundred or so families were evicted when the wealthy landlord returned from exile in Miami in the 1990s after the fall of the Sandinistas. Who knows where those people are now? A young bloke named Luis used to let me ride his horse around the mountains. When the Contras attacked a nearby co-op, Luis handed me a Kalashnikov and intimated that I should use it if he fell. Things like that remain embedded in my consciousness. (The Contras didn't attack our co-op, although the dark nights were sometimes filled with faraway gunfire.) Where is Luis now? Where are any of the ardent revolutionaries I met then, now? I return fifteen years later as a stranger, a tourist, totally unconnected; it's disconcerting to walk the land where I once felt part of a great struggle and now I am anonymous—my role has changed from the epic to the ordinary.

Stepping off the bus at Mercado Israel Lewites is the personal equivalent, if I may be so modest, of Neil Armstrong returning to the moon. My heart leaps. I recognize the unforgettable tropical blast of heat, the interminable dust in the air, and the aromatic smell of heavy diesel fumes mixed with the smell of tortillas cooking in makeshift roadside stalls. The hustle, the mood of urgency is strangely distinct from elsewhere in the region. It is all so familiar from my sojourn in 1990, and yet everything has changed, and changed utterly. I don't find the revolutionary hope of those times, but rather a horribly battered country reeling from years of war, the traumatic neoliberal reforms of the 90s, and now a descent into almost endemic official corruption, a political class prone to petty squabbling, shocking rates of crime, and of course migration. Remittance outlets feature predominantly in the city and townscapes.

But Still, Nicaragua Is Beautiful, If a Terrible Beauty

Let's start at the *Plaza de la Revolucíon*, the expansive park situated on the banks of Lake Managua and flanked by an awesome volcano. I stood here in February of 1990 on the eve of the elections, surrounded by a half a million red-and-black bedecked Sandinistas cheering President Daniel Ortega as he assured the multitude of an FSLN victory, and the consolidation of the revolution once a mandate was won, and the end of the Contra War. It was a sublime moment, and the massive party continued into the warm night as reggae legend Jimmy Cliff played from the stage. Surely a half-million dancing revolutionary enthusiasts couldn't fail?

Today this place is called *Plaza de la Paz*, Peace Park, and the stage is occupied by a bunch of gray-suited evangelical ministers lambasting a crowd of five thousand devotees on the evils of *Sandinismo* and the need for celestial salvation through sexual abstinence, in temperance, and faith in—what did they call Him?—Jehovah. Oh dear, I lament, the revolution is dead and gone; it's with Sandino in the grave.

Central Managua is no longer in ruins. In 1990, this area was filled with shells of buildings left from the devastating 1972 earthquake, occupied by squatter families. Now there are some pleasant parks and an open-air convention center. There's a Christmas commercial fair here, and as I peer into the enclosure all I see are multinational and franchise signs. This boulevard used to be decorated by a long line of colorful and creative revolutionary murals. They're gone, and in their place are billboards advertising Western Union, the Metro Center shopping mall, and the usual US brand names. I search for the *palapa* bar—a lovely, humble open space beneath a grass roof, where I was once part of some meetings with Cuban officials, arranging solidarity brigades going to Cuba during the crisis of 1990, in response to the fall of the Berlin Wall and the threat of a US military strike. The *palapa* has been erased and in its place stand a Cineplex and a shopping mall. Even the Intercontinental Hotel, a historical landmark once filled with international journalists, diplomats, and dignitaries from socialist countries (and, also in February 1990, international election observers) has transformed into a commonplace luxury hotel—the Crown Plaza—catering to bland, rich tourists. I remember coming here on the emotion-filled morning after the fateful election results in 1990, and randomly sharing an elevator and a quick chat with ex-US President Jimmy Carter.

Managua was like that in those days—a point of extraordinary global convergence, where one went from a meeting of barrio residents organizing local food distribution to hobnobbing with the international political jetset. Next door to the Intercontinental is the military complex where I once found myself pushing aside Bianca Jagger and Billy Bragg to get to the free salad bar during some fucking journalists barbeque. I didn't dare push aside Daniel Ortega, also lingering around the catering stand that evening, with his gang of hardcore guerrilla pals. His wife Rosary gave Irish Times journalist Michael McCaughan and I a lift home that night. It does seem a bit far fetched, that two scumbag Irish gatecrashers hitch a ride home with the nations First Lady, but it could have had a lot to do with Michael's irresistible charm. "Character gets you a long way," he explained.

Now I approach the same military quarters, and two hostile guards send me on my way. Nearby, a comely prostitute offers her services. This genuinely shocks me. In 1990, maybe due to my naiveté more than my consciousness, I never came across a sex worker. Today, sex tourism is a big thing; prostitutes linger all around the center of Managua.

I scurry over to *barrio* Martha Quezado—*Gringolandia*—where once there was a scattering of bars and cheap hotels, making it the main hangout for all the international solidarity activists, Central American guerillas and various renegades and desperados. Today it's a curious mix of backpackers and local hipster-hangouts. At the infamous Sara's Bar, where once one could sit around a merry table of serious international revolutionaries back from the front line and plotting all kinds of trouble, there is now a bunch of privileged students of Spanish and a group of Australian tourists talking about new-age spirituality. Up the street, I can't even find the Bobby Sands Bar. Maybe it's that cell phone dealers store. Or maybe it's the cobbler's. The barrio is unrecognizable; I am lost in a place where once, fifteen years ago, I spent days and nights of intrigue and adventure.

I stumble upon a place advertising itself as an Irish bar. Now here's a pleasant surprise! Lured by the prospect of a *cead mile failte* (big welcome), I take a peep. But this new bar is fancy, and populated by a hip crowd. It's a typical Irish theme bar you could encounter anywhere across the globe, with corny Guinness posters and soccer paraphernalia decorating the walls. I'm disappointed to be told by the standard gorgeous barmaid that they don't actually serve Guinness. It's not like the ramshackle Bobby Sands Bar of yesteryear, filled with provos on the run romancing heart-wrenching Salvadoran political refugees.

So I decide that this place, this pastiche representation of a global Irish bar, is a symbol of all that has changed in Managua. It's a neoliberal outpost trading a cultural brand, profiting from other people's misery. I'm saddened; this is the new Nicaragua. Once there was authentic international solidarity and people shared a common purpose, coming together in the bars at night to exchange experiences of struggle and to plot. Now there's a bunch of trendy people gathered in a commercial space to have vacuous fun.

But maybe I am getting the wrong impression. This bar is not all it seems. There is still something of an aura of clandestinity about it, and I would be well to watch my step here. Nor is the cleaned-up downtown sector all that it seems. The next day I return and realize that I've missed a sold out concert the previous night in the Ruben Dario Theater by the Meiji Godoy brothers—the bards of the Sandinista revolution. An exhibition of the paintings of Armando Morales is decorating the walls of the next-door art gallery. He portrays the Sandinista struggle in dark, brooding portraits of Sandino, the victims of Somoza dictatorship, and clandestine insurgents—pulsating with revolutionary vigor, masked, and armed. As he is an *artiste*, there are also lots of portraits of nude women with guns. The art gallery is full of people. Maybe the Sandinista legacy remains only in art and culture?

Not so. Outside the Ruben Dario Theater I am delighted to stumble upon a statue, a massive realist representation of a revolutionary worker holding a Kalashnikov sky-high. A Sandinista flag flies from his gun barrel, forty feet high. It's not so much the survival of this symbol of the revolutionary days that encourages me, but more the fact that there's a throng of people around the statue. It's a group of boisterous high school students with their teacher, who is explaining what the monument signifies, and he is all about the armed struggle and the heroic fight to overthrow the dictatorship. He reads the words engraved on the plinth—"only the workers and peasants go the whole way." The young students, all giggles and hoots, seem to appreciate the revolutionary sentiment. Nearby stands Carlos Fonsecas's mausoleum—Fonseca was the martyred founder of the FSLN, and it's an impressive structure flanked by a row of proud red and black Sandinista flags. The eternal flame that accompanied this monument in 1990 has been extinguished, but it still stands as a memory of the overthrowing of the dictatorship and it is a fresh monument, shiny and well tended, and—judging only by the array of gorgeous flowers—cherished.

Indeed, the newspapers are full of anti-dictatorship battles. The current president, a nasty piece of neoliberal work called Bolaños, is accusing the opposition Sandinistas and Liberals of fermenting a collective dictatorship to depose him. Daniel Ortega, still leading his party, is in turn denouncing Bolaños as a dictator trying to centralize state power. So the idea of dictators is the currency in the political circles. The Sandinistas failed in their revolutionary program, but the political classes are united in revulsion at the notion of dictatorship—this is one legacy of the FSLN years. Ironically enough, to a nation once plagued by sixty years of Somoza dictatorship, the "Marxist" Sandinistas brought parliamentary democracy. This explains why this prominent monument to a Marxist leader takes a central place in Managua, and why it is acceptable to all political strands—Carlos Fonseca is presented as a slayer of dictators.

But it's clear that the current-day Sandinistas have lost their revolutionary vigor and become mired in incestuous battles for political power. Today's paper shows a picture of *Comandante* Ortega pictured shaking hands with the conservative Cardenal Obando y Bravo, as he cuts a deal with his previous sworn enemy against the current embattled President Bolaños. Ortega and his cohorts in the Sandinista leadership are also scheming with the right wing neoliberals of the Liberal party, snuggling up in an anti-Bolaños orgy with the repellent party leader Gordo

Aleman, who is currently under house arrest for embezzling millions of dollars from the national exchequer during his presidency in the 90s. This kind of despicable Machiavellian political chicanery is typical of the Sandinistas today. They embrace the free market and have feathered their own nests while fatuously talking up the interests of the workers and the *campesinos*. A cartoon in *La Prensa* shows Ortega with a bag of money—"We, the Sandinista leadership, are very practical," goes the caption, "the Left for the masses, and the free market for us...."

News comes through from Chiapas, via e-mail alerting me that I need to be back there in a few days. First of all, it strikes me that when I was here before there was no such thing as e-mail. We wrote, and the postal odyssey usually took a month or so each way. Telephone costs were prohibitive, and even sending faxes was a rare occurrence. So being in Nicaragua in 1990 was really being far away from anywhere else. Now I communicate with people all over the world instantaneously with the Internet. It leads to a strange and disconcerting disconnection between past and present. I can't locate anybody I knew in Nicaragua in 1990—things have changed too much—but I have everybody I've known since I began using the internet in 1997, anywhere in the world, just a keyboard away. I search out the Salvadoran Center, where I once hung out with refugees riveted by news of the 1990 insurrection in San Salvador, but it has disappeared without a trace. I am overwhelmed to be a tourist in a place where once we were all so integrated in the urgent exigencies of the day, struggling to build a new world.

Early the next morning I leave Managua and head north for Leon, a sweltering town where fifteen years earlier I taught English to a class of Sandinista students at the university. Leon is a lovely colonial town blessed with a fantastic climate. The former Sandinista Mayor, Omar Cabezas (who wrote the quintessential guerrilla text *Fire From the Mountain*), is in the newspapers—having been elected as the parliamentarian human hights assessor. Leon is still Sandinista, but it's the new neoliberal version. Subtiava, the indigenous barrio, is as poor and wretched as before, yet the spruced-up center of town is full of fancy SUVs and franchises. Such is the path of progress—the few get rich, the majority stays the same. I am perturbed by the presence of several Sandinista museums to the Revolution. Is that it—museums? It's good that they are cherishing the memory of the struggle, but the Sandinistas still control this town. The revolution is dead and gone, it's with the neo-liberals in the grave of the bickering parliament.

The abuse of power comes as no surprise. So Ortega and his gang play the power game and cast off renegades along the way—like Sergio Ramirez, his Vice-President during the revolutionary years, who cast aspersions on the naked pursuit of political power. Ortega came close to taking power in the 2002 elections, but the US stepped in again and ensured by undisguised threat, that their man—in this case the sorry, unforgettable figure of Bolaños—got elected. The upcoming elections in 2006 may see Ortega gaining power because of the appalling economic and political failures of the neoliberals, and the current left-turning trend in Latin America. Nostalgia for his heady revolutionary past will guide the beleaguered electorate, but it remains to be seen if his potential administration, beset by chronic clientism and compromise, will affect any real progressive change.

The betrayal by the Sandinistas of their revolutionary principles also raises questions of solidarity and support. On a personal level, did my support of the Sandinista project mean that my political formation was based on a flawed principle, an untruth? Returning to Nicaragua fifteen years later, I think it is still consistent to lend support to the Sandinista revolutionary program, if not the flawed Party itself. I might well have got a little carried away with the revolutionary fervor back in the day, but the principles were sound. Unconditional solidarity for any political party or movement is a foolish stance, especially when one has no participation in the processes of decision-making or ideological direction. But one's loyalty remains to the idea and the revolutionary actions of a movement in a particular time.

NorthBound Chicken Bus Odyssey

I'm back on the chicken buses on the long crawl to Mexico.

In forty-eight hours of intense road journey, on several buses, I leave Nicaragua, pass through Honduras, and cross El Salvador and the Pacific coast of Guatemala. A perusal of the local newspapers along the road presents the usual depressing vista. In the toll of daily violent deaths, Guatemala fares better than Honduras—eight to six, but El Salvador is way ahead with thirteen murders reported in today's paper, December 21st.

There's not a lot to be said when one spends all of 18 hours in a country, and half of that on buses traversing the length of it, but El Salvador reads like the same bad script from the same shit movie. The (neoliberal) government has declared a super *mano dura* policy against the Mara Salvatrucha, and here—the birthplace, in many respects, of the gang phenomenon—the slaughter is more pronounced. I stay overnight in San Miguel, once a strategic center of the anti-guerrilla insurgency war, and it's like the war never ended. There is a palpable sense of fear lingering around the town as I search out a place to eat after sunset. The streets are deserted at 7 p.m., and random people warn me of the dangers lurking at every corner.

El Salvador dollarized its economy a few years ago, resulting in a general price hike. It's the most expensive of the Central American republics. More pressing is the issue of currency sovereignty, but the Salvadoran government has accepted a poorly colonial status as a satellite of the USA, and its (clandestine, illegal) migrant workforce in the US contributes up to half of the cash flow in the local economy.

The FMLN, the ex-guerrilla insurgency, is now the nation's second-most powerful political party; the compromises undertaken to achieve this status have been difficult. There have been three major splits in the party. By not following the same neoliberal path as the Sandinistas, the FMLN has converted itself from an outlaw force to an inside dealer with some weight. While most remnants of the 1980s revolutionary program has been shelved, the FMLN is still the only left-of-center show in town for those who feel the urge to vote. They are not on-board the government's super *mano dura* policy, denouncing it as a further catalyst for widespread violence.

The bus crossing the frontier to Guatemala is filled with

migrants. A couple of illiterate *campesinos* sitting beside me have hired street money-changers to fill out their immigration papers, in full sight of the immigration officials who are checking people's papers. Nobody gives a fuck. The peasants pay a few dollars to the hustlers and probably pay a few to the migration officials too. All the way up the isthmus they will be shelling out cash, hand over fist.

We are continualy taken off the packed chicken bus while crossing Guatemala. Cops make us line up by the bus and we are ordered to spread our legs and they pat us down, as if we are being arrested. A while later, the army comes onboard and orders us all off again. People grumble and get on with the humiliation. The third time it happens, I somewhat foolishly decided to use my privileged status to make a stand.

"Why do we have to get off the bus? This is the third time this afternoon." The cop looks at me with surprise.

"You a visitor to this country, gringo, and you are obliged to do what the authorities tell you. If you don't like it, go back to the United States."

He is a nasty bit of work, and I regret having started this. I have visions of being stranded on the roadside with this thug and his mates, the chicken bus disappearing into the mountains. But I can't back down—that will probably make it worse.

"This is no way to treat people," I say. "We have been searched twice; let us go on our way."

He grabs my passport and flicks through the pages.

"Your visa is out of date!" he says, satisfied to have caught me. Now he can have some fun!

I look at the visa stamp he is pointing at.

"Eh, that's for El Salvador, señor."

Stifled laughter can be heard around the bus. The cop is embarrassed.

He hands me back my passport, and stomps off the bus.

We roll on and some of the passengers turn to talk to me, to show their approval for my action. I am satisfied that I have indeed managed one small act of resistance on my trip. It's not much, but when there's an insane social war raging all around, it's better than nothing.

Exodus, Migration, Desolation.

This Chicken Bus Diary is not about bad roads and shit buses. The PPP (Plan Puebla Panama) analysis is that if infrastructure were improved—more highways—the region would improve. Big highways help big business. The neoliberal notion, that once a region can produce goods at a competitive rate it is realizing its potential, is flawed. As small farmers and producers are forced out of the market, big business dispossesses the locals. The end result? Where once there was a community, now there is a company.

Spending days on buses filled mostly with migrants—poor people heading north, harassed endlessly by authorities and criminal elements—is a melancholy experience. People are strong and resilient but look at their faces in repose when they try to sleep as we lurch along the rough roads—lines crease young farmers' visages. Theirs is not a sleep of confidence, but one filled with the phantasmagoria of the dangers and difficulties they will face on their journey.

Economic hardship has spurned people throughout the ages to seek better fortunes elsewhere. People have always migrated; exodus is nothing new.

But there is something more in Central America, and I understand it in light of what was happening here in November of 1989, when it looked like the Sandinistas would win the upcoming elections Thousands of guerrillas of the FMLN surrounded San Salvador, the URNG in Guatemala fought on, and the clandestine insurgency in Honduras was just waiting for the signal from the others. This region was a harbinger for a new world. Central America would lead us into the twenty-first century with the combined example of their revolutionary societies, which were neither capitalist or communist, but something different, something we glimpsed in Sandinista Nicaragua—a hope, an inspired example of a better way of organizing society from below, with more equality and more justice.

The modern-day exodus is a form of economic migration and, depressingly, the political desertion of the revolutionary idea. There is no more hope in the political idea; there is nothing left. Social disintegration, the breakdown of communities in struggle, and endemic crime—these are the logical conclusions of the neoliberal project.

The tragic failure of movements to implement the revolutionary programs propagated in the 1980s goes some way in explaining the current terrible situation in Central America. That those forces were defeated by US-promoted neoliberal capitalism is the phase of global history in which we currently live. The poignancy of the bus full of migrants (now creating a big problem for the US itself in macro terms of security, crime and clandestinity) is that it could so easily have been so different. Fifteen years on from that fateful year of 1990, we could have had a group of thriving, self-determined Central American republics premised in good education, health, and equality, heading towards regional autonomy. People would have had a reason to stay and fight.

Instead, this is a catastrophic region. Darkly violent places survive tenuously on remittances sent back from migrant family members working illegally in the US and other countries. Nicaragua, the flagship of the failed revolutionary project, is like an orphaned child fallen in with a bad gang of glue-sniffing street kids. Honduras, El Salvador, and Guatemala are mad conflict zones caught between state forces, their clandestine death squad militias and their poverty-born, violent youth delinquents—themselves products of a trigger-happy, war-traumatized society.

The old Central American staples of endemic corruption and periodic natural disasters ensure that this wretched part of the world—now cast into oblivion as the world focuses on Iraq, Afghanistan, and Palestine—remains a veritable hell, a space of near-apocalyptic hopelessness.

EPILOGUE

CONSEQUENCES

BERLIN, 2005

I'm flying back to Berlin after eleven years absence. Returning to the place that was for me both a militant *autonome* boot camp and an awakening to the seductive lure of building power-from-below in autonomous communities. From that teeming cosmopolitan sub-culture in the heart of the old weathered city, I learned that a life worth living is a life amongst people who struggle and resist. And it was the Berlin anarcho-squatting scene that gave me the wings to explore different parts of the vast globe without fear—confident in the knowledge that there are sound people everywhere, it's just a matter of going a little further to encounter them.

I have shamefully succumbed to purchasing a ridiculously cheap ticket on one of these neo-liberal airlines that function like maquiladoras of the air. Its cheap, but no fun. In the squats, we produced our own train tickets. My *companero* Robert was a master craftsman, and with his deft hand, fine documents were furnished that allowed wide and furtive travel, unlimited on the European networks.

I'm busy explaining the wonders of free rail travel to my companions—Padre Kino and Katja, Chiapas veterans—and the engaging adventures and romance that lurk everywhere on late night European trains traversing the great cities. "Stop exaggerating," says Kino the contrarian, while Katja laments the termination of that particular scam. But of course, Kino is right—it wasn't always completely free and exhilarating, the stress involved in negotiating the endless parade of ticket inspectors and guards was exhausting.

As we approach Berlin—announced by a vast ocean of twinkling lights mapped across the horizon—I remember my last tempestuous exit from this rambunctious city. Fleeing—as usual—and overwrought with anxiety. My faithful and beloved comrade Mayday accompanies me to Berlin Alexanderplatz. I accommodate myself in a musty, deserted 6-person Pullman compartment and embrace my co-conspirator farewell, as if we shall never meet again. I won't return, I can't return: my Berlin days are finished.

The clandestine life entails endless, absurd situations. This particular tale is all about a flag. Almost as a joke, but more with a sense of solidarity with the Kurdish struggle for national liberation, I hang a Kurdish flag out of my window in our squatted house in East Berlin. At this time the Kurdish flag is outlawed by the German state and to exhibit it is a "terrorist" crime. And that is why we in the squats fly the Kurdish flag—because it is like the skull and crossbones—a symbol of outlaws and resistance to the state.

Anyhow, the *Bullen* has confiscated my flag by ripping it down from atop of their riot van below my second floor balcony. The flag is gone and so too cops, and I think nothing more of it. Some time later I set off on my travels once more.

A year later I return to a stack of legal letters beginning with a summons to court for displaying "terrorist paraphernalia" and concluding with a hefty sentence in abstencia handed down by an unforgiving judiciary. I have an arrest warrant out in my name for this most bizarre and ridiculous of charges. Matze, the wise and experienced local squatter with much legal expertise, advises me to leave as quickly as possible. Robert manufactures one of his special train tickets and I am off on the late night train to Paris, and suddenly there we are, Mayday and I, interrupted, bidding farewell on an impossibly scenic Alexanderplatz platform amongst clouds of steam and the sublime architecture of old European train stations.

Ode to Clandestinity

Fleeing Berlin on the late night train to Paris—and me a fugitive with a fake ticket—is perhaps, I reflect, the most appropriate way to leave the subterranean life in Berlin and renew once more as I would, in Chiapas, Mexico. If clandestinity is about moving furtively in the shadows while keeping one step ahead of the forces of repression, law, and order then in Berlin I learned how it is a fleeting tactic to strike like lightning and retreat safely—like this surreptitious exit from the control zone. As a long-term strategy, clandestinity is about protecting ourselves, our rebel spaces and allowing the seed to germinate underground. This is a lesson learned with powerful consequences in Chiapas.

The train chugs through the long night and various ticket inspectors come through without much ado. As we approach the Belgian border I finally begin to relax. An older yuppie businesswoman shares my compartment and we begin talking and eventually, drinking and laughing together. As we pull into the last German station before the frontier, I am horrified to see that the late night platform is lined with cops. As the train pulls to a stop, I can see a cop boarding each carriage. The color drains from my face and my body tenses up.

At excruciating moments like this I always seem to remember one of Camus' lines: "…most people don't live the life they would like to live," he said, somewhat harshly, "and it's a question of cowardice." I am trying to live the life I choose and now it seems to be a question not of cowardice, but of fear—or at least dealing with fear. If cowardice shrinks the person, fear eats the soul. Garden of Gethsemane, sweating blood, these kinds of images haunt my consciousness as the cop pulls open the old sliding doors with theatrical verve. My heart sinks. He has one of those little hand held computer things with him. I'm fucked. Visions of being led off the train at gunpoint by twitching guards—not for the first time—spring to mind.

The businesswoman notices something about my fear-ridden demeanor. She begins to engage the guard in a splendidly flirtatious manner. He is suitably bowled over by the lavish attention from this handsome woman, and in the lasciviousness of the moment, he hands me back my passport without even the briefest inspection. As the love-struck guard recedes from the compartment, I sigh a breath of relief and gaze upon my knight in shinning armor. "My station," she says as we pull into the first stop in Belgium, and off she goes, one of the most unforgettable, unnamed women in my life.

The amusing after-word to this particular episode is that at the same station the woman debarks, the Flemish ticket inspector climbs on. He takes my ticket and laughs with some mirth—"This is a forgery," he says, knowingly. The train traverses Belgium for all of a half-hour before entering France. The train inspector charges me for the six-mile jaunt across Belgium and leaves with a conspiratorial wink.

Against Amnesia

The specialty of these maquiladora airlines is to deliver their cargo—or better to say, livestock—to some obscure and remote airport far outside the city. As we touch down in some forgettable and unnamed little airport outside Berlin, I reflect upon my abrupt departure eleven years ago. The unlawful manner of dealing with the charges—absconding—could have some unwelcome consequences. Most of all I remember a fleeting thought I had entertained back then—what happens, I mused, if I return in ten years time to Germany, when all this anarchy and liberation is over, and I am older and newly respectable, with a job and a family, and they arrest me for this youthful folly?

Eleven years later I am returning to Berlin and I am not a respectable family man with a job—on the contrary I am the same fucking reprobate with a penchant for anarchy. This shocks me as much as much as the prospect of being arrested upon arrival. Am I an illumined devotee or an unwavereable conservative? Is this a sign of revolutionary staunchness or blind faith?

Airports are control zones—whether in the middle of nowhere or in the center of metropolises—and they are all the same. Namely, they are visions of how neo-liberal capitalism would like all of society to be. A place where you are monitored by security personal and cameras every step of the way, a space where you are checked, searched, registered and told to stay in line. Airports are a nightmarish vision of how society could and can be run—a place where you must take off your shoes for inspection, for fucks sake.

I hate airports with a passion and this little one outside Berlin, although quaint and rustic, is as intolerable as the rest. There is a long line for immigration and I wonder why we are queuing up—between Ireland and Germany—if we are all Europeans now? I remember how when I first arrived in Berlin, I was checked by East German border guards, and they stamped my passport with some Stalinist symbol. Cold War bureaucracy; another world. The Wall is long gone now, but there are new ones springing up all over the place.

The rebel must return to their own past with a knife in one hand and a bouquet of flowers in the other. My past here in Berlin reminds me of how freedom can be, but it also presents me with a threat. A past filled with the memory of glorious possibilities—how we lived in our free spaces, how we began to organize collectively and with passion!—but also how life in the shadows, illegal and clandestine, presents certain consequences that need to be negotiated. A certain feeling of dread creeps over me as I queue for immigration—fear and loathing—waiting to go through the gate of state officialdom. These anonymous people in uniform have the sublime power of taking people away and dispatching them as their office dictates. Standing in line at the airport, passport in hand, the sense of being an outlaw takes hold of me—and of being small before power.

The immigration, or possibly security, officer takes my passport and pumps the details into his computer. He waits, confident in the knowledge that he is in total control. A look of minute suspicion crosses his visage. He beckons his colleague over and she looks slightly perturbed as she assesses the details on the screen. They converse quietly in hushed tones and glance at me as if I am some kind of anomaly. Is it my criminal history, or my clandestinity, which doesn't quite register in the scheme of things? But suddenly, fear leaves me, and I smile down upon these bureaucrats with a newfound rebel confidence. As if to say—I am proud to be a miscreant in your system, so fuck you! After an inordinately long time—and with a suspicious but uncertain stare—the official hands me my documents and I am on my way, unfazed and free as a bird.

Walking We Ask Questions; Sometimes We Change the Plot

There I go telling stories, even in the epilogue of the book. This was intended to be a short summation of the book with a poetic epitaph as a means of conclusion. Nothing ever turns out as it should. Indeed, this isn't even the book that I had intended to write. *Clandestines* began its life as a radical political tract that would graph the trajectory of resistance movements from anti-imperialism to anti-capitalism.

Starting with the anti-imperialist struggles for national liberation (Ireland, Kurdistan, Nicaragua) it was to critique the shortcomings of these movements from an anti-authoritarian position. By taking inspiration from the formative years of the autonomous movement in Europe, squatting in Berlin, and a reading of anarchism, the book was to plot the emergence of the new movement against capitalist globalization. The pivotal moment was to be the Zapatista uprising of 1994, which inspired so many with its participatory democracy and new formulation of revolutionary politics, a renewal of global struggle and resistance.

That book has yet to be written, and I fear I would not do justice to the significance of the theme. Instead I have written a book of rebel tales, about traveling politically and engaging enthusiastically with people of changing circumstance and cultures of resistance. This book is about searching for the revolutionary in everyday lives, and a map for delving into some of the more shadowy and uncharted moments and movements of recent history.

Why write rebel stories instead of political theory or analysis? First of all—obviously—it's easier, and writing becomes a joy, not a chore. Secondly, I realized my impulse to write came not from the urge to pontificate, but to communicate. Here Eduardo Galeano's observations in his essay "In Defense of the Word" are useful: "Our writing is informed by a desire to make contact, so that readers may become involved with words that come to us from them, and that return to them as hope and prophecy."

I think the history of this era—basically the 90's—will be written with a grudging nod to the anti-authoritarian, anti-capitalist movements that emerged after the fall of the Berlin Wall and the demise of the communist influence on global struggle. Here and amongst the wider protest movement, hope was nourished despite the official proclamation announcing the "end of history," and the struggle for a better world was renewed.

And what was life like below deck, in the engine room, and the crew's mess on this ship of resistance? These are the stories that need to be told too. How do we live, side-by-side, how do we treat each other? From where springs solidarity and mutual aid? Where is freedom and how best to overcome our despair? I'm not sure, but I think I know where to look for the answers.

A Tale is More Precious than All the Wealth of the World

When we emerge from the rustic airport outside Berlin, a balmy autumnal evening embraces us. And we are greeted by the unwelcome news that Katja's car—which she left here a week ago when she set off to visit Ireland—has been stolen. Shortly, the cops arrive on the scene, and they begin their investigation by questioning Katja as if she was somehow party to the crime. The irony is not lost upon me that we have only been in Germany for ten minutes and the police are already interrogating us. It seems apt. An excessively bureaucratic cop approaches me—notebook and pencil in hand—and begins to ask for my personal details. I look at him somewhat bemused, somewhat bewildered, and say to him what I wish I could always say to figures of authority and officialdom—No!

Sure enough, the cops won't give us a lift to town, and we are left on the side of the quiet road outside the now deserted airport eighteen miles from the city. Soon enough, as fate would have it, a kindly mechanic in an old Eastern-bloc truck picks us up and we get to ride into Berlin in the high, decrepit cabin of this relic of another era. "Keeps your heads down," he beckons as we approach the city—in respect of the vagary that it is illegal to have more than one passenger in this class of vehicle.

Breaking the law, we arrive back in Berlin—Clandestines forever.

FURTHER READING

Zapatistas, http://struggle.ws/zapatista.html
Anarchism, http://struggle.ws/revolt.html

CREDITS

Institute for Anarchist Studies. The IAS was established as a nonprofit foundation in 1996 in order to support the development of anarchism through a grant-giving program for radical writers. To date, the IAS has funded over fifty projects by authors and translators from around the world.

The IAS has grown significantly since its inception. In addition to supporting projects like the Latin American Archives Project, coordinating a Speakers Bureau, and cosponsoring the annual Renewing the Anarchist Tradition conference, the IAS also publishes a biannual magazine, "Perspectives on Anarchist Theory," as a forum in which to frame, explore, and debate questions of significance to contemporary anarchist theory and practice.

The IAS relies entirely on contributions from generous individuals around the world to be able to carry out its programs. Contact them at: www.anarchist-studies.org

Photo credits:

Introduction courtesy of Tim Russo

1. Sex and the Berlin Wall courtesy of Umbruch Bildarchiv
2. May the Road Rise to You courtesy of Umbruch Bildarchiv
3. Portrait of the Last Autonomen photos courtesy of Síabhra Durcan
4. Twilight of the Armed Struggle courtesy of Bryan Meade
5. Civilization and its Discontents courtesy of Niels Barmeyer
6. The Making of a Rebel courtesy of Jim Collins
7. High Sea Adventures courtesy of Timo Russo
8. The Resurrection of Vampiro photos courtesy of Tim Russo
9. Looking Back on the Sandinista Revolution photos courtesy of Ian Gordon
10. Three Cuban Tales photo courtesy of Victor Blue
11. Tales from the Vanquished Pier photos courtesy of Tim Russo
12. A Carnival of Dreams-The Passion of the Brazilian Left courtesy of Tim Russo
13. Diez de Abril photos courtesy of Tim Russo
14. Chicken Bus Diaries courtesy of Tim Russo

Epilogue

Consequences—Berlin 2005 courtesy of Tim Russo

Author photo courtesy of Timo Russo

Umbruch-Bildarchiv Berlin

“Against the underexposure of the left movement.”

http://www.umbruch-bildarchiv.de

email: post@umbruch-bildarchiv.de

Eddie Yuen is co-editor of *Confronting Capitalism: Dispatches from a Global Movement* (Soft Skull Press 2003). He teaches in the MA program in Activism & Social Change at New College of California in San Francisco.

Simone F. Schmidt lives in Toronto, and spends parts of her days rendering scenes of torrential rains flooding Tom Flanagan's home in pen and ink. She would like some mail.
schidt@gmail.com

Timo Russo is an independent photographer, radio journalist and organizer based in Mexico. His work can be viewed at www.globalaware.org.

Ramor Ryan is a rebellious rover and Irish exile who makes his home between New York City and Chiapas, Mexico. He can be contacted at ramorx@hotmail.com

ALSO AVAILABLE FROM AK PRESS

DANNY BURNS – Poll Tax Rebellion

MAT CALLAHAN – The Trouble With Music

CHRIS CARLSSON – Critical Mass: Bicycling's Defiant Celebration

JAMES CARR – Bad

NOAM CHOMSKY – At War With Asia

NOAM CHOMSKY – Chomsky on Anarchism

NOAM CHOMSKY – Language and Politics

NOAM CHOMSKY – Radical Priorities

WARD CHURCHILL – On the Justice of Roosting Chickens: Reflections on the Consequences of U.S. Imperial Arrogance and Criminality

WARD CHURCHILL – Since Predator Came

HARRY CLEAVER – Reading Capital Politically

ALEXANDER COCKBURN & JEFFREY ST. CLAIR (ed.) – Dime's Worth of Difference

ALEXANDER COCKBURN & JEFFREY ST. CLAIR (ed.) – Politics of Anti-Semitism, The

ALEXANDER COCKBURN & JEFFREY ST. CLAIR (ed.) – Serpents in the Garden

DANIEL & GABRIEL COHN-BENDIT – Obsolete Communism: The Left-Wing Alternative

EG SMITH COLLECTIVE – Animal Ingredients A–Z (3rd edition)

VOLTAIRINE de CLEYRE – Voltarine de Cleyre Reader, The

HUNTER CUTTING & MAKANI THEMBA-NIXON – Talking the Walk: A Communications Guide for Racial Justice

HOWARD EHRLICH – Reinventing Anarchy, Again

SIMON FORD – Realization and Suppression of the Situationist International: An Annotated Bibliography 1972–1992

YVES FREMION & VOLNY – Orgasms of History: 3000 Years of Spontaneous Revolt

BERNARD GOLDSTEIN – Five Years in the Warsaw Ghetto

AGUSTIN GUILLAMÓN – Friends Of Durruti Group, 1937–1939, The

ANN HANSEN – Direct Action: Memoirs Of An Urban Guerilla

WILLIAM HERRICK – Jumping the Line: The Adventures and Misadventures of an American Radical

FRED HO – Legacy to Liberation: Politics & Culture of Revolutionary Asian/Pacific America

STEWART HOME – Neoism, Plagiarism & Praxis

STEWART HOME – Neoist Manifestos / The Art Strike Papers

STEWART HOME – No Pity

STEWART HOME – Red London

KATHY KELLY – Other Lands Have Dreams: From Baghdad to Pekin Prison

JAMES KELMAN – Some Recent Attacks: Essays Cultural And Political

KEN KNABB – Complete Cinematic Works of Guy Debord

KATYA KOMISARUK – Beat the Heat: How to Handle Encounters With Law Enforcement

RICARDO FLORES MAGÓN – Dreams of Freedom: A Ricardo Flores Magón Reader

NESTOR MAKHNO – Struggle Against The State & Other Essays, The

G.A. MATIASZ – End Time

CHERIE MATRIX – Tales From the Clit

ALBERT MELTZER – Anarchism: Arguments For & Against

ALBERT MELTZER – I Couldn't Paint Golden Angels

RAY MURPHY – Siege Of Gresham

NORMAN NAWROCKI – Rebel Moon

MICHAEL NEUMANN – The Case Against Israel

HENRY NORMAL – Map of Heaven, A

HENRY NORMAL – Dream Ticket

HENRY NORMAL – Fifteenth of February

HENRY NORMAL – Third Person

FIONBARRA O'DOCHARTAIGH – Ulster's White Negroes: From Civil Rights To Insurrection

DAN O'MAHONY – Four Letter World

CRAIG O'HARA – Philosophy Of Punk, The

ANTON PANNEKOEK – Workers' Councils

BEN REITMAN – Sister of the Road: The Autobiography of Boxcar Bertha

PENNY RIMBAUD – Diamond Signature, The

PENNY RIMBAUD – Shibboleth: My Revolting Life

RUDOLF ROCKER – Anarcho-Syndicalism

RUDOLF ROCKER – London Years, The

RON SAKOLSKY & STEPHEN DUNIFER – Seizing the Airwaves: A Free Radio Handbook

ROY SAN FILIPPO – New World In Our Hearts: 8 Years of Writings from the Love and Rage Revolutionary Anarchist Federation, A

MARINA SITRIN – Horizontalism: Voices of Popular Power in Argentina

ALEXANDRE SKIRDA – Facing the Enemy: A History Of Anarchist Organisation From Proudhon To May 1968

ALEXANDRE SKIRDA – Nestor Mahkno – Anarchy's Cossack

VALERIE SOLANAS – Scum Manifesto

CJ STONE – Housing Benefit Hill & Other Places

ANTONIO TELLEZ – Sabate: Guerilla Extraordinary

MICHAEL TOBIAS – Rage and Reason

TOM VAGUE – Anarchy in the UK: The Angry Brigade

TOM VAGUE – Great British Mistake, The

TOM VAGUE – Televisionaries

JAN VALTIN – Out of the Night

RAOUL VANEIGEM – Cavalier History Of Surrealism, A

FRANCOIS EUGENE VIDOCQ – Memoirs of Vidocq: Master of Crime

MARK J WHITE – Idol Killing, An

JOHN YATES – Controlled Flight Into Terrain

JOHN YATES – September Commando

BENJAMIN ZEPHANIAH – Little Book of Vegan Poems

BENJAMIN ZEPHANIAH – School's Out

HELLO – 2/15: The Day The World Said NO To War

DARK STAR COLLECTIVE – Beneath the Paving Stones: Situationists and the Beach, May 68

DARK STAR COLLECTIVE – Quiet Rumours: An Anarcha-Feminist Reader

ANONYMOUS – Test Card F

CLASS WAR FEDERATION – Unfinished Business: The Politics of Class War

CDs

THE EX – 1936: The Spanish Revolution

MUMIA ABU JAMAL – 175 Progress Drive

MUMIA ABU JAMAL – All Things Censored Vol.1

MUMIA ABU JAMAL – Spoken Word

FREEDOM ARCHIVES – Chile: Promise of Freedom

FREEDOM ARCHIVES – Prisons on Fire: George Jackson, Attica & Black Liberation

FREEDOM ARCHIVES – Robert F. Williams: Self Respect, Self Defense, & Self Determination

JUDI BARI – Who Bombed Judi Bari?

JELLO BIAFRA – Become the Media

JELLO BIAFRA – Beyond The Valley of the Gift Police

JELLO BIAFRA – High Priest of Harmful

JELLO BIAFRA – I Blow Minds For A Living

JELLO BIAFRA – If Evolution Is Outlawed

JELLO BIAFRA – Machine Gun In The Clown's Hand

JELLO BIAFRA – No More Cocoons

NOAM CHOMSKY – American Addiction, An

NOAM CHOMSKY – Case Studies in Hypocrisy

NOAM CHOMSKY – Emerging Framework of World Power

NOAM CHOMSKY – Free Market Fantasies

NOAM CHOMSKY – Imperial Presidency, The

NOAM CHOMSKY – New War On Terrorism: Fact And Fiction

NOAM CHOMSKY – Propaganda and Control of the Public Mind

NOAM CHOMSKY – Prospects for Democracy

NOAM CHOMSKY/CHUMBAWAMBA – For A Free Humanity: For Anarchy

WARD CHURCHILL – Doing Time: The Politics of Imprisonment

WARD CHURCHILL – In A Pig's Eye: Reflections on the Police State, Repression, and Native America

WARD CHURCHILL – Life in Occupied America

WARD CHURCHILL – Pacifism and Pathology in the American Left

ALEXANDER COCKBURN – Beating the Devil: The Incendiary Rants of Alexander Cockburn

ANGELA DAVIS – Prison Industrial Complex, The

NORMAN FINKELSTEIN – An Issue of Justice

JAMES KELMAN – Seven Stories

TOM LEONARD – Nora's Place and Other Poems 1965–99

CASEY NEILL – Memory Against Forgetting

CHRISTIAN PARENTI – Taking Liberties: Policing, Prisons and Surveillance in an Age of Crisis

UTAH PHILLIPS – I've Got To know

UTAH PHILLIPS – Starlight on the Rails CD box set

DAVID ROVICS – Behind the Barricades: Best of David Rovics

ARUNDHATI ROY – Come September

VARIOUS – Better Read Than Dead

VARIOUS – Less Rock, More Talk

VARIOUS – Mob Action Against the State: Collected Speeches from the Bay Area Anarchist Bookfair

VARIOUS – Monkeywrenching the New World Order

VARIOUS – Return of the Read Menace

HOWARD ZINN – Artists In A Time of War

HOWARD ZINN – Heroes and Martyrs: Emma Goldman, Sacco & Vanzetti, and the Revolutionary Struggle

HOWARD ZINN – People's History of the United States: A Lecture at Reed College, A

HOWARD ZINN – People's History Project

HOWARD ZINN – Stories Hollywood Never Tells

DVDs

NOAM CHOMSKY – Distorted Morality

NOAM CHOMSKY – Imperial Grand Strategy

STEVEN FISCHLER & JOEL SUCHER – Anarchism in America

ARUNDHATI ROY – Instant Mix Imperial Democracy

HOWARD ZINN – Readings from Voices of a People's History

FRIENDS OF AK PRESS

Each year AK Press publishes the finest books, CDs, and DVDs from the anarchist and radical traditions. The Friends of AK Press is a way in which you can directly help us to keep the wheels rolling and these important projects coming.

As ever, money is tight since we do not rely on outside funding. We need your help to make and keep these crucial materials available. Friends pay a minimum (of course, we have no objection to larger sums!) of $20/£15 per month, for a minimum three month period. Money received goes directly into our publishing funds. In return, Friends automatically receive (for the duration of their membership), as they appear, one FREE copy of EVERY new AK Press title. Secondly, they are also entitled to a 10% discount on EVERYTHING featured in the AK Press Distribution catalog, on ANY and EVERY order. We also have a program where groups or individuals can sponsor a whole book.

Please contact us for details:

AK Press
674-A 23rd Street
Oakland, CA 94612
akpress@akpress.org
www.akpress.org

AK Press
PO Box 12766
Edinburgh, Scotland EH8 9YE
ak@akedin.demon.co.uk
www.akuk.com